D1607908

READING DANTE'S STARS

READING
DANTE'S STARS

ALISON CORNISH

YALE UNIVERSITY PRESS
NEW HAVEN AND LONDON

Designed by Mary Valencia. Set in Garamond Old Style and Michelangelo type by
The Composing Room of Michigan, Inc.
Printed in the United States of America by
Bookcrafters, Inc., Chelsea, Michigan.

Library of Congress Cataloging-in-Publication Data
Cornish, Alison, 1963–
    Reading Dante's stars / Alison Cornish.
       p.   cm.
    Includes bibliographical references and index.
    ISBN 0-300-07679-7 (alk. paper)
       1. Dante Alighieri, 1265–1321. Divina commedia.   2. Dante Alighieri,
    1265–1321—Knowledge—Astronomy.   3. Astronomy, Medieval, in litera-
    ture.   4. Cosmography in literature.   I. Title.
    PQ4401.C67   2000
    851′.1—dc21   99-39103

A catalogue record for this book is available from the British Library.

The paper in this book meets the guidelines for permanence and durability of the
Committee on Production Guidelines for Book Longevity of the Council on
Library Resources.

10 9 8 7 6 5 4 3 2 1

FOR
PAOLO, SOFIA, AND GIACOMO

CONTENTS

ACKNOWLEDGMENTS

In addition to the financial assistance provided by a Fulbright grant to Italy and a Yale University Morse Junior Faculty Fellowship, this book has been touched by the wealth and generosity of many minds. Jeffrey Schnapp was my first teacher of Dante. John Freccero was the inspiration of *lungo studio e grande amore.* Conversations with Giuseppe Mazzotta at Yale sustained the project. Albert Ascoli, Robert Hollander, and Christopher Kleinhenz supplied advice, comments, and criticism on several chapters. Zygmunt Barański, Robert Durling, and David Quint read the whole thing, as did Chauncey Wood, whose good eyes and excellent judgment came at just the right moment. Special thanks to Jenya Weinreb, Ana-Maria López-Anderson, and Leah Chang for their help in the final stages. I am grateful to colleagues and students at the University of Michigan for their warm reception of Dante and me. Theodore Cachey, Jr., and Christian Moevs also provided opportunity to air some of these ideas in that stronghold of Dante studies in neighboring Notre Dame. I would also like especially to acknowledge the friendship, encouragement, and intellectual standards of revered Italianists Krystyna von Henneberg, Eileen Reeves, and Marvin Becker, as well as the constant support of my parents, Judson and Christine Cornish. It is to my husband, Paolo Squatriti, and to the children we share, Sofia and Giacomo, that I dedicate this book.

READING DANTE'S STARS

Introduction

Astronomy had an exalted status in the Middle Ages. Dante explains that its superiority is due to the nobility of its subject matter, which is the circulation of the heavens, and to its high degree of certitude deriving from the perfect regularity of that movement.[1] Culminating the secular curriculum of the liberal arts, this final discipline of the Quadrivium bordered divine science, or theology. In his formulation of a hierarchy of learning in "divine and human readings," Cassiodorus had suggested that astronomy could lift minds aloft, "even unto the stars," in the sense that the goal of secular science is ultimately to leave the earth behind and head for heaven.[2] The astronomical textbooks of Dante's time often claimed that their high-ranking subject had just such an uplifting effect. Robert Anglicus, for example, in his commentary on John of Sacrobosco's *Sphere,* declared that because this science instills admiration for the work of the Creator, it becomes, "as Ptolemy says in the beginning of the *Almagest,* a road leading to God."[3] Dante's space voyage recounted in the *Paradiso,* one of several medieval astral journeys to wisdom modeled on Cicero's *Dream of Scipio,* is a dramatization of this notion. Contemplation of the stars, moreover, offers consolation for earthly injustice, as suggested in a letter attributed to Dante in which the indignant exile refuses to return to his native city on humiliating terms, for he can, after all, still gaze upon the mirrors of the sun and stars and contemplate, under any sky, the sweetest truths.[4]

There are more than one hundred passages explicitly invoking astronomical learning in Dante's *Commedia,* many of which are in prominent places, such as at the beginning of new cantos. Stars also punctuate the poem, because the word *stelle* furnishes the final rhyme of each of its three principal parts, *Inferno, Purgatorio,* and *Paradiso.* The entire last third of the narrative is plotted across the template of the physical heavens, and the basic form of the universe with its concentric revolutions is a model for the arrangement of sinners orbiting Satan at the rotten nadir of Hell, and of penitents in Purgatory spiraling up the mountain at whose summit lies the garden of first innocence. Many descriptions of the stars fall under the category of astronomical periphrasis, a standard embellishment of poetic diction that serves to tell time or set the scene.[5] Others function as a term of comparison in some of Dante's most dazzling similes and metaphors.

This detail and abundance of astronomical material have inspired both enthusiasm and repugnance. The earliest commentators on Dante's poem seem to have shown no surprise at it. Only in the fifteenth century, beginning with Antonio Manetti, did the physical plan of the universe in the *Commedia* come under separate scrutiny.[6] The problem was subsequently taken up by Cristoforo Landino, Alessandro Vellutello, and Pierfrancesco Giambullari; and even Galileo Galilei took Dante as an eyewitness authority for a scientific discourse on the spatial layout of Hell.[7] Interest in the poem's astronomical precision reached its peak toward the end of the nineteenth century, particularly with the work of the astronomer and dantologue Filippo Angelitti, who used modern methods of calculation in order to prove the scientific rigor of Dante's astronomical data.[8] The most useful guides in English to Dante's astronomy remain those of Edward Moore (1903) and Mary Acworth Orr (1913), neither of whom worries overmuch as to why the poet might have had such a penchant for this discipline.[9] As Chauncey Wood noted in his study of astronomy in Chaucer, to explicate this material from the technical point of view is not the same as probing its poetic function.[10]

Benedetto Croce's 1921 essay defining the poetry of Dante was in part a reaction against fastidious investigations of the moral and physical topography of the *Commedia*. Croce derided meticulous penal codes as well as diligent reckonings of distance and time traversed during the journey that naively treated the poem's astronomical observations as if they corresponded to real, not imaginary, events. He argued that to consider the *Commedia* a great medieval monolith of physics, ethics, and theology actually detracted from the unity of the work by attempting to mold it to structures lying outside its poetry. This analysis led to his notorious separation of the poetry of the *Commedia,* discernible to anyone with "eye" or "ear," from its elements of structure.[11] Such a distinction between *poesia* and *nonpoesia* gave comfort to subsequent indifference to the theological, allegorical, and scientific challenges of the poem, sanctioning the all-too-common temptation to skip over anything remotely erudite or technical. Croce approved Giambattista Vico's claim that the way to "enter into the spirit" of the poem was to disregard any moral, and above all, scientific implications.[12]

Indeed, even after the reader acquires the requisite technical apparatus, Dante's astral musings often remain hard knots, which, however beautiful, can seem indifferent to the human drama or moral lesson at hand. His grand meditations on the appearance or functioning of the celestial wheels seem to provide lovely but gratuitous backdrops. Even the apparently pedestrian purpose of those that indicate date and time is frequently frustrated by their ambiguity. Perhaps under the shadow of Croce's proscriptions, the sheer quantity of astronomical references in Dante's works has prompted apologies even from some of the manuals dedicated to explaining them. For example, Giovanni Buti and Renzo Bertagni, the painstaking authors of a *Commento astronomico alla Divina Commedia,* openly admit that "astronomy has nothing to do with poetry."[13] Only relatively recently has the poetic success of Dante's astronomical passages been the subject of critical attention. Ilvano Caliaro, in particular, has tried to appreciate the aesthetic merits, or "poetry," of Dante's astronomy.[14] Yet without essential links to their context, the astronomical passages may well deserve condemnation as excessive displays of erudition, however much they may appeal to some literary tastes.

Each of the chapters in this book is devoted, therefore, to establishing the connection between those moving lights, undisturbed and far away, and the local concern of the narrative or thematic moment to which they are attached. The task at hand is not to collect and explicate examples of Dante's use of astronomy, as the handbooks do so well, but rather to demonstrate how specific astronomical references illustrate, support, or dramatize the poetic, moral, theological, or philosophical problems at issue in the context in which they appear, and how they provide visual parallels to the strategy of representation currently at work.

The thesis of this book is that Dante's astronomy is quintessentially poetic, providing a meditation not only on the poem's meaning, but on its mode of expression.

The inherent affinities between astronomy and poetry may have been more apparent within a universe and a literary aesthetic both somewhat different from our own. Insofar as the celestial spheres produce music, as they move at separate intervals and in proportion to each other, they are governed by some of the same rules that apply to the composition of poetry, as Dante defines it both in his treatise on language, the *De vulgari eloquentia,* and in his treatise on philosophy, the *Convivio.*[15] The sweet sound of poetry is what is always lost in translation, which is why, Dante says, Homer was never translated and why the Psalms are bereft of music. It is clear, however, especially in a philosophical treatise dedicated to expounding their sense, that poems also consist in something that survives the shattering of their apparent harmony. Beneath the surface beauty of his own *canzone* is something Dante calls its "goodness."[16] It is the "truth hidden under the beautiful lie," and a good composer, as he explains in his first poetic anthology, the *Vita nuova,* should know how to "undress" his verses.[17] For medieval readers, the pleasure of the text was supposed to consist largely in the delicate removal of this outer veil, because things stated figurally delight and move the affections more than they would naked, as Augustine had occasion to put it.[18] The doctrine underneath such coverings was not thought to be harmful to poetic effect, but rather part of its essence, because poetry was "in the service of wisdom," meant to "express intellectual truth."[19] Dante says that the best kind of verse deserving the best language should also convey the best concepts arrived at through acquired knowledge (*scientia*) and innate genius (*ingenium*).[20] This definition of poetry is by no means universal. Francesco De Sanctis thought that it was Dante's great error to have confused poetry and science. According to the Romantic critic, greater virtue, truth, and perfection do not make for greater poetry, as Dante thought, because the abstraction of science is incompatible with the concreteness of images demanded by art.[21] Yet De Sanctis' notion of art as the "idea hidden in the image" can actually serve as a fair description of Dante's astronomical science, as well as his poetry, because stars are supposed to be a concrete representation of eternal ideas, the most accurate exemplum of the spiritual order that governs the world. Even if their music, like poetry in translation, is inaudible to us, their luminous choreography invites us to uncover their message and to follow their example. This moving spectacle is, moreover, the most sublime expression of love, the default subject of popular lyric in general, as well as the theme of that monument of vernacular poetry which is the *Commedia.*

Because it was a commonplace to speak of the universe as a book (*omnis mundi creature / quasi liber et pictura / nobis est*), Dante's insistent descriptions of it have been taken as part of a poetic rivalry with God.[22] If not trying to outdo the supreme artist, Dante's invocations to the heavens might at least be aiming to appropriate the stability and authority of the universal frame.[23] Yet in a world presumed ultimately to make sense, calling attention to the firmament as text has the concomitant effect of exposing the created universe to the risks of fiction and to the imperative of interpretation. In such a context, the student of natural philosophy must seek to understand not only how the whole mechanism functions, but also what good it is. The working analogy is not so much that the book we read is like the book of the cosmos, claiming similar perfection and truth, but that the world is very much like a poetic composition, needing to be read, and therein lies not a guarantee of divine integrity, but a whole lot of room for individual doubt, error, and difference of opinion. The specular notions of book as universe and the universe as book place demands on the readers of both. Dante's astronomy is therefore not simply aesthetic; it is also ethical, and the difficulty in understanding his use of it lies not so much in defects of our technical knowledge, but rather in a stubborn ambiguity that can be dissipated only by the assumption of different points of view.

One could start with the word *stelle,* the "stars" that Dante chose to bind together the three parts of his *Commedia.* Because the same word suggests something different each time, the triple repetition constitutes a kind of equivocal rhyme, in which the meaning of the same word shifts according to context. Distant stars glimpsed upon a narrow exit from Hell (*e quindi uscimmo a riveder le stelle*) are not the same as stars sighted as a proximate destination from the earth's highest mountain (*puro e disposto a salire alle stelle*), which differ in turn from stars reviewed from the perspective of a journey that has gone far far beyond them (*Amor che move il sole e le altre stelle*).[24] The *Commedia*'s disproportionate attention to that most legible part of the physical world can be said to function, in fact, along the lines of the poem's other addresses to the reader, demanding not assent but choice.[25] What Dante's stars dramatize is that understanding the natural world and the meaning behind it requires an essentially arbitrary or willful act of interpretation on the part of its interested observers. The glance at the heavens in the poem almost always presents a hermeneutic challenge, for which an acquaintance with the basic precepts of the science is but a prerequisite. Dante's descriptions of the stars tend to foreground the possibility of equivocation, the risks of reading and its ethical stakes.

Judson Boyce Allen has argued that in the Middle Ages most of what we would call "literature" or "poetry" came under the heading of ethics. What he terms the "ethical poetic of the later Middle Ages" involves the recognition, codified in Averroes' version of Aristotle's *Poetics,* that the purpose of writing fictional works is to praise or blame, and that the goal in reading them is not to know the truth, but to become good.[26] Certainly that was Dante's aim, according to the author of the Epistle to Cangrande, who stipulated that the poem belonged to the category of philosophy known as *morale negotium* or ethics.[27] As John Dagenais has remarked, medieval texts "engaged the reader . . . as in a series of ethical meditations and of personal ethical choices. They required the reader to take a stand about what he or she read."[28]

It is worth wondering to what extent the individual reader was free to make up her own mind, when texts (particularly privileged texts) might have been thought to have precise meaning or even hierarchical layers of different meanings. Guidelines for medieval readers attempting to make sense of sacred books encouraged as well as circumscribed some degree of hermeneutic liberty. In *On Christian Doctrine,* the most influential treatise on reading in the West, Augustine established the lesson of charity as a kind of limit within which any number of interpretative solutions might flourish. "Whoever finds a lesson there useful to the building of charity, even though he has not said what the author may be shown to have intended in that place, has not been deceived, nor is he lying in any way."[29] To put it another way, when presented with a choice, the reader is advised to opt for the good. Insofar as Dante's astronomy begs interpretation and not just learning, it is a dramatic and insistent argument for the affinities between living and reading, which are both ethical activities requiring the making of decisions.

In this light, the proposed resemblance of poem to cosmos also contains some correlatives to modern notions of how literature functions. It is a commonplace of reader-response criticism of the past decades that readers are invested with the burden of producing meaning out of a text. This obligation makes all the more unsettling Paul de Man's observation of "undecidability." According to de Man, the grammar and the rhetoric of any text can produce (at least) two contradictory meanings, between which it is impossible to choose by rational means.[30] Yet in his *Ethics of Reading,* J. Hillis Miller insisted that this "impossibility" of reading was also an "imperative" and, in terms reminiscent of scholastic debates about free will and divine foreknowledge, called the reader's response both "necessitated" and "free."[31] More recently still, the morality of reading has passed from the individual to the social and political sphere. Ross Chambers, for example, argues that reading has the power to produce change in what people desire, which is, "in the long run, the way to change without violence the way things are."[32]

Whatever the modern perspective, medieval reading surely entailed ethical responsibility, even if Augustine's hermeneutic limit of charity meant that the moral sense to be gotten out of a sacred text was overdetermined at the expense of its apparent literal meaning, or "grammar" (as de Man would call it). To say that texts are ethical does not prevent them from being ambiguous; it simply means that the unavoidable task of the reader is to "disambiguate," as Lee Patterson puts it. If all texts are ultimately undecidable (and therein, for Patterson, lies the medieval "anxiety of reading"), the task is insurmountable without some equivocation or arbitrary leap of judgment warranted not by the text but by the reader's own desire or faith.[33] As the individual chapters in this book show, Dante's often puzzling presentation of aspects of the cosmos, God's "other" book, demands or at least foregrounds the possibility of just such an interpretative leap.

Readers of the *Commedia* cannot be reassured too often that the poem's astronomy is really relatively simple, using broad concepts that would have been evident to any educated person, and in many instances respecting a popular view of the stars at the expense of scientific precision.[34] Although fond of rehearsing the names of stars and constellations, as were the classical poets, Dante rarely invokes arcane terminology and grossly simplifies the complex apparatus of medieval astronomical theory. Rather than impressing us with the minuteness of his calculation, the poet seems bent upon exposing the large strokes of the cosmic design, the quintessential simplicity of the celestial mechanism, product of the best of all possible minds, that lies behind whatever irregularities appear in the variegated surface of the sky.

Because this grand scheme is nonetheless necessarily foreign to modern readers, who are familiar with a cosmos of a different shape altogether, it is useful to sketch at least the outlines of the now "discarded image."[35] We must take for granted, for example, the earth's stability and the heavens' whirl. We must imagine surrounding us in every direction the hierarchy of nested planetary spheres moving independently of one another against the steady backdrop of the fixed stars. We must keep in mind the two motions of the seven wandering stars as they roll daily over our heads from east to west and slip backward, each at its own rate, through the band of constellations known as the Zodiac. We must be aware that this constellated path lies askew with respect to the poles of the universe (what we now account for by the earth's tilted axis) so that the sun, for example, wends its way south until midwinter and then spirals northward until the summer solstice.

More important, as readers of Dante's supposed cosmos we are asked to recall that there is no optimum vantage point on earth from which to witness this celestial chorus. From the perspective of the northern hemisphere the planets are always seen toward the south, whereas the reverse is true from the opposite side of the earth. Summer and winter and night and day come to different inhabitants of the globe at different times, without the slightest interruption or irregularity in the stars' preordained dance. The simple fact that our spherical abode circled by the sun experiences different hours of the day at different times, and the same hour at different times, underlies the veritable celebration of time-telling in the *Purgatorio*—Dante's spin on the most traditional function of astronomical periphrasis in poetry.

As for astrology, one need only concede its fundamental tenet: that heavenly bodies have some influence on bodies on the earth, as seen in the response of plants to the annual northern return of the sun, or measured in the constantly changing tides, or imagined in the apparent sympathy between the phases of the moon and the rhythms of women's physiology. The complex of celestial influences taken together is, in medieval cosmology, what lies behind the diversity of natural processes, what Dante called the "government of the world."[36] Astrology accounts for physics. The efficacy of heavenly revolutions stops short, therefore, of determining rational human actions, because the soul is above nature. This book does not investigate Dante's rich use of associations available in astrological lore, as Richard Kay has systematically done for the cantos of the *Paradiso* set in the planetary spheres themselves.[37] Whereas the stars may well be portents or determinants of earthly vicissitudes and bodily or temperamental passions, the significance of the planets and constellations Dante puts on display in his poem usually have more to do with their being models of beauty, order, and justice. Rather than determining human behavior, the stars picked out by the poet to adorn his text would seem to serve as standards for moral conduct, along the lines of Boethius' recollection of his studies in philosophy: "I studied nature's mysteries with you, when you mapped the courses of the stars for me with your geometer's rod, when you formed my moral standards and my whole view of life according to the norm of the heavenly order."[38]

As objects of scientific investigation, celestial bodies have the supreme advantage of being at once consistent and concrete, perfect and perceptible, "mutable but incorruptible," as Bonaventure says.[39] Their perpetual movement is unalterable, like divine things, but sensible, like things in the material world. This combination of permanence and visibility made Ptolemy oppose Aristotle in claiming that astronomy, not theology, was the surest of sciences. Physics cannot hope for reliable knowledge of material things that are always in flux, and theology deals with things that can never be seen or understood.[40] Astronomy is, moreover, the best introduction to divine science because it helps to "sharpen the eyes of the mind and intellect to consider those things whose movements most resemble the divine in their moderation, balance, and lack of excess." Finally, following Plato, Ptolemy goes so far as to claim that this science has an essential practical value in encouraging honest comportment and virtuous behavior.[41] "And therefore this science causes the person who patiently learns it to love this celestial beauty, it leads him to persevere in divine studies, it binds him to that which is similar to his own soul as regards its goodness of form, and it likens him to his creator."[42]

Part of the encyclopedic scope of the *Commedia* is its assumption of coherence between the way the cosmos is laid out and the way we are expected to behave in it. Far from the fatalistic determinism of judicial astrologers that threatens to eliminate free will, the astronomical passages of the *Commedia,* virtually without exception, confront the reader with a choice between interpretative options that are morally weighted. Familiar constellations do not dictate our actions, but rather serve, as Dante says, to "remind people of what they ought to do."[43] The literariness of the heavens suggests that the problem of reading is the problem of life: both require us to decide how we want to see it and to evaluate our own position in it.[44] For the poet of punishment and reward, the heavens' call is not just to science, or even to contemplation of eternal truths; it is an invitation to virtue:

> Chiamavi il cielo, e 'ntorno vi si gira,
>   mostrandovi le sue bellezze etterne,
>   e l'occhio vostro pur a terra mira. (*Purgatorio* 14.148–150)

[The heavens call to you and revolve about you, showing to you their eternal beauties; and your eye is still gazing upon the earth.]

The stars are real bodies that exert a physical influence on other bodies in the world below. Their beauty, however, affects the mind. The early medieval encyclopedist Isidore of Seville concluded his etymology of *astronomia* first by warning that some people, stricken by the beauty and brightness of the stars, with blinded minds have fallen into an astral perdition (*lapsus stellarum*), as they endeavor to foretell future events. By contrast, following Cassiodorus, he ends by saying that with astronomy the philosophers lead the seven liberal arts up to the stars, removing minds from obsession with earthly things and placing them in contemplation of things on high.[45]

In spite of Ptolemy's arguments for the unique certainty of his science, the ancient astronomers, when they looked at the stars, aimed to "save the appearances"—that is, to construct the simplest hypothesis that could still account for all the phenomena, with no claim to its actual correspondence to the real structure of the universe. The certainty of the visible motions is thus fraught with the uncertainty of their interpretation—the arbitrariness of theories required only to conform to appearances, or the insidiousness of those intended to foretell the uncertain future. These beautiful things are capable, as Isidore's summation admonishes, of leading minds either to perdition or to supernal contemplation and virtuous behavior. To turn the astronomers' guideline around, these are appearances that can save as well as damn. Dante's stars are portents of readability. The chapters that follow chart a navigation of those constellations, woven into the fabric of a fictional drama of salvation.

CHAPTER ONE

The Allure of the Stars
Vita nuova, Convivio, Commedia

One of the most important and original things about Dante's literary project is his recuperation of sensual, earthly love—a love incited by pleasure, particularly of the eyes—as salvific and educational. The beauty of poetry, like that of a woman, is similarly co-opted for the project of seeking truth. As Dante says of the first philosophical poem in the *Convivio,* even if people miss its allegorical meaning, they will meditate at least on its beauty (*ponete mente almen com'io son bella*). In general, we might say that just as Dante uses Beatrice, a real woman of supreme physical attractiveness (*sommo piacere*), as the vehicle for his salvation, so he employs vernacular poetry (whose traditional subject is erotic) as the vehicle of his message. Dante's continual recourse to astronomical imagery derives from an analogous notion: the stars, *quelle cose belle,* are perfect and unchanging yet also visible and, indeed, supremely beautiful. They have a physical influence on the body, but more important, they suggest to the mind an invisible and far superior reality. This is what Beatrice has in common with the astronomical heavens: both seduce the mind "beyond the widest-turning sphere."[1]

The celestial spheres, which will provide such a rich repertory of images in the *Commedia,* also play a prominent role in Dante's earlier works. One of the novelties of the so-called "sweet, new style" was to incorporate scientific learning into the conventions of love poetry. In the *Vita nuova,* philosophy enhances the lyric form in praise of a lady. In the *Convivio,* which explicitly supersedes the youthful *libello,* philosophy *is* the lady, into whose service erotic lyrics are now pressed. Then in the *Commedia,* the beloved Beatrice of the poet's adolescence will return triumphant, supplanting philosophy on the mental itinerary toward God. Both Beatrice and Lady Philosophy are explicitly linked with the mech-

12

anism of the heavens in ways that establish the structural and metaphorical importance of astronomy for the educational journey motivated by
love. The narrative of the *Vita nuova* is framed by references to the nine
moving heavens, with whom Beatrice is said to have a miraculous relationship. In the *Convivio,* the domain of Lady Philosophy is expressed
in an extended analogy between the sciences and the ten heavens. Finally, in the *Paradiso,* Beatrice will escort her lover up through the planetary spheres by reflecting them in her eyes. What astronomy might have
to do with love and learning, with erotic desire and the philosophical
quest, is the concern of this chapter.

In the *Vita nuova,* astronomical references mark pivotal moments in
the narration, beginning with the "nine times that the heaven of light
had returned almost to the same point" when Beatrice first appeared to
the poet.[2] Her death is presaged in a dream by cataclysmic occultations
such as those that accompanied the Crucifixion—darkened sun and dis-
colored stars that seem to weep.[3] Yet her actual death is passed over with
a cryptic silence, marked only by the seemingly cold comparison of
Arab, Syrian, and Christian calendars, in all of which the number nine
miraculously appears.[4]

The putative "friendship" between Beatrice and the number nine
(*amico di lei*) is constructed by the prose portion of the narrative, where
Dante rather creatively reckons the season of their meetings, the date of
her death, and the hour of some of his dreams. At their first encounter,
she is almost at the beginning of her ninth year and he is almost at the
end of his. Nine years pass before he sees her again, at the ninth hour of
the day, and dreams of her in the "first of the last nine hours of the night."
The lover's apocalyptic hallucination of her death is said to occur after
he has been sick nine days, and her actual demise is dated in multiples
of nine according to the various calendars. Most curious of all, in an epistolary poem in which the poet reports that he listed the sixty most beautiful women of the city, Beatrice's name appears, miraculously, not in
first place, but in ninth.[5] The lady's citation in a literary composition of
the poet's own making is, then, endowed with the same fatality as the
date and time of her manifestations in the world of sense experience and
the world of dreams. Moreover, human methods of reckoning time,
whose arbitrariness Dante's learned comparison of different calendars

puts in evidence, are given the same pregnant possibilities of signification as the visible heavens that mark time and influence corruptible
things.

Dante will go on to suggest that the reason so many "nines" crop up
in his preceding narrative has something to do with the number of the
astronomical spheres that rotate around the earth. "A reason this number was so great a friend of hers could be that since, according to Ptolemy
and according to the Christian truth, nine are the heavens that move,
and, according to accepted astronomical opinion, the said heavens op-
erate down here together according to their habit, this number was her
friend in order to let it be understood that at her generation all nine of
the mobile heavens were perfectly aligned."[6] This assertion is based on
the assumption of astrological influence on corporeal things in the physical world, including Beatrice's most perfect physique. Dante's allusion
to a perfect astral coordination is similar to his later statement that, as
astrologers can demonstrate, a perfect disposition of the heavens took
place at the moment of Christ's birth.[7] He goes on to say that Beatrice
is the number nine, at least metaphorically speaking (*questo numero fue
ella medesima; per similitudine dico*).[8]

Through the number nine, Beatrice is thus identified with the astronomical heavens that are both the natural instruments of physical generation and the sensible signs of providence. She is associated not with
the stable tenth heaven of the Empyrean beyond the largest turning
sphere, where she is said to reside after her death, but with the realm of
astronomy, for "nine are the heavens that move." Movement is what distinguishes the science of astronomy, the *scientia motuum,* from its sister
mathematical arts.[9] Hugh of St. Victor, for example, specifies that
"geometry is occupied with immobile magnitude, astronomy with mobile . . . for geometry is not concerned with movement but with space.
What astronomy considers, however, is the mobile—the courses of the
stars and the intervals of time and seasons. Thus, we shall say that without exception immobile magnitude is the subject of geometry, mobile
of astronomy, because, although both busy themselves with the same
thing, the one contemplates the static aspect of that thing, the other its
moving aspect."[10]

The science of astronomy is limited to measuring, quantifying, and predicting these motions. Yet the philosopher schooled in Aristotelian cosmology is also concerned with explaining *why* they move—with finding, in other words, the *principium motus*.[11] That explanation, as Dante well knew, had everything to do with love. Linking Beatrice with celestial motion is another way of expressing her identity as love, as he has Love declare in the *Vita nuova*: "And whoever wants to understand most subtly would call that Beatrice 'Love' for the great similarity that she has with me."[12]

All movement is caused by love. Aristotle's First Mover sets the cosmos in motion by being desired. Albert the Great explains, "The first immobile mover moves as it is desired and loved" (*sicut desideratum et amatum*).[13] For Aristotle, local motion—the circular displacement of quintessentially perfect bodies—is the primary motion, from which all others derive.[14] This concept is familiar to us from the last line of the *Paradiso: Amor che move il sole e le altre stelle.* God is the "love that governs heaven" (*amor che 'l ciel governi*), the celestial mechanism is "the wheel that You, by being desired, make eternal" (*la rota che tu sempiterni / desiderato*).[15] In his profession of faith in the sphere of the fixed stars, the pilgrim says that he believes in "one God, alone and eternal, who, unmoved, moves the whole heaven through love and desire" (*io credo in uno Dio / solo ed etterno, che tutto il ciel move, / non moto, con amore e con disio*).[16] This turning of the spheres, what Dante called *circular natura,* is what brings about all other "movements," which for Aristotle meant every kind of change in size and quality, as well as change in place.[17]

Love is the principle of movement tending toward a beloved end, as Thomas Aquinas put it: *principium motus tendentis in finem amatum.*[18] This principle makes the behavior of material things (earth's love of lowness, for example) analogous to human appetitive faculties.[19] This is what Virgil means in his lecture on love in the *Purgatorio* when he says that neither Creator nor creature was ever without love.[20] The complex of motions visible in the astronomical heavens must all be explained by love. The study of the stars, the *scientia motuum,* is therefore of innate erotic interest.

It is, at the same time, of intellectual interest, because Aristotle had reasoned that "the First Mover causes motion as something intelligible and something appetible, for these alone cause motion without being moved."[21] Averroes in his *gran commento* explains that "the first mover imparts motion the way desirable and pleasant things move us, because they seem good."[22] We terrestrial animals do not always desire the things that we know to be good, because we know through our intellect but are attracted to pleasant things through our senses. In contrast, more perfect creatures, who have no need of sensation, find desirable only those things that they know to be good. In fact, for them, there is no distinction between the pleasant and the comprehensible: *voluptuosum et intellectum est idem in eis.*[23] Dante's ideal of a love compatible with reason finds a tangible model in celestial motion, where the intelligible and the desirable perfectly coincide.[24] Averroes, like a good Peripatetic, believes that the celestial spheres are animated; they have souls, which enable them to desire their movers. For Dante, the celestial spheres are simple, perfect bodies that function as instruments for the angels who turn them. Aristotle's identification of the intelligible with the appetible is true, then, for Dante's angels, who love more the more they know.[25]

Because Aristotle believed that all moving things were moved by other things that moved, in order to eliminate an infinite regress of causes he had to posit a starting point for this causal chain. This was his unmoved mover, who moved the most perfect movable things simply by being known and desired. But because Aristotle was unable to reduce the complexity of observed astronomical variations to a single motion, he had to posit a series of unmoved movers, or intelligences, which his Arab and Christian commentators would later identify with the angels of their religion.[26] What the mover-intelligence loves and knows in the First Mover is then unfolded (*explicatur*) corporeally through the celestial wheels, and received materially by the generable and corruptible things of our lower world.[27] A purely intellectual desire is translated downward through corporeal movement. The celestial spheres, then, make love visible.

Guido Guinizelli perceived the erotic potentiality of this cosmology

in his "Al cor gentil," sometimes considered the manifesto poem of the
dolce stil nuovo:

> Splende 'n la intelligenzïa del cielo
> Deo Criator più che 'n nostr' occhi 'l sole:
> ella intende suo fattor oltra 'l cielo,
> e 'l ciel volgiando, a Lui obedir tole
> così dar dovria, al vero,
> la bella donna, poi ch 'n gli occhi splende
> del suo gentil, talento
> che mai di lei obedir non si disprende.[28]

[God the Creator shines in the intelligence of heaven more than the sun in
our eyes. She (the intelligence) understands her maker beyond the heaven,
and obeys him as she turns it. So should indeed the beautiful lady, shining in
the eyes of her gentle (lover), give him the desire never to cease obeying her.]

Guinizelli's comparison is not between the lady and an immaterial intelligence (although at the end he will try to excuse his audacious analo-
gies by her resemblance to an angel) but rather between the lady and
the ruler of the universe: God shines in the intelligence of a sphere (*in-
telligenzïa del cielo*), who understands its creator beyond the physical
universe (*intende suo fattor oltra 'l cielo*) and thereby turns its heaven in
obedience to Him.[29] In the same way, the beautiful lady shines in the
eyes of her lover (*'n gli occhi splende / del suo gentil*), a desire which never
tires of obeying her (*talento / che mai di lei obedir non si disprende*). In
this erotic cosmology, the noble heart, the subject of the poem, is
likened to an angel; the lady to God. Desire is the motive force of the
dynamic.

Guinizelli also compared his lady to a star because she awakened love
only in a gentle heart already naturally disposed to love, just as a star can
give special properties to a stone made precious by the purifying action
of the sun:

> Foco d'amore in gentil cor s'aprende
> come vertute in petra preziosa,
> che da la stella valor no i discende

anti che 'l sol la faccia gentil cosa;
poi che n'ha tratto fòre
per sua forza lo sol ciò che li è vile,
stella li dà valore:
così lo cor ch'è fatto da natura
asletto, pur, gentile,
donna, a guisa di stella, lo 'nnamora. (lines 11–20)

[The fire of love is kindled in a gentle heart as is virtue in a precious stone, for the power will not descend from the stars into the stone before the sun has prepared it as a noble thing. After the sun's energy has extracted all base properties from it, the sun gives it power. Thus the heart that nature has made elect, pure, and noble, the lady like a star causes to fall in love.]

In a polemic improvement on Guinizelli's concept in the sonnet that forms chapter 21 of the *Vita nuova*, as Kenelm Foster and Patrick Boyde point out, Beatrice is said to have an even more miraculous effect on those who see her, because she herself renders gentle and disposed to love everything she sees:[30]

Ne li occhi porta la mia donna Amore
per che si fa gentil ciò ch'ella mira.

[My lady carries Love in her eyes so that whatever she looks upon becomes noble.]

As he clarifies in the prose commentary, Dante's *gentilissima* is able to awaken love not just in the proverbial gentle heart, but also in hearts where love does not even lie dormant. In other words, she has the power to actualize love where it did not previously exist even potentially, through the miraculous operation of her eyes and mouth: "This lady reduces this potentiality to act according to the most noble place of her eyes; and in the third I say the same thing regarding the most noble place of her mouth . . . since she has the power to make noble everything she sees, and this is inasmuch as to say that she infuses the potentiality of Love where there was none."[31] Beatrice's effect on those who see her is more universal and more miraculous than Guinizelli's lady, who enamors "in the manner of a star" only those hearts that are already noble.

Beatrice is said to awaken love even in ungentle hearts not yet naturally inclined to love, thereby operating not like a star but more like the sun itself—or like the whole complex of moving spheres, which Dante calls "circular nature."

Beatrice is repeatedly called an angel, both in the *Vita nuova* (*Questa non è femmina, anzi è uno de li bellissimi angeli del cielo*) and in the *Convivio* (*un'angela che in cielo è coronata*).[32] In Dante's cosmology, angels turn the celestial spheres, which shape material things by reducing potency to act. Albert the Great, who was virtually alone in refusing to identify Aristotle's mover-intelligences with angels, compared the transformational effect of the celestial spheres to human artistry: "Just as our own active intellect, through our spirit, gives the form it wants to material things by means of our hands or instruments, in the same way the active intellect that moves the orbs and their stars, conveys form through these luminaries. Through their light, it translates form into matter, which it moves, thus drawing matter from potency to act."[33] Like a celestial intelligence, or angel, Beatrice brings forth the potential for love, and then reduces that potency to act by means of the superlative nobility of her eyes and by the sweet speech and miraculous smile of her mouth. She seems to be something come from heaven to earth for the purpose of displaying a miracle (*una cosa venuta / da cielo in terra a miracol mostrare*).[34] Beatrice's looks share with celestial phenomena not only their power to effect change in inferior beings, but also their unique capacity, as the only incorruptible things apparent to the senses, to make perfection visible.

Because of their equation of intellect and desire, the nine moving heavens prove to be an essential figure of comparison for both the philosophically inspired love story in the *Vita nuova* and the erotic account of philosophical learning in the *Convivio*. The first canzone of the *Convivio*, "Voi che 'ntendendo il terzo ciel movete" (You who move the third heaven by understanding), seems pointedly to supersede the first canzone of the *Vita nuova*, "Donne che avete intelletto d'amore" (Ladies who have intelligence of love). The local Florentine ladies who know something about love in the earlier book are plainly outclassed by the mover-intellects of the philosophical treatise, who are responsible for promoting love in the whole universe by an act of pure intelligence.[35]

The *Vita nuova* as a whole, one might say, is a book dedicated to understanding love; whereas the *Convivio* takes on the evangelical task of promoting the love of understanding.

In the allegorical exposition of "Voi che 'ntendendo," the heavens become sciences (Venus is rhetoric); the movers, authors (Boethius and Cicero); and the planets, their books (the *Consolation of Philosophy* and *On Friendship*).[36] With an elaborate allegorical scheme linking disciplines and heavens, the astronomical order becomes the template for the organization of knowledge. The metaphoric bond of love, study, and the sight of the stars is protracted through the work, most memorably when Dante recounts in the third book that at the time he composed "Amor che nella mente mi ragiona" his excessive reading had led to eye trouble, which made the stars look blurry like a letter bleeding into a damp page.[37] Astronomy is thus not just a part of the domain of philosophy; it is the constant metaphor both for the miraculous effect of the beloved on the lover and for philosophical activity as a whole.

In the *Vita nuova,* Beatrice was said to work her miraculous transformations through the phenomena of her eyes and mouth. In the *Convivio,* Philosophy is also said to have a body; she is "visibly miraculous," with a "sensible beauty" that men's eyes can experience daily.[38] Like all beautiful and noble ladies, she manifests through her body the goodness of her soul, most especially through the "balconies" of her eyes and mouth.[39] The eyes of Philosophy are her certain demonstrations of truth, which he calls sweet and ineffable manifestations, capable of stealing instantly the minds of men.[40] Her smile signifies her persuasions, in which the interior light of wisdom displays itself as under a veil.[41] Morality, Dante says, is the beauty of Philosophy, and wisdom is its body. Just as the beauty of a body results from the good arrangement of its parts, so the beauty of wisdom, the body of Philosophy, results from the proper alignment of moral virtues. This beauty gives wisdom a sensible "pleasure," or appearance.[42] Like Beatrice, who renders hearts gentle and thereby capable of love, so the miraculous effect of Philosophy's sensible beauty is one of moral progress, not only for those who are already disposed to love virtue and knowledge (*là dovunque è della sua potenza seminata per buona natura*), but even for those who live in miserable ignorance.[43] The paradigm remains the same: the lady's marvelous looks (*mirabile piacere*) produce a moral change, an ennobling effect, and finally a degree of beatitude in those who gaze upon her.

The already superlative Beatrice (*tanto gentile e tanto onesta pare*), is eclipsed in beauty, honesty, and nobility by her new rival, Philosophy, (*bellissima ed onestissima figlia del re del universo*). Beatrice, as we have seen, is associated with the nine heavens that move, the heavens that activate potentialities in the material world. Lady Philosophy, *donna di queste scienze,* governs all ten. In the *Convivio* the nine moving heavens are distinguished by their capacity to narrate the number, order, and hierarchies of angels, while the tenth immobile spiritual heaven of the Empyrean announces the immutable stability of God. Dante seems to maintain the limits of Beatrice's domain in the *Commedia,* where she returns to escort her charge from the surface of the earth and through all nine material heavens, but yields him to another guide on their entrance in the Empyrean.

As Joseph Anthony Mazzeo perceived, in the *Commedia* this "virtuous operation" of the lady's looks is returned to the source of the metaphor. In the fictional universe of the epic poem, the stars become the visible trace of immaterial reality; the stars are, as it were, the eyes of God.[44] In the *Paradiso,* the stars, carried by the celestial wheels, are what Beatrice now clearly reflects in her eyes. The effect of seeing these beautiful eyes is, as it was in the *Vita nuova,* transformative; it is the mechanism for the pilgrim's translation upward through each successive sphere (*da cielo in ciel*). This advancement brought about by the "lights" of the beloved (*le sue luci*) is, as it was in the two earlier works, described as a moral change:

> E come, per sentir più dilettanza
>   bene operando, l'uom di giorno in giorno
>   s'accorge che la sua virtute avanza,
> sì m'accors'io che 'l mio girare intorno
>   col cielo insieme avea cresciuto l'arco,
>   veggendo quel miracol più addorno. (*Paradiso* 18.58–63)

[And just as, by feeling greater pleasure in doing good, a man is aware that day by day his virtue advances, in the same way I became aware that my turning together with heaven had increased its arc, when I saw that miracle more adorned.]

The description of Beatrice as a "more adorned miracle" recalls the verse in "Voi che 'ntendendo" in which Philosophy was described as an adornment of miracles: *di sì alti miracoli adornezza*. In the prose commentary on that verse, Dante explained that it was because of this lady's marvelous adornments (*adornamenti de le maraviglie*) that men first fell in love with her, as the Philosopher seems to say in the beginning of the *Metaphysics,* because marvels become adorned when their causes are seen.[45]

In the passage in the *Metaphysics* to which Dante is alluding, among the primary marvels Aristotle says gave impetus to the beginnings of philosophy are celestial phenomena, such as the passions of the sun, moon, and stars: "Philosophy arose then, as it arises still, from wonder. At first men wondered about the more obvious problems that demanded explanation; gradually their inquiries spread farther afield, and they asked questions upon such larger topics as changes in the sun and moon and stars, and the origin of the world."[46] Albert the Great in his commentary on this passage enumerated among such marvels the phases of the moon and its eclipses, the way the sun's path is inclined obliquely to the plane of the equator, how it passes through a quarter of the Zodiac in unequal periods, why it becomes eclipsed, how it makes equal the times of generation and corruption of earthly things, the way some stars move independently from the constellations, each with its own proper motion with respect to the poles of the Zodiac combined with a daily rotation with respect to the poles of the world—and other such things that cause a person ignorant of the science of the stars to marvel.[47] The most striking marvelous adornments of the universe are celestial bodies; their beauty lies at the origin of all philosophical investigation.

Astronomy is at the threshold between secular and divine science, because the stars are the only incorruptible visible things. Essential mediators of divine wisdom, they alone are capable of displaying perfectly regular patterns to the eyes. The sight of the heavens is the culmination of the liberal arts and the origin of philosophical speculation. The study of the stars, while deficient as a goal in itself, is nonetheless a fundamental stage in the philosophical or spiritual quest for divine truths. In Dante's essential paradigm of love as knowledge, the visible splendors of the sky are equivalent to the sensual, corporeal delights of the beloved. Beatrice shares with the astronomical heavens miraculous adornments that cause men to advance in knowledge and virtue. While alive, and in her special condescension to meet Dante in the *Commedia,* her sensible beauty (*sommo piacere*) is of a comparable order of perfection.[48]

Just as the lover's meditation on the reflections of the celestial wheels in Beatrice's eyes becomes the vehicle for ascent, the astronomical references throughout the *Commedia* are an invitation to make the same journey. With each deliberate description of the stars and their movements, the reader is made to stand before the universe in one of its myriad manifestations, as the lover stands before the beloved. As the astronomical references become more and more abstract, separated from the direct observation of real celestial bodies, they elevate the mind by degrees from earthly to celestial things. Nowhere is this dematerialized and disembodied astronomy more readily apparent than in the poet's direct address to the reader in *Paradiso* 10, where he exhorts us to gaze fixedly upon the intersection of the two great movements of the universe:

> Leva dunque, lettore, a l'alte rote,
>   meco la vista, dritto a quella parte
>   dove l'un moto e l'altro si percuote;
> e lì comincia a vagheggiar ne l'arte
>   di quel maestro che dentro a sé l'ama. (*Paradiso* 10.7–11)

[Lift then your sight with me, reader, to the high wheels, straight to that place where one movement strikes the other; and there begin to look with longing on that art of that Master who loves it within Himself.]

This exordium of *Paradiso* 10 is an amorous invitation to the reader, currently staring down at Dante's own art, the verses on the page, to look up with longing on the divine art displayed by the celestial wheels. The early commentators, beginning with the poet's son, had no trouble recognizing this exhortation as a metaphor for contemplation, because, as Paul had implied, intellects can gaze upon the invisible things of God through the visible things that are made (Romans 1:20).[49] Dante envisions the reader as a student (*Or ti riman lettor, sovra 'l tuo banco*), for whom the visible order of celestial motion has been proposed as a mere taste (*ciò che si preliba*) of something he cannot yet understand.[50] By contemplating what rotates visibly in space (*per loco si gira*), where he cannot but savor something of God (*sanza gustar di lui*), the reader becomes like one of the lovers of philosophy described in the *Convivio,* none of whom fully enjoy their beloved, but who content their longing (*vaghezza*) by gazing upon her.[51]

The term *vaghezza* and its cognates are charged with astronomical as well as erotic connotations, since the planets, or wandering stars, are often called *stellae vagae.* Dante exploits these resonances elsewhere in his poem, referring to the northern constellation of Ursa Major (made up of fixed, not wandering, stars) as fond (*vaga*) of her daughter, Ursa Minor; and to the sun as making love (*vagheggia*) to Venus alternately from the brow and from the nape, as the smaller planet appears as a morning or evening star.[52] In canto 10, the action of longing (*vagheggiar*) is ascribed to the desirous attitude of the enamored neophyte as he begins to contemplate the rational order that lies behind the celestial pattern.

In the mind's itinerary toward God narrated in the *Commedia,* punctuated by astronomical descriptions, the look up at the stars (*riveder le stelle*) is the beginning of the journey toward them (*salire alle stelle*). The sight of them enables the "heart set on the love of learning and true wisdom," as Plato said, to adjust the "circuits in his head according to the harmonies and revolutions of the world."[53] For Dante, the goal is achieved when the desire and will of the individual is moved directly, and no longer through splendid intermediaries, by the love that moves the sun and the other stars:

> Ma già volgeva il mio disio e 'l *velle,*
>   sì come rota, ch'igualmente è mossa,
>   l'amor che move il sole e l'altre stelle. (*Paradiso* 33.143–145)

[But already my desire and will were being turned, like a wheel that is equally moved, by the love that moves the sun and the other stars.]

Unsurpassed in beauty, transformative in their influence, stars are the indispensable tools of poetic expression for someone who, like Dante, insists on describing intellectual and moral progress in terms of an amorous scenario.[54]

CHAPTER TWO

THE DATE OF THE JOURNEY

The first canto of each of the three canticles of the *Commedia* contains a description of time. At the start of the *Inferno,* when Dante's pilgrim emerges from the dark wood, we learn that the season was spring:

> Temp'era dal principio del mattino
> e 'l sol montava 'n sù con quelle stelle
> ch'eran con lui quando l'amor divino
> mosse di prima quelle cose belle. (*Inferno* 1.37–40)

[It was the beginning of the morning and the sun was climbing in the company of those stars that were with it when divine love first moved those beautiful things.]

Then, at the start of the *Purgatorio,* when he comes forth from the bowels of the earth onto the shores of the new mountain, there is a gorgeous description of the predawn hour, the trembling of the sea's surface suffused with the color of oriental sapphire:

> Lo bel pianeto che d'amar conforta
> faceva tutto rider l'orïente
> velando i Pesci ch'erano in sua scorta. (*Purgatorio* 1.19–21)

[The beautiful planet that comforts loving made the whole East smile, veiling the Fishes that were trailing her.]

Finally, at the start of the *Paradiso,* as the pilgrim prepares to lose contact with the earth altogether, Dante reminds us of the sun's position with respect to the great circles on the imagined armillary sphere of the universe:

> Surge ai mortali per diverse foci
> la lucerna del mondo; ma da quella

che quattro cerchi giugne con tre croci,
con miglior corso e con migliore stella
    esce congiunta, e la mondana cera
    piú a suo modo tempera e suggella. (*Paradiso* 1.37–42)

[The lamp of the world rises to mortals through different inlets; but it issues forth with better course and a better star from that one that joins four circles with three crosses, and it tempers and seals the worldly wax more to its fashion.]

This opening time-reference of the *Paradiso* restates in abstract geometrical terms the same seasonal moment described in the first canto of the *Inferno*. It is this kind of technical precision that sets Dante's temporal descriptions notoriously apart from those of his poetic predecessors.

Dante's time-references refer not just to the natural cycles of celestial objects, but to a particular, unrepeatable moment in linear time.[1] If "Seventy is the sum of our years," as the Psalm says, then the midpoint of the journey at which Dante found himself in a dark wood would refer to the year 1300, when he was thirty-five years old.[2] His presumed descent into Hell therefore occurred when he was roughly the same age as Christ was when he died on the cross, at the summit of his natural lifespan.[3] The significance in Dante's own life of the year 1300, the year he entered politics, is attested to by his early biographer Leonardo Bruni, who quotes from a letter of the poet's, now lost: "All my calamities and misfortunes had their reason and beginning from the inauspicious assemblies of my priorate, for which, even if unworthy in prudence, I was nonetheless worthy in faithfulness and age."[4] The year 1300 was also seen as a crucial turning point for the city of Florence itself. Giovanni Villani relates that in 1300, when he went down to Rome for the Jubilee and saw the great and ancient things of that city, then on the wane, he had the idea of writing a history of his native Florence, which was then on the rise.[5] And 1300 was the first Roman Jubilee year, a year of special indulgences granted to visitors to the holy city, proclaimed by Pope Boniface VIII apparently in response to an overwhelming popular expectation for a special grace in this *centesmo anno*, this centenary year, as both Boniface in the bull announcing the Jubilee and one of Dante's characters,

Cunizza, refer to it.[6] The significance of the year 1300 for the date of the journey is thus rich in personal, local, ecclesiastical, and popular associations, and it is therefore understandable that the findings of Filippo Angelitti, an astronomer and Dante enthusiast in the late nineteenth century, that this date is really 1301 should have been met with resistance, dismay, and even "terror."[7]

Dante's indications have long been known to be inconsistent with the real astronomical situation of 1300. Already in 1544, Pierfrancesco Giambullari had pointed out that the moon was full not on the night between Thursday and Good Friday 1300, as Dante implies, but some three days before.[8] The 1595 Crusca edition of the *Commedia* tabulates positions for all the planets, showing that Venus, which appears so splendidly before dawn on the first day in Purgatory, was actually an evening star during the presumed date of the journey.[9] Starting in 1897, Filippo Angelitti used the "certainty" of mathematical formulas to calculate the actual positions of the planets in Dante's lifetime, thereby exposing the date of 1300 as a collective misreading. Because the positions of the planets alluded to in the poem correspond much better to the spring of 1301, he argued that that must be the date of the journey.[10] All the other chronological indicators in the poem needed to be reinterpreted in light of these calculations, because the "undeniable and absolute certainty" of scientific truths, especially astronomical ones, was to be preferred over the more "malleable" data of history and politics.[11]

Edward Moore's response to Angelitti was to chalk up Dante's apparently erroneous astronomical details to the prerogative of poetic license, as "he was a poet first and an astronomer afterwards."[12] Mary Acworth Orr, author of a monograph on Dante and the early astronomers, remarked graciously that "no one will dispute a poet's right to arrange his skies as he thinks fit," but she offered as a possible escape the recent discovery of a widely disseminated almanac, in which the planetary positions for 1301 could easily have been interpolated for the year 1300.[13] The inconsistencies could thus be reduced to the status of a clerical error. Far from being the firmest facts for dating the narrative, as Angelitti proclaimed, the astronomical references have been seen as inescapably fictitious, either willfully or unintentionally. Patrick Boyde resolves the issue by calling the date of Dante's journey an "ideal Easter" and noting his propensity to "depart from the truths of physical science in order to obtain the higher truths of ethics and theology."[14]

Dante's astronomical signposts, seen as either chronological anchors or red herrings, inhabit that ambiguous space between verisimilitude and visionary narrative that is the source of time-worn polemics over the truth-value of his poem. The problem of the date of the journey, however antiquated and fastidious it might appear, leads inexorably back to the *Commedia*'s audacious claims to reality, which led Charles Singleton to quip that the "fiction is that the fiction is not a fiction."[15] The problem of the date of the narrated journey arises because of this fiction's peculiar claims to historicity. Or, to put it another way, it arises out of the conflicts among various authorities—historical, scientific, ecclesiastical, and poetic—that Dante's fictional cosmos pretends to reconcile. This is because all dates, and most especially the date of Easter with which Dante's narrative is connected, are always artful reconciliations of the apparently divergent threads of reality. All dates are, in effect, fictions; and this is one of the things Dante's art has to say about the world.

A date is a shorthand method of counting and dividing up the unrelenting revolutions of various celestial bodies around the earth. Whether we date from the Annunciation or Incarnation, the beginning of a regime, a new religion, or the holding of an Olympiad, the number assigned to a year reflects the revolutions of the moon or the sun or, from a post-Copernican point of view, the earth. Only since the invention of atomic clocks in the 1970s (controlled by caesium-oscillators, which are much more regular than any natural motion) has time-telling become totally detached from astronomical observation.[16] As we in the modern world are well aware, the present date is an extremely relative notion. What day it is depends upon where the sun is with respect to our horizon (or time zone, we would say). Our system of months is based on the apparent cycles of the moon, which are incommensurable with the cycles of the sun, on which the seasons depend. Traditionally, dates are based on, but are tragically incompatible with, various astronomical periods, so that our reckoning of time is always short or long of the mark. This "imperfect correspondence of conventions to phenomena" is, as a scholar of medieval astronomy and literature has written, "what astronomical sciences are all about."[17]

The errors, approximations, and conventions inherent in any system of time-reckoning always entail an uneasy compromise. In 1265 Roger Bacon defined the science of time as attempting to reconcile the observed motions of natural objects with human consensus or whim: "The science of time is the science of differentiating and enumerating times that arise from movements of external bodies and human laws. The authors call this *compotus,* after *computare,* because it teaches us how to compute time by means of its parts. This division and designation occurs in three ways; in the authors' *compoti* some things are designated by nature, some by authority, and some merely by custom and caprice."[18] A good example of "custom and caprice" (*usus et voluntas*) is the fact that on the Italian peninsula in Dante's time, what year it was depended on what city you were in, because cities differed as to whether the year of Our Lord was reckoned from the nativity (December 25) or from the circumcision (January 1) or, as was the case in Florence, from the Incarnation (March 25).

Dante clearly delighted in the spectrum of possible ways of computing time. At the beginning of the *Vita nuova,* he tells us how old he was when he first met Beatrice by counting the times the sun had returned roughly to the same point—a fairly conventional way of saying that he was nine years old. Yet Beatrice's own age at the same time is given, in more arcane language, as a fraction of the lengthiest (and what Dante will later call the most "divine") revolution in the universe: "She had been in this life for so long that in her time the starry heaven had moved toward the east one twelfth of one degree, so that almost at the beginning of her ninth year she appeared to me."[19] In Dante's time, the "nearly imperceptible" eastward rotation of the sphere of the fixed stars, estimated at one degree every hundred years, explained the phenomenon known as the precession of the equinoxes.[20] Beatrice's miraculous existence is thus quantified as a portion of the largest measure of all, the gradual shift of the starry heaven—a phenomenon for whose direct observance, as one of the most basic medieval textbooks noted, no mortal's lifespan is sufficiently long.[21]

In his commentary on "Voi che 'ntendendo" and in the first stanza of "Io son venuto," Dante will date other amorous encounters, appropriately, by Venus, the planet of love.[22] The inhabitants of Dante's Hell tend to tell time by the moon, those of Purgatory by the sun. In the *Par-*

adiso, Dante's ancestor Cacciaguida dates his own birthday (the labors of his mother) in relation to the incarnation of Christ (that day that "Ave" was pronounced) by the periods of Mars.[23] Perhaps most original of all is Beatrice's method of predicting the era of a general correction of human morals by means of the inconsistency then evident in the Roman calendar. She prophecies that "before January becomes all unwintered, due to the percent neglected down there (on earth), these supernal wheels will rain down the good fortune which is so eagerly awaited."[24] Because the Julian calendar year was twelve minutes too long (roughly the hundredth part of a day), the spring equinox kept coming earlier each year, having already slipped back from March 25 to March 13 in Dante's time. Without calendar reform, it would have continued to do so until (after some 6,500 years) it would occur sixty-five days early, before the beginning of January. It is fitting that Beatrice uses a human computistical error (the "neglected percent") to measure the outside temporal limits of human moral error.[25]

All calendars are imperfect, and yet they all endeavor to give an accurate account of the way things really are. No reader can forget that bizarre moment near the end of the *Vita nuova* when the fact of Beatrice's death is coldly dated according to three different calendars: "According to Arabic custom, her most noble soul departed in the first hour of the ninth day of the month; and according to Syrian custom, it departed in the ninth month of the year (because their first month is Tisirin, which for us is October); and according to our custom, her soul departed in that year of our indiction, that is in the year of Our Lord, in which the perfect number (that is, ten) had completed nine turns in that century in which she was placed in this world, and she was of the Christians' thirteenth century."[26] Dante's recourse to an array of different calendrical systems calls attention to the supremely arbitrary nature of human methods of reckoning time. At the same time, it suggests that such chronometers, like the celestial phenomena they imperfectly represent, are nonetheless the bearers of profound significance. The "true" time of Beatrice's death is to be ascertained from the chronological measure, or combination thereof, that best expresses the number nine, "her special friend." The arbitrariness of calendrical conventions does not diminish their significative value.

The significant use of dates is something Dante learned from historiographic, not poetic, models.[27] One of Dante's most privileged historical sources, Paulus Orosius' fifth-century *History Against the Pagans,* at times seems to reduce itself to a mere series of dates. Orosius' purpose, at the behest of Augustine, was to refute the pagan charge that the temporal coincidence of Rome's present calamities with the success of the Christian faith was a sign of the disastrous effects of the new state religion. Making no claim to completeness, Orosius is content to position the landmark episodes in Roman history in relation to the vicissitudes of other dynasties. His schematic chronological ordering of the events is meant in itself to elicit an alternative meaning from the jumble of the past. Dates are not just cognitive anchors; they are arguments.[28] The fact that apparently isolated things occurred, as he repeatedly points out, "in the same year," is an indication of their providential purpose. By juxtaposing different chronologies he discovers, for example, that Babylon's fall and Rome's liberation from the despotism of the Tarquin kings were simultaneous: "Indeed, it was as if the one fell and the other rose at the same instant: while Babylon endured foreign rule, Rome for the first time began to resent the arrogance of her own princes. Babylon, like a person awaiting death, bequeathed an inheritance, for which Rome, though still a minor, presented herself as heir; and as the rule of the East fell, the rule of the West arose."[29] In Orosius' vision of the succession of empires, the comparative duration of each of these dynasties is also taken as highly persuasive: "To these arguments, I now add the following proofs to make it clearer that God is the sole ruler of all the ages, kingdoms, and religions. The Carthaginian Empire, from its founding to her overthrow, lasted a little more than seven hundred years; the Macedonian, from Caranus to Perses, a little less than seven hundred. Both, however, came to an end in the number seven, by which all things are decided."[30] The most important chronological proof of God's well-laid plan for the limited duration of successive empires was the coincidence of the birth of Christ with the *pax romanum,* the interval of Rome's peaceful hegemony under Augustus: "Neither is there any doubt that it is clear to everyone from his own knowledge, faith, and investigation, that it was by the will of our Lord Jesus Christ that this City prospered, was protected, and brought to such heights of power, since to her, in preference to all others, He chose to belong when He came, thereby making it certain that He was entitled to be called a Roman citizen according to the declaration made in the Roman census list."[31]

Orosius strongly suggests that knowing the date of an event in relation to that of another can be a key to the meaning of history. Dante embraced the providential coincidence of Christ's birth with the year of the census, not as an apology for Christianity as was Orosius' intent, but as evidence of Rome's exalted role in salvation history. In contrast to Orosius' unrelenting critique of the Roman past, its iniquities, violence, and corruption, in the *Convivio* Dante calls Rome's illustrious citizens (from Brutus to Caesar) divine, and views her imperial hegemony as the "perfect disposition of the earth."[32] In keeping with this historical method, Dante draws attention to the simultaneity of events in Jewish and Roman history. Fudging Orosius' dates by about sixty years, Dante claims that David was born at exactly the same time that Aeneas came from Troy to Italy, in other words, that Rome and Mary's kingly ancestor were born together.[33] The phrase *David nacque e nacque Roma* ("David was born and so was Rome"), is not simply chronologically descriptive, it is evidence; it explains the sense of history.

Moreover, because dates are an abbreviation of certain planetary configurations, which were known to everyone to be the proximate cause of physical generation and decay, dates are in a tangible sense the causes of events. Where Orosius was content to call attention to the rare moment of political order into which Christ chose to be born, Dante logically assumes that this perfect disposition of the earth mirrored the perfect disposition of the planets on that occasion. Just as historians can assure us of the first phenomenon, so astrologers can demonstrate the second: "And, incidentally, it should be mentioned that, since the heavens began to turn, they had not been better disposed than at the time their Maker and Governor descended from on high—as astrologers can demonstrate with their art."[34] The specification of "since the heavens began to turn" implies the standard assumption that March 25 was the anniversary of the creation of the world, as well as of the Annunciation, and the now erroneous Roman date for the spring equinox. Dante suggests that all the planets, not just the sun, were in optimal alignment at Christ's incarnation, just as they were at the first moment of their existence. One might therefore recall with some measure of amazement Dante's similar claim in the *Vita nuova,* that the nine moving heavens were perfectly disposed at the time of Beatrice's conception.[35]

The date of Dante's journey in the *Commedia* is also portrayed as a propitious moment. The sun is close to the point of the spring equinox, rising, as the poet puts it in the *Paradiso,* with better course and better stars, to make a better imprint on the earth and living things.[36] In the first full-blown time-reference of the *Commedia,* he states moreover that the sun was in the company of those same stars that were with it at the creation, "when divine love first moved these beautiful things."[37] Yet it is precisely this opening claim that establishes the wholly fictional and conciliatory nature of Dante's skies.

As Hipparchus had noted long ago (ca. 150 B.C.), because the tropical year is slightly shorter than the sidereal year, the sun does not return at exactly the same season to exactly the same portion of the sky, but to progressively more western points along the path we call the Zodiac. The equinox occurs when the sun, moving along this path, intersects the celestial equator (an imaginary belt around the earth's middle), causing night and day to be of equal length all over the world. In Dante's time, this intersection could no longer be observed in the first point of the constellation Aries, as it had been by the ancients, or "under the Ram," as it endured in the popular imagination, but several degrees into Pisces, the preceding sign.[38]

Dante was not just aware of this phenomenon of precession of the equinoxes; he even used it to quantify Beatrice's existence at the beginning of the *Vita nuova.* It must have been perfectly evident especially to Dante, then, that if it is springtime at the start of his journey, there is no way the sun can appear with the same stars that accompanied it at the springtime of creation. Drifting back through the Zodiac at the rate of one degree in a hundred years, in the some 6,500 years since the beginning of the world, the equinox would now be sixty-five degrees (more than two full Zodiacal signs) away from where it started.[39]

The patently false astronomical description of spring at the start of the poem yokes the date of the journey to the anniversary of the creation at the expense of scientific precision, rendering the beginning of the world and the beginning of the journey astronomically identical. It is a fiction, but a fiction that has the combined authoritative weight of popular imagination and religious symbolism.[40] The stars and planets observed during Dante's narrated journey belong to a very special sort of fiction, whose truth-value is far greater than any observed or retrospectively calculated astronomical data. This fiction, if we may call it that, is the calendar date of Easter.

Christ's Passion, which took place during the Jewish Passover, was commonly thought to have occurred on the historical anniversary of creation. The fifth-century Gaudentius of Brescia, in his *Paschal Tract on the Exodus,* declared that "the Son of God, through whom all things were made, raised the fallen world by his resurrection on the same day and at the same time when he created it from nothing, in order that all things in heaven and on earth might be reformed by Christ."[41] Already in the first century, the Jewish philosopher Philo of Alexandria, whose interpretation of Passover would dominate the Christian understanding of Easter, viewed the spring equinox appointed to the Jewish feast as an artistic rendering of the world's beginning—"a likeness and portraiture of that first epoch in which the world was created." The month in which the feast of unleavened bread is celebrated is called the first month "because in a sense it is an image of the primal origin reproduced from it like the imprint from an archetypal seal."[42]

In some traditions, Christ was thought to have risen from the dead at the precise moment of the equinox. As one fourth-century writer put it, "Christ rose again at the spring equinox, at the full moon, on Sunday, which we recognize as corresponding to the beginning of the world as Genesis relates."[43] Yet because the hours of daylight begin to grow longer than the hours of the night only after the moment of the equinox, the Christian feast would eventually be excluded altogether from that date. Another early Christian text asserts: "During this equinoctial concurrence between the sun and the moon, the paschal festivity is not to be held, because as long as they are found in this position, the power of darkness has not yet been overcome."[44]

The concern with the time of the year and the time of the month in the paschal celebration stems from Moses' instructions to the people of Israel in the book of Exodus to commemorate the Passover "in the first month," the month that was called Nisan after the Babylonian captivity, "from the evening of the fourteenth day and until the evening of the twenty-first day," in other words, starting from the evening after the first full moon of the spring season.[45] According to Philo, the full moon served to give Passover twenty-four hours of continuous illumination: "The feast begins at the middle of the month, on the fifteenth day, when the moon is full, a day purposely chosen, because then there is no darkness, but everything is continuously lighted up as the sun shines from the morning to the evening, and the moon from the evening to the morning, and while the stars give place to each other, no shadow is cast upon their brightness."[46] Gregory of Nyssa shows his debt to this Jewish symbolism in his fourth-century Homily on Easter: "Before the rays of the setting sun totally disappear, the moon which illumines the world is seen at the other horizon. But before the moon has finished its night journey, the brightness of the day already mingles with its remaining light. Thus, darkness is completely excluded from that night of the full moon, because of the mutual succession of the sun and the moon, evening and morning."[47]

The Christian Passover is further complicated by its adherence not just to the time of the year and the time of the month, but to the day of the week. The fact that Christ was reported to have risen on a Sunday, the *dies Domini* and the first day of the week, further reinforced the symbolic reenactment of creation inherent in the paschal celebration. Thus, in addition to the criteria of the spring equinox and the full moon, the Church was also bound to observe the *triduum,* the three days of "the Lord's crucifixion, rest in the grave, and resurrection," as Friday, Saturday, and Sunday. Augustine remarks that "the Jews keep the Passover from the 14th to the 21st of the first month, on whatever day that week begins. But since at the Passover at which the Lord suffered, it was the case that the Jewish Sabbath came in between His death and His resurrection, our fathers have judged it right to add this specialty to their celebration of Easter."[48] Yet because of this insistence on Sunday, the full moon, like the spring equinox, was also eventually excluded from all Easters and reduced to a fiction. At the Council of Nicea in 325, where the problem of dating Easter was one of the main ecumenical disagreements at issue, the Dominical observance (that is, observing Easter on Sunday no matter what the age of the moon) finally overrode the Quar-

todecimans' rigid association of the feast with the fourteen-day-old
moon on whatever day of the week it happened to fall. The reaction
against the Quartodeciman heresy fomented a general hostility to the
idea of celebrating the Pascha at the same time as the Jews. In fact, in order to avoid any accidental coincidence of the two holidays, one of the
firm post-Nicene rules for dating Easter in the West was that it should
under no circumstances coincide with the full moon, even if it meant
postponing it to the following Sunday.[49] The real full moon, the essential factor in determining the date of the Jewish Passover, was thus per-
manently displaced from the celebration of the Christian Easter. In order to maintain in spirit the Mosaic provision, Nisan 14 was thus
extended virtually for seven days, that is, until Nisan 21. Any day within
this week could be regarded as the full moon and hence suitable for
Easter.[50] Gregory of Nyssa indeed declares that the phenomenon of un-
interrupted light at the full moon should be extended metaphorically to
the whole "week" of a person's life: "so that all the days of their lives they
may celebrate one bright and shadowless Passover."[51]

The full moon that Philo had said made Passover a feast of "one continuous day," becomes, in the observance of the Christian Passover, as it
were, anecdotal. Its nocturnal illumination is substituted by the artificial light of the paschal candle lit during the Easter vigil.[52] Indeed, the
fact that the Easter moon would now always be past full began to take
on its own symbolism. With moonlight viewed as a mark of the devil or
a kind of "bastard light," the moon's diminished state was sometimes
seen as indicative of Christ's victory.[53] Yet in the famous letter to Januarius explaining the reason for Easter's variable date, Augustine used
the astronomers' understanding of the lunar phases in order to embrace
the waning moon as a positive symbol. The increase and decrease in the
moon's light depends on its approach toward and retreat from the sun.
A waxing moon corresponds to its increasing distance from the sun,
whereas a waning moon is a sign of a rapprochement between the two
lights. In the same way, Augustine suggests, the soul of man, "receding
from the Sun of righteousness," acquires more light as regards the things
that are beneath it, but "becomes more and more darkened in its deeper
and nobler powers; but when the soul begins to return to that unchangeable wisdom," the more the light of the soul turns to the things

that are above, "and is thus withdrawn from the things of earth; so that it dies more and more to this world, and its light is hid with Christ in God."[54]

Augustine's letter in response to Januarius' question as to why it is that we do not celebrate Easter, like Christmas, every year on the same day, is concerned in part with refuting the claim that in its paschal observance the Church was worshipping the sun and the moon. He is thus in the odd position of justifying the cosmological components of the sacrament of Easter, while at the same denying that they have any special significative capability: "Whensoever illustrative symbols are borrowed, for the declaration of spiritual mysteries, from created things, not only from the heaven and its orbs, but also from meaner creatures, this is done to give to the doctrine of salvation an eloquence adapted to raise the affection of those who receive it from things seen, corporeal and temporal, to things unseen, spiritual and eternal."[55]

Augustine begins his response by clarifying that the difference between Christmas and Easter is that the first is merely commemorative, whereas Easter is also sacramental: "Therefore we observe Easter (*pascha*) in such a manner as not only to recall the facts of the death and resurrection of Christ to remembrance, but also to find a place for all the other things which, in connection with these events, give evidence as to the import of the sacrament." The essential significance of this sacrament, as can be seen from its proper etymology, is that of a radical change, or journey, what Augustine calls *transitus*. As he explains both in the letter to Januarius and in a commentary on the Gospel of John:

Pascha is not a Greek word, as some people think, but Hebrew. Yet in this noun there is a providential coincidence of the two languages. Since in Greek, *paschein* means "to suffer," it has been thought that pascha meant "passion." . . . But in the original language, that is in Hebrew, Pascha means *transitus* (passover). The people of God, indeed, celebrated Passover for the first time when, fleeing from Egypt, they passed over the Red Sea. . . . In the same way we are liberated from the slavery and ruin of Egypt and we make a most salubrious journey, from the devil to Christ, from this unstable world to the most stable kingdom. We pass over, indeed, to God who endures, in order that we not pass away with the passing world.[56]

A reformed astrologer, Augustine warns that celestial luminaries are not to be considered any more significant than any other visible creature, from whom God is pleased to borrow apt similitudes for the representation of divine mysteries. Yet he goes on to suggest that even the constellation in which the sun travels in this season might be part of God's eloquence: "If, however, the name of Ram (*Aries*) could be given to that portion of the heavenly bodies because of some correspondence between their form and the name, the word of God would not hesitate to borrow from anything of this kind an illustration of a holy mystery."[57] What the African father is no doubt alluding to, albeit delicately, is the association between the ram in the thicket, which Abraham was permitted to sacrifice in place of his son Isaac, and Christ as sacrificial victim, crucified in the evening while the paschal lambs were being slaughtered: "Who was that ram by the offering of which that sacrifice was completed with typical blood? For when Abraham saw him, he was caught by the horns in a thicket. What, then, did he represent but Jesus, who, before He was offered up, was crowned with thorns by the Jews?"[58]

Dante's troublesome stars must be seen against this rich background of paschal symbolism and chronometry. His opening fiction, of the sun in the company of those stars that were with it when divine love first moved those beautiful things, may not correspond perfectly with astronomical observation, but serves as a mimetic re-presentation of the world's creation, honoring the popular association of the Ram with spring, and even, perhaps, Augustine's subtle connection of the constellation with the ram sacrificed by Abraham. Similarly, Dante's moon, said to be of some help to him the night he passed in the dark wood, is full on Maundy Thursday, in agreement with the ecclesiastical calendar, if not with the astronomical facts. And it is waning, as he conspicuously points out, on the nights that follow, appearing as a slice or a bucket.[59]

One of Angelitti's principal objections to 1300 as the date of the journey is that in that year the "real" moon was full not on the Thursday before Easter, but on the preceding Tuesday.[60] He could not understand, he said, what the ecclesiastical calendar had to do with it. Siding with Angelitti, Orr joked that an "ecclesiastical" moon would have been of little use for planning a journey. But Orr misses the point because, for a journey such as this one, for the allegorical *transitus* that is the sense as well as the date of the *Commedia,* the paschal moon is of far greater use.

It is clear even from the foregoing brief review of the tradition that Nisan 14 or the real full moon had long ago been reduced by the Church fathers to a state of mind, extended for seven days (or indeed for the whole metaphorical week of a man's life) and replaced in the annual celebration by the artificial light of the paschal candle. In fact, whereas the Jews were limited to one Passover per year, early Christians sometimes gloated that they were able to celebrate it three or four times a week, or more often if they liked, that is, whenever they partook of the Eucharist.[61] More important still, whenever an individual soul emerges from the grip of sin and voluntarily turns toward God, it is, in a true sense, Easter: "Who is it that celebrates Pascha, if not those who pass from the death of their sins to the life of the just?"[62]

Finally, the liturgical blessing of the Easter candle on the Saturday night vigil itself contains a strong rationale for Dante's third astronomical "error"—the "cornerstone" of Angelitti's arguments rejecting the traditional date of the journey as 1300—that is, the description of Venus as a morning star in the Purgatorial predawn scene. Because the planet Venus (fortunately) does not figure into the computation of Easter, there would seem to be no "paschal Venus" to justify Dante's decision to contradict the facts. Although he may well have the poetic license to rearrange his heavens however he wishes, and the appearance of Lucifer is certainly an obligatory topos of dawn for Dante's poets, it is also demanded, in a sense, by the Easter liturgy.[63]

The prayer said during the benediction of the paschal candle during the night of the Easter vigil, known as the Exultet, looks forward explicitly to the coming morning, with these verses: "Let the morning star (*lucifer matutinus*) find the flames (of this candle), that morning star that knows no setting, that *lucifer* that shone serene on the human race once it re-emerged from Hell."[64] Lucifer is a name that can refer to Christ, as Rhabanus Maurus in the ninth century explained, "since he rose again at dawn, and overcame the cloud of our mortality with the brilliance of his light. For which it is right that it is said through John, *Stella splendida et matutina.* Since appearing alive after his death, he was made a morning star for us; since by his own example he gave us a foretaste of our own resurrection, which the light to follow indicates."[65] As another medieval commentator put it, the bright morning star of the Apocalypse signifies great love, *magna charitas,* announcing the day, that is, our future happiness, accomplished by Christ's resurrection in the morning.[66] In the representational eloquence of the *Commedia,* the light of Lucifer could hardly fail to shine serenely on Dante's pilgrim once he came forth from Hell on Easter morning, reenacting Christ's resurrection from the dead— whatever the position of Venus recorded in the astronomers' tables.

In one of his Easter vigil sermons, Augustine declares that although the annual feast would seem to repeat periodically what we know to have happened only once in truth, the historical fact and the commemoration of it are not to be opposed as truth and falsity, "as if the latter lied and the former spoke the truth."[67] In another context, he distinguishes between two kinds of falsehoods, "one which involves things that are not possible," such as a statement that seven plus three equals eleven, and another "which involves things that are possible but nevertheless do not exist," such as a statement that it rained on January 1, even though it did not.[68] As the example itself illustrates, dates can easily fall into the second category of falsehood, the realm of plausible untruths—what we would call fictions.

The date of Dante's journey entails a number of astronomical falsehoods. His vernal equinox, his full moon, and even his morning star are not "mere" fictions, but constitute an imitation of the larger fiction of Easter's sacramental commemoration. Every Easter date is in effect an approximate imitation, a *mimesis,* as the Greeks would call it, of the first Easter, in which the equinox, Sunday, and the full moon were made to coincide perfectly.[69] This analogy between literary representation and liturgical celebration may be less evident to us than it was to a fourth-century homileticist, who felt called upon to justify the late date of Easter one year in this way: "People are shocked that Easter comes with such irregularity, at least as regards its season. But it is not a shocking thing to the wise. You have seen how poetic compositions . . . have some short verses and some long. The ignorant are amazed that they are so clumsily arranged; but the artist, who knows the harmony of meters, sees the regularity of his art, even if his verses look irregular."[70]

Dante's journey takes place at Easter. The journey itself, at whatever historical time we decide it took place, *is* Easter, that is, a Pascha, or *transitus*, "from Hell to heaven, from death to life, from worse to better, from sin to sanctity, from vice to virtue, from old age to infancy."[71] Petrarch surely understood this when he pretended to have met Laura on Good Friday, April 6, 1327, when that date was actually a Monday—although people are less scandalized, it seems, to discover that Petrarch was disingenuous than to discover that Dante was.[72]

Dante had, indeed, a ferocious love of the truth, combined with great erudition and a special predilection for the science of the stars. His fiction, at once "realistic" and symbolic, tries to get at the truth of a concrete, individual, and historical experience. To superimpose a personal experience of conversion or transit onto the chronological template of the Easter celebration is to exemplify the truth of the paschal mystery itself and to make sense, perhaps, of one's own autobiography. The date of Dante's journey is not a choice between science and falsehood, nor simply a "fictionalization of the truth," which is trivially true of every literary text, but rather a reflection on the cosmos as fictional, as the artificial work of genius. This is what it means to read the cosmos like a book, and to take harvest from our reading.

CHAPTER THREE

THE HARVEST OF READING
Inferno 20, 24, 26

Celestial phenomena are almost totally muted in Dante's *Inferno,* because Hell affords no view of the sky. Yet Virgil, Dante's guide, continues to be aware of the movements of the planets and is able to track the passage of time with surprising accuracy from under the ground. This uncanny ability smacks of the supernatural or necromantic powers with which the Latin poet was often credited in the Middle Ages.[1] There is also, however, a much humbler sort of reader of the stars foregrounded in the *Inferno.* Deep in the regions of fraud, we find three farmers set in relation to the legible heavens and marked as symbolic alternatives to rash sailors, deluded soothsayers, and even a certain perplexed classical poet. Farming is comparable to reading in that it requires the interpretation of signs with the goal of bringing forth fruit. The agricultural use of astronomical knowledge might be said to lie behind Hugh of St. Victor's metaphor of one's studies as a "field of labor," which, "well cultivated by your plough, will bear you a manifold harvest."[2] The star-gazing farmers of Dante's Hell establish the status of the *Commedia*'s astronomy as fruitful reading material, even in the blind prison of the *Inferno,* where the sweet light no longer strikes our eyes.

Dante could find a literary model for useful scrutiny of the visible heavens in the *Georgics,* Virgil's poem about farming. The Roman agricultural song begins by announcing its intention to discuss "under what star to turn the earth." The "bright lights of the world" that "lead the year sliding through the sky" give "sure signs" to the experienced husbandman and to the competent navigator, as to when to plough and when to set sail.[3] Michael Putnam notes that in the *Georgics* the Zodiac "offers crucial stability" in the "sustained parallel between the farmer and the seafarer."[4] These two professions are traditionally linked through their shared reliance on fundamental astronomical learning. Indeed,

they provide examples of the honest uses of a discipline often suspect for its futility or fraud. Cassiodorus remarked that astronomy was not to be despised if from it we learn "the proper season for navigation, the time for ploughing, the date of the summer's heat and of the autumn's suspected rains."[5] Farmers and sailors are not only the original astronomers but also model readers of many other natural signs, upon which their lives depend.

Reading the stars is, of course, also the occupation of professional astrologers, with which Italy was well furnished in Dante's time. Despite some inconsistency in terminology, there was always an acknowledged distinction between the study of the stars' order and motion (*ratio stellarum*) and the science of the stars' significance (*significatio stellarum*). Dante uses the same word, *astrologia,* both for what we would call astronomy and for what is sometimes specified as "judicial" astrology, because it involves judging propitious or inauspicious occasions. There is no question that Dante, like most educated people of his time, believed that the stars influenced the earth, had various effects on the growth and decay of plant and animal life, and could even incline human temperaments one way or another.[6] Although human reason is, to be sure, above the stars, the success of much astrological prognostication can nevertheless be explained by the fact that most people simply follow their passions, as Thomas Aquinas pointed out.[7]

In the *Convivio,* Dante blithely asserts that our life and every living thing here below is caused by heaven, and that nature's seemingly infinite variety is due to the constantly changing disposition of the constellations. He even goes so far as to say that our minds, inasmuch as they are grounded in our bodies, are differently disposed depending on the circulation of heaven.[8] The length of a human life can be compared to an arc, because the shape describes the path from rising to setting of the planets that influence the whole of it.[9] Love is undoubtedly aroused by the revolutions of the heaven of Venus, as the ancients rightly inferred—although the pagans mistook the planet for a deity.[10] So, too, Dante repeatedly implies, his own literary and intellectual talent derived from his being born under the constellation of Gemini (*gloriose stelle, o lume pregno / di gran virtù*), probably to be identified with the personal star (*tua stella*) that Brunetto Latini implies might lead him to literary glory, and with the good star (*stella bona*) that might aid his careful genius, as the poet himself implies in the canto of Ulysses.[11]

Moreover, Dante seems to have believed that major events involving large numbers of people would be brought about and also presaged by particular planetary conjunctions. Just as the perfect disposition of the heavens mirrored the optimal terrestrial government at the time of Christ's birth, so untoward planetary configurations are associated with the degradation of present-day customs.[12] In "Poscia ch'Amor," the poet laments that grace and courtesy have swerved away from the world because of the state of the heavens (*Ancor che ciel con cielo in punto sia, / che leggiadria / disvia cotanto*), and in "Tre donne intorno al cor mi son venute" the virtues have been reduced to begging because men have encountered the rays of such a sky (*che sono a' raggi di cotal ciel giunti*).[13] In his epistolary invectives, Dante forecast upcoming revolutions in store for the contemporary world, which he claimed to know through "truth-telling signs" (*signis veridicis*), because "through the movement of heaven, the human intellect is able to understand its mover and His will."[14] Many of Dante's early commentators were convinced that the prophetic utterances scattered through the *Commedia,* such as the cryptic *veltro* and the *cinquecento diece e cinque,* referred to an imminent great conjunction of Saturn and Jupiter—*già stelle propinque.*[15] In the *Purgatorio,* Dante exhorts the heavens to hasten the arrival of the mysterious individual who will chase off the ancient she-wolf:

> O ciel, nel cui girar, par che si creda
> le condizion di qua giù trasmutarsi,
> quando verrà per cui questa disceda? (*Purgatorio* 20.13–15)

[O heaven, through whose turning it appears to be believed that conditions down here are transformed, when will come the one before whom she will flee?]

Beatrice, moreover, encourages us to expect prodigious political vicissitudes to "rain down" from the supernal wheels:

> raggeran sì questi cerchi superni,
> che la fortuna che tanto s'aspetta,

le poppe volgerà u' son le prore,
sì che la classe correrà diretta;
e vero frutto verrà dopo 'l fiore. (*Paradiso* 27.144 – 148)

[These supernal wheels will irradiate such that the fortune that is so long awaited will turn the sterns to where the prows are now, so that the fleet will run straight; and true fruit will follow upon the flower.]

Her mixed metaphor of ships and fruit-bearing flowers follows inevitably from the double role of the stars—as guides and as causes. Stars steer attentive sailors to port, but they also bring forth fruit from well-tended plants, as farmers well know.

THE FARMER AMONG THE SOOTHSAYERS

Belief in the impact of the stars on human affairs cannot therefore be the criterion on which such astrologers as Michael Scot and Guido Bonatti are condemned to the fourth subcategory of fraud.[16] Their punishment seems instead to be motivated by their concerted, and usually well-paid, efforts to avert or avoid the predicted effects of planetary motion. To put it in the most general terms, the soothsayers are in Hell not for trying to read nature's signs, but rather for reading them perversely—in much the same way, perhaps, that Francesca's eternal predicament is caused not so much by the book that she curses in canto 5, but rather by her uncircumspect use of it. The whole canto of the soothsayers has recently come to be seen as a meditation on correct and incorrect ways of reading, particularly as regards classical literature.[17] Indeed, Dante's epic predecessors contribute four of the seers of antiquity named in the *bolgia*—Tiresias from Ovid's *Metamorphoses,* Amphiaraus from Statius' *Thebaid,* Arruns from Lucan's *Pharsalia,* and Manto from Virgil's *Aeneid.* Virgil's text comes under particular scrutiny, as he is made to recant at length the account of Mantua's origins he gave in his epic. Dante's conspicuous re-reading of the *Aeneid* in the context of supernatural divination not only serves to contrast Virgil's *alta tragedìa* with his own *comedìa,* but also to differentiate the Italian poet's prophetic role from Virgil's vocation as *vates,* or prophet.[18]

Among the various pagan prophets and diviners of note, Dante has

Virgil point out the aged seer Arruns, who discerned terrifying omens of civil war at the start of Lucan's *Pharsalia*. In the Roman epic, Arruns' expertise is primarily in the Etruscan arts of extispicy (the inspection of animals' entrails), augury, and the interpretation of lightning bolts, leaving the "secrets of heaven" and astrological prediction to the learned Figulus:[19]

> So they decided to follow the ancient custom and summon
> Seers from Etruria: the eldest of these, named Arruns,
> Lived in the otherwise abandoned city of Luca.
> This was a man well schooled in interpretation of omens—
> Motions of thunderbolts and veins, still throbbing, of entrails,
> Also the warnings of birds by special flight or behavior.[20]

Whereas Lucan imagined Arruns holed up within the walls of a deserted Etruscan city, Dante depicts his dwelling as a cave in the mountains. The tight, dark ditch, or bolgia, around which the seer now trudges, with his head contorted over his rear end, contrasts with the magnificent panorama of sea and sky he once had from up there:

> Aronta è quel ch'al ventre li s'atterga,
>   che ne' monti di Luni, dove ronca
>   lo Carrarese che di sotto alberga,
> ebbe tra' bianchi marmi la spelonca
>   per sua dimora; onde a guardar le stelle
>   e'l mar non li era la veduta tronca. (*Inferno* 20.46–51)

[Arruns is that one who backs up against the other's belly, who in the hills of Luni, where the Carrarese who lives below does his weeding, had a cave for his lodging among the white marble, from where his view of stars and sea was never impeded.]

Omitting the examination of entrails, Dante prefers to characterize Arruns' divinatory activity as a prolonged gaze into the stars and over the sea. His topographical positioning of the seer's cave, high above the fields, introduces the figure of a peasant, totally alien to Lucan's text, that serves to make a marked moral contrast. The simple peasant of Carrara is intent on working the earth (*ronca*) with the hope of making it bring forth fruit, while the famous augur has his attention fixed on the signs and portents visible in the sky and over the horizon.

This incidental farmer inserted into the canto of the soothsayers actually has a common analogue in various indictments of astrology and other arts of divination. In his discussion of the value of astronomy as a liberal art, Cassiodorus differentiated its advantageous uses for navigation, ploughing, planting, and harvesting from its investigation in order to know one's fate, which is contrary to faith. He recommended that passages treating astrological prediction not only should not be read, but should be ignored as if they had never been written.[21] On the same theme, John of Salisbury invokes a farmer's proverb taken from Horace, saying that "he who puts his faith in dreams and augury will never be free of worry," but goes on to vouch for the "authenticity and value of those signs which have been conceded by divine ordinance for the guidance of man."[22] These are signs learned not through books but through experience, and are to the help of working men rather than philosophers: "Consequently farmer and sailors, as the result of certain familiar experiences, infer what ought to be done at any particular time by conjecturing the state of the weather to come from that which has preceded."[23]

A common source for both Cassiodorus and John of Salisbury would have been Augustine's belittling assessment of astronomy in the *De doctrina christiana,* where the profit of this science in the reading of Scripture is reduced to calculating the phases of the moon in order to celebrate the Lord's Passion: "Although the course of the moon, which is relevant to the celebration of the anniversary of the Passion of Our Lord, is known to many, there are only a few who know well the rising or setting or other movements of the rest of the stars without error. Knowledge of this kind in itself, although it is not allied with any superstition, is of very little use in the treatment of Divine Scriptures and even impedes it through fruitless study [*infructuosa intentione*]; and since it is associated with the most pernicious error of vain prediction it is more appropriate and virtuous to condemn it."[24] As we saw in the previous chapter, Augustine was at pains to defend the special coincidence of astronomical events in the commemoration of the Passion as significant parts of God's eloquence, while distancing himself from astrological prognostication in general. In his letter to Januarius, he explicitly differentiates the "fruitless study" of astronomy from its valuable use by husbandmen and navigators. "Who cannot perceive the difference," he asks, between the "useful observation of the heavenly bodies in connection with the weather, such as farmers or sailors make; or in order to mark the part of the world in which they are and the course which they should follow—and prying into the future?"[25] Dante's juxtaposition of Lucan's seer, Arruns, with the simple Carrarese peasant is therefore not wholly without precedent, as farmers are traditionally cited as fruitful readers of the stars in contrast with immoderate seekers of hidden things.

In terms that recall Hugh of St. Victor's agrarian metaphor cited at the beginning of this chapter (*o lector . . . tibi fructum referet*), Dante explicitly likens his reader's task in the canto of the soothsayers to the art of husbandry. He admonishes us to ponder for ourselves how, if God lets us "take harvest from our reading," he could have looked dry-eyed on such deformations of "our image":

> Se Dio ti lasci, lettor, *prender frutto*
> *di tua lezione,* or pensa per te stesso
> com' io potea tener lo viso asciutto,
> quando la nostra imagine di presso
> vidi sì torta, che 'l pianto de li occhi
> le natiche bagnava per lo fesso. (*Inferno* 20.19–24)

[If God lets you, reader, *take harvest from your reading,* now think for yourself how I could have kept my face dry when I saw up close our image so twisted that the tears of the eyes bathed the cheeks of the buttocks down the crack.] (emphasis added)

The punishment, or *contrapasso,* of the fourth bolgia consists in a severe form of infernal palsy that has turned the heads of the damned all the way around toward their backs. Looking ahead is now denied them because of their excessive desire to see into the future while alive:

> perché volse veder troppo davante
> di retro guarda e fa retroso calle. (*Inferno* 20.38–39)

[Because he wanted to see too far ahead, he looks behind and makes a backward path.]

The sinners rotate eternally around their circular ditch with a monstrous retrograde motion, "backing up" against the belly of their neighbor (*quel ch'al ventre li s'atterga*), the way the concave celestial spheres fit closely one inside the other, or, as one early commentator remarked, the way one student of divination follows closely on the books of his predecessor.[26] Virgil's emphatic scorn in canto 20 for Dante's tears of pity at seeing the weeping of the horribly deformed soothsaying sinners wash down their buttocks (*Qui vive la pietà quand' è ben morta* [*Inferno* 20.87–93]) has been taken as a marked rejection of the popular medieval legends that had transformed the Roman poet into an occultist wiseman and sorcerer.[27]

An extirpation of supernatural ambitions also seems to be the purpose of his long digression, taking up more than a third of the canto, on the origin of his native city, Mantua, in which he directly contradicts the account given in his own "high tragedy." In the *Aeneid*, Ocnus, "son of prophesying Manto," is said to have founded Mantua, giving it walls and his mother's name. As Teodolinda Barolini reminds us, he appears as a hero coming to the aid of Aeneas in the war against Turnus, with the image of Mincius, the river god and son of Lake Benacus, on the prows of his ships.[28] The essential difference between this version of Mantua's founding and its emendation in *Inferno* 20, aside from the elimination of the prophetess' son, is the removal of all taint of the supernatural. Mincio is no longer a river god but simply a river, not born of Lake Garda but formed by its overflow. The city's founders gather together along the swamp where Tiresias' daughter had "left her empty body" and called it Mantua "without further augury" (*senz' altra sorte*).

If the story of the city's founding by Manto's son in the *Aeneid* served to imbue Virgil's birthplace with a heritage of divination, prophecy, or *vaticinatio*, closely associated with his claim to poetic inspiration, as Robert Hollander has argued, here in Hell Dante has him give a purely naturalistic history of the place, consisting primarily of a description of the waterways that descend from Lago di Garda to form the Mantuan marsh. Indeed, the description of the lake they both call Benaco is perhaps derived from not from the heroic epic, but from the agricultural poem, the *Georgics*.[29] Virgil's digression in canto 20 is a lesson on geography as he traces the natural hydraulic system of northern *Italia bella* at the foot of the Alps, a system that feeds the lake from, Virgil thinks (*credo*), more than a thousand springs. He focuses on the variability of names as the water spills out from Lake Benaco to become the river that is called Mincio until it falls in with the Po. Mantua is located in a flat area not far down the river's course, where the water spreads out to form a marsh that smells bad in the summertime.[30]

The prolonged river-narrative is not only nonheroic; it borders on the unpleasant. It provides a demystified reading of the landscape in a canto that is all about reading. This becomes evident from Virgil's striking insistence on the truth of this account, which might otherwise seem unremarkable and even off the subject. With considerable irony, Dante has his teacher instruct him to reject a passage in the *Aeneid,* a poem that he knows by heart (*che la sai tutta quanta*), and which he may well have regarded as divinely inspired and even prophetic. Dante declares that all other stories of Mantua's founding (presumably also and especially the one in the *Aeneid*) will henceforth be for him reduced to "spent coals," not unlike the extinguished power of the sorceress in the revised story of Mantua's origins, who left of herself only her "empty body" by the swamp where the city subsequently rose.[31] Dante's obedience to Virgil in the canto thus requires his repudiation of Virgil's own poem; his faith in what he says here in the fourth bolgia of fraud inside Dante's *comedìa* requires that he treats what he said in the *alta tragedìa* as a "lie that defrauds the truth." In this literary competition, if that is what it is, the focus on water in the ancient poet's amended etiology of his city may also be particularly significant because of the association of rivers and their sources with literary originality and eloquence.[32] By reducing the *Aeneid*'s mythologized and mantic personifications to indifferent topographical facts (a lake, a river, a marsh), Virgil's lengthy correction of his own text might be seen as a kind of antidote to the sin punished in this bolgia, which involves "reading too much into" natural phenomena.

If the relevance of Virgil's dull geographical digression to the sin of divination is that Dante wants to distance the Roman poet from his medieval reputation as supernaturally inspired *vates*, it is all the more striking that this canto in particular should close with one of his intuitive, and to that extent mantic, readings of the stars:

> Ma vienne omai, ché già tiene il confine
>   d'ambedue gli emisferi e tocca l'onda
>   sotto Sibilia Caino e le spine;
> e già iernotte fu la luna tonda . . . (*Inferno* 20.124–127)

[But come now, because Cain with his thorns (the moon) already holds the border of both hemispheres and touches the waves beneath Seville—and just the other night was the moon full.]

This is a time-reference of the infernal sort; it uses the moon instead of the sun, and moreover implies sunrise by speaking of moonset. From the perspective of Jerusalem, which shares Hell's chronological standard, when the moon is full the sun rises just as the moon sets in the west (here indicated by Seville). In the days that follow, it sets steadily later in the morning. At this point in the journey the setting of the moon would indicate an hour of about half past seven in the morning.

Commentators have contrasted Virgil's popular, even superstitious anthropomorphization of the moon as Cain with Beatrice's scholastic disputation on the qualities of the same planet in *Paradiso* 2. Yet, because the temporal indication is accurate, according to the fictional astronomy of the journey Virgil speaks the truth about the stars even without seeing them, presumably by the light of reason alone. The moon itself, here said to have been of some help to Dante during the night of his solitary travails in the dark wood, might be associated with just the kind of limited, secular knowledge Virgil represents. Augustine linked the moon with knowledge, in contrast with the sun of wisdom in a reformulation of Psalm 18 (*Caeli enarrant gloriam Dei*): "Shine ye over all the earth; and let the day enlightened by the sun utter unto day a speech of wisdom; and night, enlightened by the moon, show unto night a word of knowledge. The moon and stars shine in the night, yet doth not the night obscure them; seeing they give that light unto it, in its degree."[33] In Purgatory, in fact, Virgil will conspicuously defer to the guiding authority of the sun itself, which at the start of the *Inferno* was defined as leading people aright by every path (*che mena diritto altrui per ogni calle* [*Inferno* 1.18]):

> 'O dolce lume a cui fidanza i' entro
>   per lo novo cammin, tu ne conduci'

dicea 'come condur si vuol quinc'entro.
Tu scaldi il mondo, tu sovr'esso luci:
    s'altra ragione in contrario non ponta,
    esser dien sempre li tuoi raggi duci . . . ' (*Purgatorio* 13.16–21)

["O sweet light, whom I trust as I enter on the new road, you guide us," he
said, "as one ought to be guided through this place. You warm the world and
give it light: if no other reason contradicts them, your rays should always be
guides."]

In conclusion, the canto of the soothsayers contrasts straightforward
and useful interpretations of visible phenomena with the sin of divination, or perverse reading of natural signs. Virgil is pivotal to this issue,
as poet (of nature and agriculture as well as of history and myth), as
renowned necromancer, and as sage. As always, Dante characterizes Virgil as an immensely knowledgeable but often limited reader. Just because
he avoids being condemned to this very bolgia for his popularly supposed occult powers does not mean that in his observation of the world
he did not make mistakes, or miss out on the big picture. This is the characterization of Virgil, and of the best of classical antiquity in general,
that will develop over the course of the *Commedia*. In the *Inferno,* it is
the unassisted gaze of the pagan mind that seems to be the target of its
few astronomical references, to each of which is attached the figure of a
farmer.

THE FARMER IN WINTER

As in the canto of the soothsayers, Virgil himself also seems to be the
specific target of the long rustic comparison at the start of *Inferno* 24.
The astronomical opening of this simile, which Robert Hollander has
gone so far as to dub Dante's Georgic, takes inspiration from Virgil's advice to shepherds to feed their goats with leafy plants in midwinter, "at
the time when the cold Waterbearer (Aquarius) is now setting, sprin-
kling the departing year" (*iam cadit extremoque inrorat Acquarius
anno*).[34] Whereas for the Romans the sign of Aquarius marked the end
of the agricultural calendar (*extremo . . . anno*), as Hollander points out,
Dante turns it around to presage the approaching end of winter, a time

when the sun "tempers its locks," in the early part of the liturgical year (*giovanetto anno*):

> In quella parte del giovanetto anno
>   che 'l sole i crin sotto l'Aquario tempra
>   e già le notti al mezzo dì sen vanno . . . (*Inferno* 24.1–3)

[In that part of the young year when the sun tempers its locks beneath Aquarius and nights head toward the south . . .]

Dante calls attention, moreover, to the lengthening of the days after the winter solstice as the nights "head south" and the sun wends its way back toward the north.[35]

The opening lines of Dante's simile cast the near dead of winter in hopeful language, altering not the season, but the way it is viewed. The rest of the simile that the astronomical periphrasis introduces goes on to stage a parallel reassessment of the hibernal landscape. In early February a shepherd who has no stock of hay is distressed to see the ground all white, as if it were covered with snow:

> quando la brina in su la terra assempra
>   l'imagine di sua sorella bianca,
>   ma poco dura a la sua penna tempra
> lo villanello a cui la roba manca,
>   si leva, e guarda, e vede la campagna
>   biancheggiar tutta; ond'ei si batte l'anca,
> ritorna in casa, e qua e là si lagna,
>   come 'l tapin che non sa che si faccia. (*Inferno* 24.4–11)

[When hoarfrost copies on the earth the image of his white sister—but not for long does his pen stay sharp—the farmer who is short of provisions rises and looks and sees the countryside all whitened; at which he slaps his thigh, turns back into the house, and here and there complains like some poor wretch who knows not what to do.]

When the hoarfrost (which was only impersonating its white sister) soon melts and the world alters its appearance, the simile's agrarian protagonist then gathers back his hope and, taking up his staff, drives his sheep out to pasture:

poi riede, e la speranza ringavagna,
veggendo 'l mondo aver cangiata faccia
in poco d'ora, e prende suo vincastro
e fuor le pecorelle a pascer caccia. (*Inferno* 24.12–15)

[. . . and then goes out again and gathers up new hope on seeing that the world has changed his face in so short a time, and he takes his staff and drives out his flock to pasture.]

The passage narrates an extended parable of misreading, or double take, beginning with the winter constellation from Virgil's *Georgics* now being read as a sign of imminent spring. The peasant misinterprets not only the pattern in the sky, but the pattern on the ground—hoarfrost's counterfeit of snow—and then completely alters his mood, regarnering hope, when he sees that the world has "changed its face." Even the simile's use of equivocal rhyme, words that look the same but mean different things (*tempra, tempra; faccia, faccia*), is a formal reflection of the deceptive appearances central to the region of fraud.[36]

The explicit tenor of the simile is Dante's initial distress at seeing the perturbation of his master upon discovering in the last canto the duplicity of devils (*elli è bugiardo e padre di menzogna*). As Margherita Frankel has noted, the revelation that devils do not always mean what they say comes on the heels of Virgil's stunned amazement at the body of Caiaphas crucified on the ground. Caiaphas' verdict sealing Christ's fate, to let one man suffer for the sake of the people (*porre un uomo per lo popolo a' martiri*), is expressed in a clear echo of Virgil's own *Aeneid*, where Jupiter concedes to let just one Trojan die in place of many: *unum pro multis dabitur caput*. This shocking twist to what must have seemed in the context of the Roman epic a positive trade-off, followed by the apparently astonishing discovery that the devil is "the father of lies," upsets Virgil to the point that he stalks off.[37] This is the perturbation that occasions the agrarian simile of canto 24. It is a crisis provoked not just by fraud, but by Virgil's apparent inexperience with black cherubim and tricksters of the sort he encountered in the circle of barratry, and by his amazement that even his own words might have been deceptive, or at least subject to a radically different interpretation.

Dante's shepherd in the simile may not be a good reader of Virgil's

Georgics, because he failed to stock up on leafy plants in winter and has a curious way of interpreting the constellations (why shouldn't a farmer expect snow in early February?). Nonetheless, he does not give up hope. Virgil, in contrast, as a virtuous pagan assigned to Limbo, is defined as someone who lives "without hope" (*che sanza speme vivemo in disio*).[38] Because Dante's pastoral image, unlike Virgil's in the *Georgics,* is inevitably charged with the spiritual resonances of Christ's words to Peter ("feed my sheep") as well as with Abraham's unwavering trust that "the Lord will provide," it constitutes an implicit criticism of Virgil's pastoral abilities, following on his rather embarrassing incompetence in dealing with some mischievous devils.[39] The farmer is better, the simile would seem to imply, than the poet of farming; not because he is better equipped or skilled or more experienced, but because he reads the signs of nature hopefully rather than astutely. It is a critique not of Virgil's know-how but of his attitude, which colors all he sees.

THE FARMER IN SUMMER

In the canto of the soothsayers, the sinister clairvoyance of an Etruscan magus is contrasted with the simple diligence of the Carrarese who works the land below. In canto 24, it is Virgil, the great sage, who is implicitly held up for comparison with a mere peasant. A third such contrast is apparent in canto 26, in the simile of the *villano* that introduces Dante's first glimpse of Ulysses.[40] In this passage, the two famous Greek heroes of the Trojan war now burning in the gullet of the eighth ditch are reduced to the status of bugs, or fireflies, seen from a great height by a farmer resting on a hillside:

> Quante il villan ch'al poggio si riposa,
>   nel tempo che colui che 'l mondo schiara
>   la faccia sua a noi tien meno ascosa,
> come la mosca cede a la zanzara,
>   vede lucciole giù per la vallea,
>   forse colà dov' e' vendemmia e ara:
> di tante fiamme tutta risplendea
>   l'ottava bolgia, sì com'io m'accorsi
>   tosto che fui là've 'l fondo parea. (*Inferno* 26.25–33)

[Just as the farmer, resting on the hillside in the season when he who lights the world hides his face from us the least, when the fly yields to the mosquito, sees fireflies down in the valley where he perhaps harvests and ploughs—with as many flames was the eighth ditch resplendent, as I realized as soon as I was where I could see the bottom.]

In this simile, the farmer's complete repose on a summer evening as he rests from his labors (the spring ploughing and the autumn harvest) could not be further removed from the damned sailor's impetuous rush across the ocean (*de' remi facemmo ali al folle volo*).[41] As commentators, beginning with the poet's son Pietro, have noticed, Ulysses' mad dash to the other side of the globe, resulting in the infernal torment of a tongue of fire, recalls the comparison, in the Epistle of James, of unrestrained speech to unguided ships and horses:

If anyone does not offend in word, he is a perfect man, able also to lead round by a bridle the whole body. For if we put bits into horses' mouths that they may obey us, we control their whole body also. Behold, even the ships, great as they are, and driven by boisterous winds, are steered by a small rudder wherever the touch of the steersman pleases. So the tongue is also a little member, but it boasts mightily. Behold, how small a fire—how great a forest it kindles! And the tongue is a fire, the very world of iniquity. The tongue is placed among our members, defiling the whole body and setting on fire the course of our life, being itself set on fire from hell.[42]

Because Dante emphatically associates the virtue of hope with James's epistle when he meets the apostle in Paradise, its presence in *Inferno* 26 underscores Ulysses' presumption as a failure of hope.[43] The only portion of this New Testament text that was conventionally interpreted as indicative of hope is the image of the farmer's patience in the epistle's final exhortation, which Dante had translated in his *Convivio:* "Behold the farmer who awaits the precious fruit of the earth, patiently holding out until it has received both the early and the late" (*Onde dice santo Iacopo apostolo nella sua Pistola: "Ecco lo agricola aspetta lo prezioso frutto de la terra pazientemente sostenendo infino che riceva lo temporaneo e lo serotino"*).[44] Hence Dante's *villano,* awaiting the fruit of his land in the summertime between the early (spring ploughing) and the late (fall har-

vest) labors, is surely a figure of hope analogous to James's *agricola*. This
agrarian figure who introduces the all-important encounter with
Ulysses, tragic alter-ego of the poet, exemplifies that virtue of certain expectation (*attender certo*), as Dante defines hope to Saint James in *Paradiso* 25, that the presumptuous Ulysses totally lacks.[45]

The two figures are also opposed in the very different ways they are
depicted as viewing the stars. While the farmer's existence is regulated
by the seasons of the year, determined by the movements of the sun—
the summer heat, the autumn harvest, the spring ploughing—the Greek
sailor, despite his intention to circle the globe in pursuit of the sun (*dietro al sol*), marks time by the lunar phases:

> Cinque volte racceso e tante casso
>   lo lume era di sotto dalla luna
>   poi ch'entrati eravam nell'alto passo. . . . (*Inferno* 26.130–132)

[Five times was kindled and five times snuffed the light under the moon since
we had entered on the deep way . . .]

Moreover, Ulysses makes the fatal navigational mistake of abandoning
his pole star by crossing over into the southern hemisphere from which
it can no longer be seen:

> Tutte le stelle già dell'altro polo
>   vedea la notte e il nostro tanto basso
>   che non surgea fuor del marin suolo. (*Inferno* 26.127–129)

[The night already saw all the stars of the other pole, while our own was so
low that it never rose above the surface of the sea.]

The symbolic tenor of Ulysses' lost polar star is articulated in the ex-
change between a ship's governor and a failed leader in book 8 of Lucan's
Pharsalia. In his nocturnal flight from the scene of the lost battle, Pompey distractedly consults the boat's helmsman on the navigational use of
the stars. The pilot explains: "We do not follow those sliding stars that
course over the starry heaven and that, because of their continual motion, deceive poor sailors: but rather that pole that never sets and never
submerges itself in the waves, illumined by the two Bears, is the one that

guides our prows."[46] The sailor's nighttime disquisition on the stars is clearly less about astronomy or navigation than about governance. Unlike the sure pilot following his single pole, Pompey is wavering and indecisive, hovering, as in Lucan's description of the sun on that same evening, between two hemispheres "neither entirely in the region from whom he was hiding his light, nor in one to which he was showing it."[47] Dante's farmer, by contrast, is troubled by no such uncertain celestial displays, as he enjoys the sun at its maximum, even at dusk, in the season when it least "hides its face."

Dante's relaxed agrarian spectator may also owe something to the three humble witnesses to Icarus' ill-advised flight across the sky described in Ovid's *Metamorphoses:* "Some fisher, perhaps, plying his quivering rod, some shepherd leaning on his staff, or a peasant bent over his plough handle caught sight of them as they flew past and took stock still in astonishment, believing that these creatures who could fly through the air must be gods."[48] Like Ovid's fisherman, shepherd, or farmer, Dante's *villano* is an implicit observer, from a safe distance, of Ulysses' tragic fate, which, like Icarus' mad flight, also ends in flames. Ovid's observers look up in amazed admiration at creatures that resemble gods, whereas what Dante compares to the farmer's fireflies surveyed way down in the valley are in fact damned souls who in life were very close to gods. Explicitly compared with the eager pilgrim (*sì com'io*), the farmer's posture of illumined patience in fact contrasts with Dante's precipitous desire to see Ulysses inside the flame, and serves instead as a warning to the poet as he writes (to restrain the impetus of his genius so that it will not run where virtue does not guide it), as well as to the inevitably curious reader as he reads.[49]

All three of Dante's farmers encountered in the region of fraud in some way constitute a critique of the classical world. Yet the choice of an agrarian figure to counter the strained vision of the diviners, the shortcomings of Virgil as pastor, and the insane flight of Ulysses to the other side of the world might well derive inspiration from Virgil's own poem on agriculture, which explicitly defines the restful life of the farmer as ignorant of fraud (*at secura quies et nescia fallere vita*).[50] In the *Georgics,* commonly cited as an authority in such astronomical handbooks as Sacrobosco's *Sphere* and Macrobius' commentary on Cicero's *Dream of Scipio,* the farmer is exalted to the status of someone whose knowledge of natural phenomena gives him power over nature. The ostensibly humble subject of the poem thereby becomes cognate with the poet's own aspirations, as Philip Hardie has observed. When, at the end of the second book, the poet declares blessed those who have "been able to win knowledge of the causes of things" and asks the "sweet Muses" to show him "heaven's pathways, the stars, the sun's many lapses, the moon's many labours," this request for information about celestial movement can also be read as a prayer to know not just the path *of* heaven, but the path *to* it.[51] All quests for knowledge translate into journeys; and some, like Ulysses', fail.

Like the canto of Ulysses, the first book of Virgil's agricultural poem also leads from a peaceful portrait of rural life into a violently contrasting image of headlong, precipitous disaster. From a discussion of "sure signs" given by the sun and stars for farming and navigation, the poet shifts to a recollection of the terrible portents announcing disastrous political events in recent Roman history. At Caesar's assassination, witnesses observed an eclipse of the sun, barking dogs, howling wolves, ominous birds, eruptions of volcanoes, bloated rivers, horrifying entrails, freakish lightning, and comets. Virgil magnificently juxtaposes the peace of rural life with the rage of these past wars by imagining a future time "when in those lands, as the farmer toils at the soil with crooked plough, he shall find javelins eaten up with rusty mould, or with his heavy hoes shall strike on empty helms, and marvel at the giant bones in the upturned graves."[52] An appeal for an end to bloodshed concludes the book, depicting contemporary strife as a chariot run wild, not unlike Dante's image of Phaeton (*quando Fetòn abbandonò li freni*) or, for that matter, of Ulysses (*de' remi facemmo ali al folle volo*): "Impious Mars rages over the entire globe, just as when chariots burst from the starting gates. They pick up speed and, uselessly holding the reins, the driver is carried along by his horses; the chariot does not respond to his commands."[53]

In Dante's *Inferno* astronomical knowledge is presented under the humblest possible aspect, exalting the farmer as a fruitful reader of the stars, of which Hell's damned have totally lost sight. A correct understanding of nature's signs, most vividly legible in the pattern of the heavens, was for Dante, as for Virgil, a powerful symbol of poetic aims. Virgil in his *Georgics* exhorts the Muses to give him the kind of knowledge of nature possessed by happy husbandmen, ignorant of their blessings but far from the clash of arms, bearing the last trace of Justice since she altogether left the earth.[54] But it is only as Dante's guide that he emerges temporarily from his permanent prison to see the stars again. In the *Inferno,* Dante's peasants, tied to the land but with a view of the heavens, provide a counterpoint to those whose excessive curiosity leads them to interrogate the stars and navigate uncharted seas, rather than to wait and hope. Ironically enough, the poet whose praise of rural life would have been a fundamental model for Dante's agrarian figures, is himself cut off from the celestial panorama and, from a Christian point of view, from the farmer's essential virtue: hope. The journey to the stars narrated in the *Commedia* is accomplished not by straining toward them, but by descending in the opposite direction, into the very earth.

CHAPTER FOUR

ORIENTATION
Purgatorio 9

Purgatory is another place, an inhabited world parallel to but different from and better than our own. Like all utopias, it is "an invitation to perceive the distance between things as they are and things as they should be."[1] In Dante's invented geography, this distance is quantifiable spatially and temporally, as he calculates nine hours' difference between Italy and the isolated mountain in the unexplored seas of the southern hemisphere. The penitentiary island also gives a fourth cardinal point to the globe, as it lies opposite Jerusalem and ninety degrees from the delta of the Ganges on one side and an equal quadrant from the straits of Gibraltar on the other. The sun, passing over one of these sites every six hours, thus never sets on the attention of the reader. Augustine had occasion to remark that "at the time when night is with us, the sun is illuminating with its presence those parts of the world through which it returns from the place of its setting to that of its rising. Hence it is clear that for the whole twenty-four hours of the sun's circuit there is always day in one place and night in another."[2] Dante gives these places names. Because they are on opposite sides of a common horizon, when it is sunset in Eden, the place of original sin, it is dawn in Zion, the place of its redemption.[3] Such temporal symmetries bolster the sense of "simultaneous eschatology" in Dante's representation of the afterlife, yet he also takes pains throughout the narrative to juxtapose the local time of his journey among the dead with what time it would have been "here," where the poet wrote and the reader, presumably, reads.[4] In this respect, the multiple time-references of *Purgatorio* amount to a utopian gesture, inviting us to compare the corrective world of Purgatory with our own present state and to examine the distance between the two.[5]

Purgatory has in one sense a vantage point similar to our own, because it rises out of the same ocean as our inhabitable continent, yet be-

cause things also look different from down under, the astronomical details of the second canticle help to transform a purely secular outlook.
Purgatory is a kind of *mundus inversus,* or world-upside-down, similar
to our world but inverted, turned around. There are different stars visible to the southern hemisphere, "never seen except by the first people."
But our pole star, which is always above our heads, and many other familiar constellations never make an appearance down there.[6] Virgil was
credited with observing this peculiarity of living on a spherical earth in
his *Georgics,* as Macrobius noted in his astronomical gloss to Cicero's
Dream of Scipio: "The south pole, on the other hand, once buried from
our sight, as it were, by the location of our abodes, will never show itself
to us, nor the stars with which it is undoubtedly adorned. And this is
what Virgil, knowing nature's ways full well, meant when he said, 'One
pole is ever high above us, while the other, beneath our feet, is seen of
black Styx and the shades infernal.'"[7] For Dante, as for Virgil, the stars
that adorn the other pole are now seen only by the dead, but by those
hopeful of salvation, not by the residents of Hell. Their description in
the *Purgatorio* makes the perspective of this otherworld visible to us as
readers.

The location of Dante's terrestrial paradise at the top of the mountain is an amalgamation of various medieval opinions. Peter Comestor
assumed that it was in an extremely high place, almost touching the circle of the moon. Aquinas thought that it was below the equator, and
hence somewhere in the southern hemisphere. Bede described it as an
uninhabited place, secret and hidden, across an expanse of land or sea
and inaccessible to men. Because Jerusalem is the center of the inhabitable land, Dante's antipodal Eden fulfills Walafrid Strabo's notion that
it is as remote as possible from our world.[8] By fixing Eden along the same
axis as Satan (stuck in the center of the earth) and Jerusalem, Dante spatially aligns the pivotal human events of sin, punishment, redemption,
and expiation.

This arrangement, alluded to in the last canto of the *Inferno,* becomes
clear only when Dante's protagonist reemerges from the bowels of the
earth and stops to catch his breath partway up the steep base of the purgatorial mountain. In order to rest and to get his bearings, he turns
around and sits down with his guide, to face east where they can see the

way they came up (*vòlti a levante ond'eravam saliti*). This view is a help-
ful one, Dante says (*che suole a riguardar giovare altrui*), although it is
not clear from his words whether he refers to the review of the distance
climbed that consoles weary hikers, or the orientation toward the east
that helps people figure out where they are.[9] At any rate, the first impression is one of disorientation, as the pilgrim is astonished to observe
the sun toward the north (*tra noi e Aquilone*) and hitting them on their
left shoulders (*che da sinistra n'eravam feriti*), just as Lucan's Arabs mar-
veled to see the shadows of trees going to the left when they left their
home south of the equator.[10]

In spite of the advantage of their magnificent panorama, the ensuing
lesson in reorientation depends less on sense-observation than on the
imagination. "Imagine Zion," Virgil instructs, "and this mountain sit-
uated on the earth such that they have one and the same horizon, but
two different hemispheres."[11] Because the two peaks of Purgatory and
Zion are on opposite sides of the equator, the tilted road of the Zodiac,
which Phaeton negotiated disastrously when he tried to drive the chariot of the sun, lies between them, to the south of one and to the north
of the other (Fig. 1).[12] Dante shows his grasp of the geography lesson
when he responds by remarking on how the ancient Hebrews used to
see the "diameter of the highest motion, which is called 'equator' in some
discipline," just as far to the south, toward the hot climes, as from here
it appears toward the north.[13] The explicit reference to the way the Jews
"used to see" the equator spatially connects the present state of the purgatorial souls, seeking liberty from sin, with the past history of the Jews,
in particular their exodus from captivity in Egypt, which is recalled by
the song of the arriving penitents. The allegorical significance of Dante's
fictional geography is thus pointedly allied with this central Christian
allegory of exodus.[14] As the present chapter will show, the astronomical
time-references of the second canticle are involved in this fundamental
strategy of allegorical comparison.

The prominence of temporality in Dante's *Purgatorio* has often been
noted. As Jacques LeGoff has amply shown, the very origins of Purgatory as an idea are wrapped up with notions of time.[15] Dante's conspicuous attention to the passage of time in this part of his poem has caused
it to be described as the canticle of nostalgia.[16] The stars Dante puts in

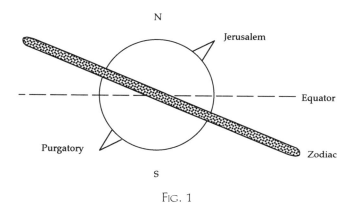

FIG. 1

the southern hemisphere are said to be a joy to that antipodal sky as they are a bereavement for ours, as they were seen only by Adam and Eve (the first people) and contribute to what Charles Singleton termed the "lament for Eden."[17] The pathos of temporal distance that suffuses the second canticle is perhaps best epitomized in the famous image of valediction that opens the eighth canto:

> Era già l'ora che volge il disio
> ai navicanti e 'ntenerisce il core
> il dì ch'han detto ai dolci amici addio;
> e che lo novo peregrin d'amore
> punge, se ode squilla di lontano
> che paia il giorno pianger che si more. (*Purgatorio* 8.1–6)

[It was now the hour that turns the desire of sailors and softens their hearts the day they have bid farewell to their sweet friends; and that pierces the new pilgrim of love, if he hears a ringing from afar that seems like the day lamenting its own death.]

Nostalgia presumes the mental juxtaposition of two temporal moments, as in the sentiment expressed in a popular song, *Penso a Napoli com'era, penso a Napoli com'è* ("I think of Naples as it was; I think of Naples as it is"). In *Purgatorio* this poignant chronological differential is spatialized by the measurable time-difference between two points on the globe—

between, for example, the location of the soul doing penance on the mountain and the distant resting-place of the body it has now abandoned.

Whereas in Hell time was told primarily by the movements of the unseen moon, in Purgatory it is told directly by the sun.[18] In fact, the pilgrim's own body serves as a kind of gnomon, casting a lone shadow across the face of the mountain. Even in the absence of that shadow, in the thick, black smoke of the terrace of wrath, the purgatorial souls differentiate Dante's mortality from their own state, remarking that he is "one who still tells time by calends."[19] By contrast, the inmates of Purgatory mark out time by completing revolutions on each terrace of penance during the daylight hours, coordinating, that is, their moral actions with the cycles of the sun.[20] With its numerous astronomical time-references, the *Purgatorio* asks its readers to tell time by keeping in mind not only the four conveniently placed points on the global dial, as it were, but also their own position in relation to the rest of the system. If nothing else, Dante's multiple chronometers illustrate that in this life, too, what time it is depends as much upon where you are, as observer and subject, as where the sun is. Through the inclusion of the point of view of the reader, Dante's repeated insistence on the chronological gap between "here" and "there" solicits the juxtaposition of this world with the next, which is perhaps the essential point of all Christian allegory.

The allegorical method of reading the past has been taken as an indication of the medieval lack of a sense of history, the insensibility to anachronism, rendering all times present.[21] Yet certain other kinds of allegorical procedure, which have been described as the "elimination of time," have also been contrasted with biblical typology precisely on the basis of temporality.[22] According to one definition, Hellenistic allegory is atemporal, whereas Judeo-Christian typology is primarily concerned with comparing the two "times" of the Old and New Testaments, with how both prefigure events still to come, and with how all these times bear on the immediate relation between God and the individual soul.[23] Typology, or *allegoria in factis,* is distinguished by its insistence on the historical, and hence chronological, truth of its literal level.

Much has been made in the second half of the twentieth century over whether or not Dante meant his text to be read according to the four levels of biblical typology, as the Epistle to Cangrande would seem to suggest.[24] There is no consensus even among those who consider Dante's *Commedia* as an "allegory of the theologians" as to what should be considered the literal level of the poem. The "state of souls after death," which the epistle asserts to be the poem's literal subject, seems rather to postfigure historical and biblical events rather than to prefigure eschatological truths, as does the history recounted in the Bible.[25] There seems to be no denying, however, that episodes and images in Dante's poetic fiction do recall standard "types" of the Old Testament (most notably the historical events of Exodus) as well as their allegorical fulfillment (our redemption effected by Christ in history) as told in the New Testament. The very nature of Dante's subject matter is eschatological, but it also appeals to the reader in the allegorical level called the "moral" sense, of which Dante in his *Convivio* suggested readers of Sacred Scripture should take note "for their own good."[26] The four levels of biblical interpretation are thus discernibly echoed in the *Commedia,* whether or not we want to affirm that Dante could write or was pretending to write theological allegory.

If we follow the explanation in the Epistle to Cangrande, a typological reading of the Old Testament insists on the historical truth of the biblical narrative (as the author of the epistle puts it, "the exodus of the sons of Israel from Egypt in the time of Moses"), which nonetheless also signifies events that take place at other times: "our redemption" wrought by Christ's death in Jerusalem (which occurred in the past), the ever-present possibility of our conversion from the misery of sin to a state of grace (happening now), and the exodus of an individual soul from the "slavery of its corrupt condition to the liberty of eternal glory" (in the future). As John Freccero put it, "the advent of Christ was believed to be threefold: once, in the past, when He appeared among us in human form; again, in the present, in the soul of the convert or regenerate sinner; finally, at the end of time, in the Second Coming . . . it follows that the spiritual or allegorical sense [of Scripture] . . . is also threefold."[27]

The three allegorical senses built on the literal meaning of Scripture are known as the historical, the moral (or tropological), and the anagogical (or eschatological). Whereas the historical level of medieval exegesis has to do with the past and the anagogical with the future, the moral level concerns the present. A. C. Charity characterized the applied typology of the *Commedia* as an imperative, a call or challenge to the individual reader to be changed by the experience recounted in the text.[28] Strictly speaking, the moral significance of the plot of the *Commedia* entails the belief that, in the words of Oscar Cullman, "this entire happening takes place *for me*."[29] The personal pronoun, "me," the temporal indication, "now," and the deictic adverb, "here," are all related to this moral, present sense.

The synchronic time-references in *Purgatorio,* far from being a gratuitous display of astronomical erudition, should in fact be numbered among the poem's addresses to the reader because they call attention to her geographical context. They participate in what Singleton characterized as the "double vision" of the poem. Nowhere is this more apparent than in the most difficult time-reference in the canticle, where the sense of the text remains obscure in the absence of the reader's particular point of view. It is to this notoriously ambiguous passage, the opening astronomical scene of canto 9, that we now turn.

Even this, the most elaborate of astronomical periphrases that Dante uses to tell time in *Purgatorio,* is suffused with the pathos of temporal distance. The opening of canto 9, like the one describing departing travelers in the preceding canto, portrays a valediction. The evening hour at the beginning of canto 8 is suggested by the pangs of homesickness experienced by sailors the day they have said goodbye to sweet friends, and by the "new pilgrim of love" when he hears the distant bells of the campanile, sounding the lament of the dying day. In canto 9, it is the goddess Aurora who takes leave of her sweet friend because, in the melancholy mythology of dawn, it is her daily abandonment of her impossibly aged bedfellow that brings about the morning hour:

> La concubina di Titone antico
>   già s'imbiancava al balco d'orïente,
>   fuor de le braccia del suo dolce amico;
> di gemme la sua fronte era lucente,
>   poste in figura del freddo animale
>   che con la coda percuote la gente;
> e la notte, de' passi con che sale,

fatti avea due nel loco ov'eravamo,
  e'l terzo già chinava in giuso l'ale;
quand' io, che meco avea di quel d'Adamo,
  vinto dal sonno, in su l'erba inchinai
  là 've già tutti e cinque sedevamo. (*Purgatorio* 9.1–12)

[The concubine of ancient Tithonus was already growing white at the balcony of the East, released from the arms of her sweet friend; her forehead was glimmering with gems, placed in the shape of the cold animal that strikes people with its tail, and in the place where we were night had made two of the steps with which it climbs, and the third was already bending down its wing; when I, who still had with me some of Adam, conquered by sleep, lay down on the grass where all five of us were sitting.]

The Provençal *alba* (reputed to be the oldest of romance literary genres) is a dawn song focused on the poignant moment of lovers' parting. In Dante's image, the dawn herself, harbinger of day and unwelcome disrupter of nocturnal pleasures, also suffers daily separation from her *dolce amico*. She leaves the bed of her paramour and appears at the balcony after a night of love, her face white and her forehead adorned with gems.[30]

But because in Purgatory it is not now dawn but well into the night, this brilliant portrait is chronologically misplaced, and has thus been a source of considerable confusion and polemic since the earliest commentaries on the *Commedia*. Until relatively recently, the exordium was usually interpreted as a totally nocturnal scene, a spectacle of moonrise, which Dante has chosen to describe as aurora, a so-called lunar aurora (Fig. 2), referring to a bright glow preceding the moon (now about three nights past full) just as it is beginning to rise over the eastern horizon of Purgatory and adorned by the stars of the constellation Scorpio (*il freddo animale / che con la coda percuote la gente*). Because the mythological Aurora was always known as the legitimate spouse of Tithonus, it was supposed that Dante's term *concubina* could only refer to some other woman. The fourteenth-century commentator Jacopo della Lana was perhaps the inventor of the new mythology devised to explain this crux. He proposed that Tithonus, "like so many men of the world," had tired of his bride, the beautiful Aurora, and had become infatuated with the daughter of the Moon, also called Aurora, who became his concubine,

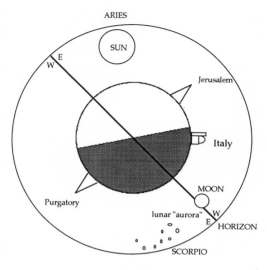

FIG. 2

or whore, and with whom he went *fornicando* from sunup till sundown while his wife was absent from his bed.[31]

Apart from what one might think of this wholly original anecdote (Scartazzini called it a *sozza imagine*), the solution involving a lunar aurora is quite incongruous with Dante's emphasis on the constant rotation of the sun around the earth.[32] Unlike Homer's rosy-fingered goddess who appears only once every twenty-four hours, Dante's Aurora is an ongoing, continuous phenomenon without beginning or end, happening constantly at successive points around the globe, indeed producing a circular continuum of dawn without interruption. In Dante's cosmology, old Tithonus, whatever the state of his virility (which Scartazzini questions), has *no time* for another mistress, as his wife is always and forever just leaving his bed.

An alternative solution to the problem depends on seeing the passage as a double time-reference, like so many others in the *Purgatorio,* even though the usual deictic counterpoint, *qui,* is missing from the description. In 1775, Bartolommeo Perazzini proposed, ostensibly for the first time, that the passage refers to two different hemispheres, one where it is night (*là ov'eravamo*), the other where it is about to be dawn.[33] When it is two or more hours into night in Purgatory (around half past eight in the evening), it is nine hours later in the time zone of Italy (around half past five in the morning), where the sun is getting ready to rise. In this reading of the poem, what is meant by "forehead" of the dawn is not the eastern edge of the sky just above the sun's first glow, but rather the opposite part of the heavenly vault, where, from the perspective of the poet and his readers, Scorpio now shimmers (Fig. 3).[34] Such a reading is supported by a similar use of the term *fronte* in the purely metaphorical dawn toward the end of the journey, when Dante recalls how he lifted his eyes to see Mary at the summit of the celestial rose: "Just as in the morning the eastern part of the horizon overcomes that where the sun goes down, so too as my eyes traveled from valley to peak I saw the highest part conquer with light the whole other face (*fronte*)."[35]

Although this interpretation makes chronological and astronomical sense, it does not explain the negative connotations of this dawn. Elsewhere called *la bella Aurora* and "bright handmaiden of the sun," here the hopeful goddess seems vilified by the pejorative label of concubine and

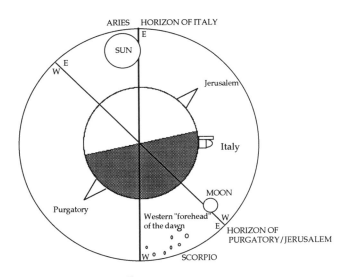

FIG. 3

by her sinister headdress.[36] Dante's *concubina* has been seen to derive from a multiplicity of sources, from Virgil's set phrase of Aurora abandoning her husband's couch (*Tithoni croceum linquens Aurora cubile*—a canonical example of descriptive periphrasis) to a passage from the Song of Songs, translated by Dante in the *Convivio* as *Sessanta sono le regine, e ottanta l'amiche concubine* (Sixty are the queens, and eighty the bed-sharing mistresses).[37] In response to attempts to soften the term into a perfectly good synonym for "spouse," such as "bedfellow" or "she who shares the couch," Gino Casagrande has traced the negative semantic valence of *concubina* from Cicero to Augustine, in whose sermons the phrase *concubinas habere non licet* (It is not licit to keep concubines) became a virtual formula.[38] Even in the *Aeneid,* the description of dawn's rising seems to reflect the ominous beginning to Dido's last day, and in the *Convivio* Dante used Solomon's "queens" and "concubines" to differentiate inferior sciences from the supreme one of Ethics: *La colomba mia e la perfetta mia.* Some have taken this resonance of the Song of Songs to show that Aurora, a pagan goddess after all, suffers by comparison to the bride celebrated in the Canticum as "my perfect dove," whether it be Mary, the Church, or, as Dante suggested, moral philosophy.[39]

Moreover, the astrological sign of Scorpio is the house of death, associated with corruption and decay of living things and with the dying sun as it moves toward the winter solstice. It is also associated with night, which it now is in Purgatory, and with sleep, which Dante now lies down to do.[40] The scorpion is an animal also associated with deceit, fraud, and treachery, as readers remember from the description of Geryon's poisonous, forked tail in *Inferno* 17. Mars and Venus rule the house of Scorpio, making it the sign that promotes adultery and concupiscence as well as violence. In astrological medicine, Scorpio has influence over both the male and the female genitalia but comes to be associated most often with female sexuality. The scorpion represents the evil woman (*mulier nequa*), the lascivious woman (*mulier fornicaria*) who inspires lust, and the very etymology of the word *scorpion* is traced to *scortum,* meaning "harlot" or "prostitute."[41] In other words, the significance of Scorpio serves to reinforce the negative, and specifically female, connotations of the *concubina.* Presumably the scorpion that hangs on the forehead of a great Renaissance lady, Elisabetta Gonzaga, in a famous portrait in the

Uffizi gallery, is not meant to impugn her virtue. Even so, at her celebrated party memorialized in Castiglione's *Cortegiano,* one of her guests
surmises that the *S* adorning her brow on that occasion has a similarly
ominous meaning ("her intimate desire to kill and bury alive anyone
who gazes at her or serves her").[42]

If the scorpion on the forehead of Aurora gives her—like the Duchess
of Urbino in the imagination of her guest—a terrifying, gorgon-like aspect, it is not entirely incongruent with the pagan tradition of the goddess. Afflicted by Venus with an insatiable sexual appetite in revenge for
a flirtation with Mars, Aurora was known in antiquity as a female
rapist.[43] This reputation is probably related to the way stars seem to flee,
or disappear, as the dawn approaches. Often depicted in ancient iconog-
raphy with arms outstretched to take hold of a young man, Aurora (or
Eos) kidnapped every one of her three lovers, Tithonus, Cephalus, and
Orion.[44] The hunter Orion brings further resonances of violence to this
mythological construct, because it was for an attempted rape that Diana created and unleashed the scorpion against him so that, as constellations, they continue to this day to chase each other around the sphere
of the fixed stars.[45] The sexual violence associated with Aurora is echoed
by the other pagan episodes of rape and kidnapping—Philomena,
Ganymede, Achilles—also recalled in canto 9 in the description of
morning that follows the opening scene of the *concubina.*[46]

Giorgio Stabile has suggested that the dawn of *Purgatorio* 9 is presented as illicit and ominous not because it refers to the pagan goddess
as opposed to a Christian, mystical awakening, but because it is occur-
ring on the other side of the earth, in the northern, fallen hemisphere
rather than in the edenic context of the purgatorial mountain.[47] If it is
the case in the *Commedia* that one hemisphere over which the sun passes
is irrevocably corrupt whereas the other remains pristine, as Stabile's interpretation implies, that was not the spirit of the worldview in the *Convivio,* where Dante also imaginatively populated two different hemispheres in order to trace the path of the sun over the course of the year.
In that text, to gloss a line in one of his canzoni referring to the sun that
circles all the earth, *il sole che tutto il mondo gira,* Dante asks his reader
to imagine two cities that would be located on the terrestrial globe by
dropping two pebbles into the ocean, one from the northern celestial

pole and one from the southern. The city at the north pole he calls Maria; the city at the antipodes of Maria he calls Lucia. The inhabitants of Maria have the northern pole star always directly above their heads, and the soles of the Lucians' feet face those of the Marians.[48] At the vernal equinox, the citizens of Maria would be able to see a semicircle of the sun revolving low on their horizon in a clockwise direction, like a mill wheel, ascending in a spiral around them, as on the threads of a screw, for about ninety-one turns. When these gyrations are completed, the sun then descends by the same path for another ninety-one days or so, until it disappears from view and begins to be seen by the inhabitants of Lucia, who would see it ascend and descend with as many turns as it did for Maria—only in a counterclockwise direction. As a result, during the dark winter months in the city of Maria, Lucia is the beneficiary of the sun's light—and vice versa.

The choice of Lucia as the city of the southern pole has been plausibly explained by her association with the winter solstice, with which her feast day coincided in Dante's time.[49] The celebration of Saint Lucy with a festival of light is thought to contrast deliberately with the fact that her day is the darkest day of the year, "the yeares midnight," as John Donne put it.[50] The city of Lucia in the southern hemisphere, where autumn is like our spring and winter like our summer, becomes a city of light when those of the northern hemisphere are shrouded in darkness. The point of this pedagogical demonstration in the *Convivio* is not solely scientific; it is also moral. The two hemispheres are not opposed as good and evil, or dark and light, but rather as the reciprocal poles of a providentially illuminated universe: *Quando l'uno ha lo giorno, l'altro ha la notte.*[51] The example serves to illustrate the point that when the sphere of the sun has made one complete trip and has returned to its starting point, every region of the terrestrial ball will have received as much time of light as of darkness. The lesson is followed by an outburst of gratitude for such divine wisdom and providence, and of contempt for the blindness of his readers, for whose utility and delight he writes, who do not lift their eyes to observe such things but keep them fixed on the mud of their ignorance.[52]

It would seem to be no accident that the astronomical digression of the *Convivio,* involving the fanciful place-name Lucia, should prove instructive to the astronomical exordium of *Purgatorio* 9, precisely at the moment that Lucy will come to transport the sleeping pilgrim up to the gates. An appreciation of the reciprocal illumination of two hemispheres learned in the *Convivio* is exactly what is needed to make sense of this difficult time-reference. The unexpected description of Aurora at the start of the first night in Purgatory, and the first time Dante falls asleep, reminds us that even though it may be night in Purgatory, it is dawn somewhere else. Indeed, it is dawn for us; it is dawn "here." And we might well be vigilant, even while the protagonist slumbers.

The aggravated difficulties of *la concubina di Titone antico,* a double time-reference that suppresses the crucial second term, have called attention to its similarity with Dante's difficult rhymes, the so-called rime petrose, one of whose thorny features is that of astronomical periphrasis.[53] In fact, the sequence of the four "stony rhymes" is meticulously oriented around the time of the winter solstice, a time when the fire of love should cool and does not, a time when the heart of the lover risks freezing over like the stony heart of his cold mistress and like the hibernal landscape around him. In the dark conceits of the rime petrose, the sun has reached the nadir of its voyage, and, from the perspective of the morbid heart in winter, there seems to be no promise of renewal. In "Io son venuto al punto della rota," unlike the sun which at this very moment is turning at the tropic of Capricorn to make its way slowly back toward the sweet new season, the lover is fixed in his deadly obsession and will not turn back.[54] The narrator of the petrose, stuck on a road that has turned to mud, is perhaps a good example of those ignorant people reproached in the passionate outburst in the *Convivio* for refusing to lift their eyes to the sun's providential illumination of the whole globe. What is lacking in the rime petrose, intent on describing the frozen state of *questo emisperio,* is a view of the world that contains more than one pole. By the same token, readings of *la concubina di Titone antico* that ignore the other hemisphere (which is, in this case, our own) are destined to see in it an exclusively nocturnal scene, a "lunar" aurora.

To think of the other side of the world at nighttime or at the winter solstice is to begin to understand the providential distribution of light in the world. Do not doubt, admonishes the Venerable Bede in his treatise on time, that even in the darkest night the splendor of the sun drenches with daylight all those spaces of the sky above the moon.[55] In the *Paradiso*, Dante will journey into those brilliant regions beyond the shadow of the earth, but already in the *Purgatorio* multiple time-references serve as a constant reminder that the alternation of dark and light is merely the impression of an individual bound to any one particular terrestrial location in a cosmos that is in reality wholly flooded with light. Bede tells us that the mutability of night and day signifies on the one hand our exile from Paradise into this vale of tears, which occurred in the past, and at the same time holds the promise of our future transfer out from the shadows of sin and into celestial joy.[56]

Like the Song of Songs, which Dante's scandalous epithet *concubina* recalls, the exordium of canto 9 emphasizes the carnal relation between husband and wife. Because Aurora and Tithonus are lovers, even if they also happen to be married, the moment of dawn is an ongoing love story. It is a story not of scandal but of pathos, deriving from the ever-increasing age of *Titone antico* with each daily parting from his eternally youthful bride. Married to an immortal goddess, only Tithonus bears the marks of time, the trace of successive dawns one after another through the ages, while Aurora reawakens each morning the same. Dante describes a cosmos in which darkness is only the temporary absence of a light shining somewhere else, where the relentless rotation of the sun makes for a continuum of dawn happening constantly at some point on earth, and where a beautiful goddess is always and forever just leaving the bed of her beloved husband—the principle of eternity linked by love to the principle of time.

At the moment described in the opening lines of canto 9, the jewels of Scorpio are visible in the "forehead" of the dawn only because they are far from her. The constellation stands out against the still-dark western regions of the sky as the sun approaches in the east. At this moment, the contrast of the jewels and the forehead is still marked but is undergoing the process of erasure, the gradual obliteration of light by light that only slightly later will dissolve it into that unimaginable image of the *Paradiso*, the *perla in bianca fronte,* a white pearl indistinguishable from the white forehead it adorns.[57] The process of purgation is the smoothing of imperfections, to "make oneself beautiful" (*ire a farsi belle*), as Dante says.[58] The sinister scorpion fading in the brow of an amorous dawn foreshadows the seven *P*'s (symbolizing *peccata,* or sins) that the pilgrim is about to receive on his forehead, and which are to be expunged progressively over the course of a three-day mountain hike. The removal of these blemishes is a process of blanching, which finds its astronomical parallel in the gradual disappearance of stars at the coming dawn. Bernard of Clairvaux interpreted the dawn as the humility that divides the "night" of sin from the new light of the just life.[59] The troublesome time-reference that opens canto 9 is thus a spectacular illustration, in natural terms, of the supernatural work of purgation that begins precisely here, when the penitent soul climbs up the three steps and through the musically creaking door to Purgatory proper.

The phenomenon of dawn depends for its very occurrence on highly contingent circumstances: the accident of the earth's shadow and an observer's present location with respect to the sun. Unlike the sun, the dawn does not exist beyond the realm of the earth. Indeed, it can be defined only in relation to something else, either the night that is passing or the day that has not yet arrived. Evanescent as the present moment itself, dawn divides two different states, the shadows from the day—or, metaphorically, as in Bernard's interpretation, the sinners from the just. It is at high noon that Dante's character abandons the surface of the earth for the regions where it is always day. Yet images of dawn do not disappear in the *Paradiso.* In fact, toward the end of the poem, the approaching final vision is introduced with a description of dawn and the stars as they fade from view:

> Forse semilia miglia di lontano
>   ci ferve l'ora sesta, e questo mondo
>   china già l'ombra quasi al letto piano
> quando 'l mezzo del cielo, a noi profondo,
>   comincia a farsi tal, ch'alcuna stella
>   perde il parere infino a questo fondo;
> e come vien la chiarissima ancella
>   del sol più oltre, cosí 'l ciel si chiude
>   di vista in vista infino a la più bella. (*Paradiso* 30.1–9)

[Perhaps six thousand miles away the sixth hour is burning, and this world is already inclining its shadow to a level bed, when the middle of the sky, which looks deep to us, begins to lighten so that stars up to that point are lost from view; and as the most bright handmaid of the sun advances further, so does the sky shut off its vistas, one by one, until even the most beautiful one is gone.]

These lines constitute a kind of unhinged, paradisiacal time-reference. Two places six thousand miles apart enjoy simultaneously noon and dawn respectively, and neither relates to what time it is in the narrative, where Dante is about to exit the most distant sphere of the physical universe to enter into the eternal space of the Empyrean. In the description of this hypothetical sky, the fainter stars begin to disappear here and there up to the zenith, until the brightest ones of all are at last obliterated (*infino a la più bella*). This dawn, too, announces a valediction, as Beatrice is about to leave the pilgrim's side and resume her place in the celestial rose.

The time-references of the *Purgatorio,* of which *la concubina di Titone antico* is the most notorious example, emphasize the temporality of this world, while they point to the elimination of time that will characterize the next. As with other invocations to the reader, Dante, by insisting on the contemporaneousness of times in a bipolar world, asks the reader to investigate what lies beneath the veil of his strange verses, or under the gem-encrusted surface of his *concubina.* Controversy over the use of allegory in the *Commedia* is centered on the letter, that is, whether Dante is claiming that his narrative is literally true. Whether or not what the author says happened to him then and there *really* happened is one question, but in the "polysemy," or system of multiple meanings, built into the text, it is the question of what is happening now to us that is the more urgent.[60] In *Purgatorio,* as in allegory, all times are made to converge onto the present. Dante's time-references are the cosmological correlative of the moral sense of Scripture insofar as they constitute an invitation to read the signs of the *liber coelestis* as they relate to "me here now."

CHAPTER FIVE

LOSING THE MERIDIAN
From *Purgatorio* to *Paradiso*

Purgatory's location makes us aware of time as a constant alternation between night and day, dark and light. Time is told on the basis of observation, not just from a single vantage point, but from several at once. *Purgatorio*'s double and quadruple chronological indicators draw attention to the radical contingency of the most obvious astronomical phenomena. Morning, noon, and night depend wholly on the point of view of the individual, on one's own present state. Reckoning the hour of the day requires a terrestrial perspective from which to gauge the sun's distance from the circle we draw around us, called the horizon, and from another passing straight over our heads, called the meridian. When we move into the third canticle, these various perspectives are lost. Astronomical references can no longer have their most common valence as indicators of time, because time-telling has no meaning without a fixed point of reference. From the moment he leaves the surface of the earth at noon on the Wednesday after Easter, Dante's protagonist is therefore no longer aware of what day or time it is throughout the celestial portion of his journey. Only when he looks back down at earth from the height of the fixed stars can he tell by the changed illumination of the globe that a certain period has elapsed. From *Purgatorio* to *Paradiso*, astronomical descriptions gradually lose their traditional, chronometric function and become metaphors for timeless realities.[1]

This shift in the meaning of stellar invocations mirrors and accompanies, I believe, the shift in poetic strategy advertised in the final portion of the work. I am alluding here to the notion that Dante's mode of representation varies according to the realm of the afterlife he is claiming to represent. Francis Newman found theological underpinnings to structural differences in each of the three canticles in Augustine's doctrine of corporeal, spiritual, and intellectual vision. Marguerite

Chiarenza corrected this view by showing that the challenge of the final canticle is to indicate an imageless, or intellectual, vision without abandoning the indispensable vehicle of poetic imagery. John Freccero has elaborated the thesis that the *Paradiso* is pure metaphor, and that the *Inferno*'s apparent sensual immediacy is fundamentally ironic.[2] This three-part poetic strategy—sensate, imaginative, intellectual—might be summarized as follows. The *Inferno* boasts a remarkable realism, where bodies seem unproblematically solid, deriving in fact from a deceptive verisimilitude. The mimetic technique of poetry and the other arts is then exposed and thematized in the *Purgatorio*, where even the fleshy-looking souls there encountered are explained as fictitious or virtual representations of now defunct bodies. In the *Paradiso* the poet renounces all claim to either explicit or implicit realistic representation, and the shades of the saints appear as lights whose very brilliance obliterates all recognizable physiognomy. To put it yet another way, the *Inferno* fraudulently describes figures and events as if they were not just representations; the *Purgatorio* honestly calls attention to the fact that it is but a representation; and the *Paradiso* vociferously denies the validity of its representations as nothing more than dim stand-ins for a really lived but inexpressible experience.

A parallel observation can be made with regard to the way celestial bodies and their movements are perceived in the three canticles.[3] In Hell Virgil unproblematically knows what time it is even though the stars are hidden from view, whereas in Purgatory Dante exposes and elaborates the whole mechanism of time-reckoning as a highly contingent play of phenomena as perceived from different locations on earth relative to the sun and stars—a relation that disappears entirely in the last portion of the journey. In *Paradiso*, the aspect of the heavens is rendered unfamiliar and alien by our traveling through them. New constellations appear, made up of happy souls, not quintessential bodies, and in the shape of spinning wheels, a cross, an eagle. Even though most of the action of the *Paradiso* takes place among them, celestial phenomena gradually become detached from the setting of the story to be invoked as similitudes, likenesses, and confessed substitutes for an indescribable vision.

Already toward the end of the *Purgatorio* chronological indicators begin to lose their descriptive function. The multiple time-reference that opens *Purgatorio* 27, for example, begins with a hypothetical clause—*si come quando:*

> Sì come quando i primi raggi vibra
>   là dove il suo fattor lo sangue sparse,
>   cadendo Ibero sotto l'alta Libra,
> e l'onde in Gange da nona rïarse,
>   sì stava il sole; onde 'l giorno sen giva. (*Purgatorio* 27.1–5)

Just as when it emits its first rays there where its Maker spilled His blood, with Spain falling under high Libra, and the waves of the Ganges burning under the noon hour, thus stood the sun; whence the day was departing.

Dawn in Jerusalem, where the sun's maker shed his blood, coincides with dusk in Purgatory, midnight in Spain, and noon in India, as we have by now learned. What is peculiar in this passage is that Dante presents the actual state of affairs, the expository reality of local and distant time, as a simile, introduced by a concatenation of conjunctions "just as when."

The exact opposite occurs in the exordium of *Purgatorio* 30, where an elaborate metaphor, equating the seven torches leading the first allegorical pageant witnessed in the Garden of Eden to the Septentrion, masquerades as just another astronomical time-reference:

> Quando il settentrïon del primo cielo
>   che né occaso mai seppe né orto
>   né d'altra nebbia che di colpa velo,
> e che faceva lì ciascuno accorto
>   di suo dover, come 'l più basso face
>   qual temon gira per venire a porto,
> fermo s'affisse. . . . (*Purgatorio* 30.1–7)

[When the Septentrion of the first heaven, which has never known setting nor rising, nor the veil of any other fog but sin, and which was making everybody there aware of his duty (just as the lower one does someone who turns the tiller to come to port) stopped still. . . .]

The seven stars of the Little Dipper not only indicate to sailors which way to turn their helms; they can themselves be compared to the tiller of a ship or, as Statius likened them, to the steering pole of a chariot.[4]

Yet here the most familiar navigational marker, which Dante qualifies as the "lower" Septentrion, has become the image of a higher constellation, the "Septentrion of the first heaven," which belongs in the Empyrean. The seven flames of the candelabra, symbolizing the seven gifts of the Holy Spirit, resemble the northern pole stars insofar as they never rise or set and, like those celestial beacons, remind people of what they ought to do morally in order to make it to safe spiritual haven (*che faceva lì ciascuno accorto di suo dover*).

The two-part pageant at the summit of Purgatory that frames Beatrice's return to earth stands out from the rest of the *Commedia* by its dependence on personification allegory of the sort elaborated in the *Romance of the Rose* and innumerable other medieval works. The procession led by these seven candelabra is also strikingly packed with astronomical comparisons. The candles themselves produce a kind of dawn in the east, appearing as a flash but growing more and more resplendent.[5] They are said to be "brighter than the moon in her midmonth in a clear midnight sky," and the colored streaks left by their advancing flames are compared to the rainbow caused by the sun and the corona around the moon to make "such a beautiful sky."[6] The winged figures representing the evangelists coming behind the twenty-four elders, who in turn stand for the books of the Old Testament, are said to follow each other in the procession "even as star follows star in the heavens."[7] Consistent with its dawnlike approach, the triumphal chariot pulled by a griffin is compared favorably with that of the sun, justly incinerated when Phaeton led it off track.[8] Finally, the seven ladies dancing on either side of the chariot representing the three theological and the four cardinal virtues will later reveal themselves as "nymphs here and stars in heaven"—glossing at last the newly rediscovered constellations of the southern pole, the four stars shining on Cato's face in the morning, and the three others coming out at night.[9]

The plethora of astronomical images associated with the allegorical parade follows no doubt from the poet's explicit request at the outset for Urania's help in describing it. The muse of astronomy is called upon for the purpose of aiding the poet in his lyrical expression of hard concepts:

> Or convien che Elicona per me versi,
>   e Uranìe m'aiuti col suo coro
>   forti cose a pensar mettere in versi. (*Purgatorio* 29.40–42)

[Now I need Helicon to pour through me and Urania to help me with her choir to put into verse things difficult to think.]

Astronomy is called in to assist at an important shift in poetic mode. Whereas the *Commedia* as a whole relies in large part on the testimony of historical personages—sinners, penitents, and saints—who both really lived in the world and now serve as *exempla* or figures of moral truths, the players in the spectacle produced in the Garden of Eden are more stiffly allegorical.[10] The candelabra, the twenty-four elders, and the four winged creatures are purely symbolic apparitions, with no reality other than what they signify, no life other than that of spectacle. Astronomy is of use already in this edenic prelude, Dante implies, because celestial luminaries are the best available images of suprasensual reality—"things difficult to think on." Astronomy thus becomes the muse of difficult poetry, a mode of signification employed in the dramatic mysteries of the *Purgatorio*'s climax.

The opacity of these allegorical pageants (whose meaning continues to feed scholarly debate) and of Beatrice's prophetic commentary upon them is openly acknowledged.[11] Beatrice in fact swears off this arcane language for the remainder of the journey, just as she and her charge prepare to abandon the surface of the earth. At this juncture, Dante's new guide echoes Christ's own cryptic iterations to his disciples just before his departure from them:

> *Modicum, et non videbitis me*
>   *et iterum,* sorelle mie dilette,
>   *modicum, et vos videbitis me.* (*Purgatorio* 33. 10–12)

[In a little while you will not see me, my beloved sisters, and then again, in a little while, you will see me.]

Zygmunt Barański has observed how the quotation from the Gospel of John introduces the whole semiotic problem, so prominent in the

Paradiso, of how divine things can be represented to mortal minds.[12] In the Gospel, these words ostensibly foretell Christ's imminent death and subsequent resurrection. Their immediate context has to do with the need for using metaphors, or speaking in proverbs, until the truth can be made plain: "These things I have spoken to you in parables. The hour is coming when I will no longer speak to you in parables, but will speak to you plainly of the Father."[13] Although with this Christological allusion Beatrice might well be intimating the future displacement of the Church or its eventual reform at the hands of some divine messenger (*messo di Dio*), by the end of the same canto she too pledges to leave off enigmatic pronouncements (such as the notorious *cinquecento diece e cinque*) and to speak from now on in plain language. When her lover complains that her "longed-for words soar out of sight," she replies that her difficult speech should be a reminder to him of the shortcomings of human reason.[14]

Astronomical references accompany these declarations. Beatrice admonishes that the teaching of the school he once followed is as distant from the divine way as is the earth from the fastest-moving heaven.[15] Her assurance that she will henceforth desist from strange prophecies in veiled speech is also marked by noticing the position of the sun, in the final time-reference of *Purgatorio*. Beatrice says:

> Veramente oramai saranno nude
>   le mie parole, quanto converrassi
>   quelle scovrir a la tua vista rude. (*Purgatorio* 33.100–102)

[Truly now my words shall be naked as much as need be in order to uncover them to your crass vision.]

In the very next lines Dante goes on to specify that the hour was almost noon when Beatrice made this vow of future candor:

> E più corusco e con più lenti passi
>   teneva il sole il cerchio di merigge,
>   che qua e là, come li aspetti, fassi. (*Purgatorio* 33.103–105)

[And more ruddy and with slower steps the sun was holding the circle of the meridian, that shows itself here and there, according to different aspects.]

The poetic significance of this otherwise gratuitous piece of chronological information may be to illustrate the promised clarity of Beatrice's speech by the sun's reaching its zenith, the maximum point of brightness during the day. Yet by making reference to the meridian, an astronomical convention that depends entirely on the point of view of the observer, this final chronological indicator also calls attention to the relativity of time-telling that we have seen throughout the second canticle.

The meridian is a celestial circle, like the horizon, which has no fixed location in the cosmos and is the mechanism that makes multiple time-references possible—hence the modern expression of antemeridian and postmeridian hours. Because it has no fixed place but varies according to the accident of the observer's position, Dante says that it moves from here to there according to different aspects: *qua e là, come li aspetti, fassi.* Macrobius explained the meridian in this way: "The meridian and the horizon are not inscribed on the sphere because they can have no precise location, but vary according to the diversity of observers and inhabitants. The meridian is the line the sun crosses when it reaches a point directly overhead, indicating midday. Because the roundness of the earth makes the aspect of localities different, the same part of the sky is not over the heads of all men; so all will not be able to have the same meridian, but each people have their own meridian directly overhead. Similarly, each individual, as he looks about him, has his own horizon."[16]

Like enigmatic speech, the meridian circle is about to be abandoned as the pilgrim and his guide prepare to leave the surface of the earth, since it is a cognitive instrument determined by terrestrial location, defined by a point that is directly over the head of someone standing on the ground.[17] A traveler through the celestial spheres no longer has a meridian, nor a horizon, and consequently no local time. Once we leave the earth, on the seventh day of the journey, the question of what time it is will no longer have much sense.[18] The meridian circle, on which the sun appears to different people on different parts of the earth at noon, is a fictional convention, by which we tell time. In the same way, the enigmatic speech of Beatrice and other prophets, not to mention all the images used by poets, is suitable and necessary to our present terrestrial condition. Beatrice's renunciation of veiled language—in favor of "nude words"—coincides with Dante's and our imminent displacement from the familiar focus of the astronomers' diagrams (the earth). The glance at the sun in relation to the meridian provides an example of the cognitive crutches humans use to understand the cosmos, with which the pilgrim must now prepare to do away. The journey to Paradise is an attempt to go beyond these conventions, to see the stars not as they pass over our head, but from the perspective of divinity that makes them move.

On the level of rhetorical style, Peter Dronke has suggested that the whole set of cantos at the summit of Purgatory, rife with personification allegory and obscure prophetic statements, belongs to the category of poetic technique that Geoffrey of Vinsauf calls *collatio occulta,* or hidden comparison.[19] Geoffrey writes:

A comparison that is made in a hidden way (*collatio occulta*) is introduced with no sign to point it out. It is introduced not under its own aspect (*vultu proprio*) but with dissembled mien, as if there were no comparison there at all, but the taking on, one might say, of a new form marvelously engrafted, where the new element fits as securely into the context as if it were born of the theme. The new term is, indeed, taken from elsewhere, but it seems to be taken from there; it is from outside and does not appear outside; it makes an appearance within and is not within; so it fluctuates inside and out, here and there, far and near; it stands apart, and yet is at hand *hic et ibi, procul et prope; distat et astat.*[20]

The distinguishing feature of *collatio occulta* is that it is concealed, that it does not identify itself as a comparison—it is something closer to a metaphor than a simile, to put it in modern terms.[21] Most striking of all, however, is that Geoffrey's characterization of this mode of expression as shifting constantly here and there (*hic et ibi*) exactly recalls Dante's description of the meridian circle: *il cerchio di merigge, che* qua e là, *come li aspetti, fassi.* One might say that both hidden speech, of the sort Beatrice now promises to renounce, and the meridian circle vary, not according to their own aspect (*vultu proprio*) but according to context, to the point of view of the observer. Because they are both accommodations befitting the limited and localized perspective of someone still tied to the earth, Beatrice's renunciation of a certain habit of signification is juxtaposed with a reference to the meridian, which she and her lover will forthwith abandon.

As Chiarenza has amply shown, the experience Dante professes to have had in the third portion of his journey may have been imageless, but its narration, like any other, depends on images.[22] Images, similitudes, and fictions of various sorts—the indispensable materials of poetic representation—will not be transcended in the *Paradiso,* but they will be openly acknowledged as "mere" accommodations, methods of condescending to the still-unbeatified human point of view. To put it in Geoffrey of Vinsauf's terms, the comparisons will be no longer "hidden," but exposed. Analogously, astronomical conventions will also continue to be invoked, but only as obvious and provisional approximations of what the spiritual cosmos is really like. We will gain an extraterrestrial perspective on the universe, not unlike what Martianus Capella's personification of astronomy describes as her own point of view in the *Marriage of Mercury and Philology.* Astronomia explains that the "great circles" devised by astronomers to facilitate their analyses of the universe have no real existence: "When we use the word 'circles' . . . we are merely illustrating the risings and setting of planetary bodies as they appear to us. I myself do not consider an axis and poles, which mortals have fastened on a bronze armillary sphere to assist them in contemplating the heavens." She further remarks that the "poles that protrude from the hollow cavity of the perforated outer sphere, and the apertures, the pivots, and the sockets have to be imagined—something that you may be assured could not happen in a rarified and supramundane atmosphere."[23] The circle of the meridian, like the heavy apparatus of an armillary sphere, is a form of condescension, a necessary fiction suited to the limited vision of an earth-bound observer.

Dante exposes this apparatus most plainly, in fact, at the very moment it is to be transcended by his protagonist in the first canto of the *Paradiso,* making conspicuous use of some of the fundamental conventions of astronomical science. The first and last time-reference of the *Paradiso,* often deplored for its abstruseness, begins by describing, from an observational standpoint, the most propitious coordinates of the sun during the year:

> Surge ai mortali per diverse foci
>   la lucerna del mondo; ma da quella

> che quattro cerchi giugne con tre croci,
> con miglior corso e con migiliore stella
>   esce congiunta, e la mondana cera
>   più a suo modo tempera e suggella.
> Fatto avea di là mane e di qua sera
>   tal foce, e quasi tutto era là bianco
>   quello emisperio, e l'altra parte nera. (*Paradiso* 1.37–45)

[The lamp of the world rises to mortals through different outlets; but from that one that joins four circles with three crosses it emerges conjoined with a better course and a better star, and it tempers and seals the worldly wax more to its fashion. Almost such an outlet had made day over there and evening here; and that hemisphere was totally white, while the other side was black.]

The passage does not accurately describe the present moment in the journey, because the sun (at whatever possible date of the journey one assumes) has by now progressed a good piece beyond the first point of Aries. It starts rather from an ideal beginning, as one is advised to do by a contemporary astronomical handbook prescribing that an examination of the heavens begin "with the sun because it is the most noble of the planets, and with Aries which is the noblest of the signs, and from noon as the nobler part of the day, and from the site of the equator, which is the middle of the world."[24] The "best course and the best star" replicate the astronomical configuration in which the world started off. The season is spring, and despite the opening verb, *surge,* denoting rising, the hour would seem to be noon (because Dante goes on to say that the hemisphere of Purgatory was now totally illumined, leaving the opposite side of the globe, where people live, all in the dark). Noon is the hour of Christ's crucifixion and hence the moment of humanity's redemption, the time of day when shadows are the shortest and light is at its maximum splendor. It was day (*mane*) over there and evening back here in Italy: *Fatto avea di là mane e di qua sera.*

Symbolically the four circles and three crosses mentioned in this passage have been thought to represent the conjunction of the four cardinal with the three theological virtues. Astronomically they must refer to four of the so-called great circles that can be drawn around the circumference of the celestial sphere to divide it in half. One of these is the equator, equidistant between the world's two poles, on which the equinoctial signs of Aries and Libra lie. Another is the ecliptic, tilted twenty-three degrees with respect to the equator. The ecliptic marks the sun's precise path through each successive constellation of the Zodiac over the course of the year, and is so called because planets can be eclipsed by the sun only when they happen onto that path (Fig. 4).

The astronomers also draw two circles through the poles, perpendicular to the equator and to each other, one through the two signs of equinox (Aries and Libra), the other through the solstitial signs (Cancer and Capricorn). These circles are called colures, which, according to John of Sacrobosco, means erect oxtails, indicating that from our limited perspective they would appear only as semicircles or arcs.[25] Macrobius imagines them as "crossing the celestial north pole and proceeding in different directions" at right angles to each other to pass through the four cardinal Zodiacal signs (Fig. 5).[26]

The only way to get four circles to make three crosses is by having one of them intersect three of the others. The sun traverses three of these great circles together once in the spring and once in the fall, since the equinox is defined as the moment when the sun, on its ecliptic path, crosses the equator. The equinox is a point that can be drawn on that circle passing through the poles and joining Aries and Libra (the equinoctial colure), the circle of the equator, and the circle of the ecliptic. To find

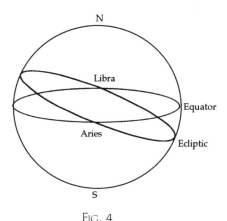

FIG. 4

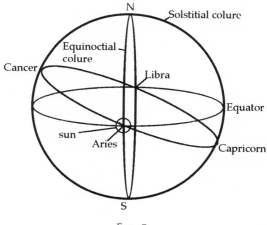

FIG. 5

a fourth circle to intersect with these, as Dante indicates (*che quattro cerchi giugne con tre croci*), one must add one of those two circles that Macrobius said cannot be drawn onto the sphere because they vary according to the observer's location, that is, the horizon or the meridian. At the equinox, the three circles joined by the sun (ecliptic, equator, and colure) will all intersect with the horizon at the moment the sun is rising or setting (Fig. 6).

In an alternate interpretation of Dante's verse, one can count three intersections not at the horizon but on the line of the meridian. Because the two colures are separated by ninety degrees, at dawn at the moment

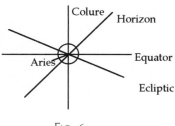

FIG. 6

of the equinox, the circle of the meridian would coincide exactly with the solstitial colure. If the sun enters the equinox precisely at dawn, Aries and Libra will lie on either side of the horizon, one rising in the east, the other setting in the west. The equinoctial colure could be imagined arching from east to west through the northern celestial pole across our backs (if we are facing south). The other colure, passing through the Zodiacal signs of the solstices (Cancer and Capricorn), the other two cardinal points of the ecliptic, could be drawn as passing vertically over our noses. The solstitial colure would be momentarily aligned, therefore, with the circle of the meridian, always located, as we have said, directly overhead. This meridian line would then be intersected by three other great circles: the horizon, the equator, and the ecliptic, in three different places (Fig. 7).[27]

Precisely because of how difficult this configuration is to explain, even with the help of pictures, this is a peculiar "time-reference," and very different from those encountered in the *Purgatorio.* It can be "observed," so to speak, only on the chalkboard, in a diagram, on the armillary sphere, or in one's head. Moreover, despite its ostensible mathematical precision, the reference is manifestly inexact, as Dante admits with his qualifying adverb *quasi,* because the sun has passed the exact

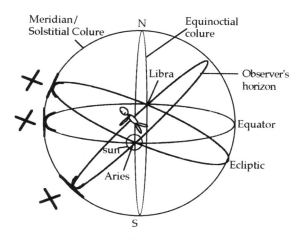

FIG. 7

point of the equinox by some weeks by the date of the journey. Paradoxically, it also seems to describe both dawn (*surge ai mortali*) and noon (*tutto era là bianco*) at the same time. Second, the crux (or rather, three cruxes) of its interpretation depends on those wholly relative great circles, which Macrobius said could not be drawn on the sphere because they depend entirely on the person doing the looking.

Paradiso begins, therefore, with an elaborately imprecise chronological indicator, which seems to collapse noon into dawn, just as in that spectacular unanchored dawn near the end of the same canticle, discussed in the previous chapter, the auroral fade-out of the stars is accomplished by the sixth hour burning some six thousand miles away (*forse semila milia di lontano / ci ferve l'ora sesta*). Such an apparent imprecision is a stumbling block only to those of us left on earth, where dawn and noon happen at distinctly different times. Down here we know what time it is with reference to meridians and horizons, and by the shadows of bodies that block the light—all of which are eliminated by the pilgrim's disengagement from the terrestrial context.

This loss of perspective, necessarily disorienting, is the astronomical correlative of a spiritual *askesis,* or removal from the world. It marks the ascent from relative and conditioned understanding to the regions of pure intellect, which, as the author of the *Asclepius* put it, is "the light of the human soul, as the sun is of the world, and it lights it more, because things illuminated by the sun are from time to time deprived of light because of the interposition of the earth or of the moon during the night."[28] At *Purgatorio*'s end, Beatrice prepares for the celestial portion of the journey by renouncing oblique speech just as the sun, standard symbol of intelligibility, is reaching its zenith. The voyage through the astral spheres thus begins at noon, at the maximum illumination, when shadows are at their shortest. In the *Paradiso,* such times of day as noon and dawn become purely metaphoric, shades appear as lights, and constellated spirits replace the vision of the stars. As objects of sense-perception, astronomical phenomena are lost from view; as dazzling but still inadequate substitutes for invisible truths, they become paramount.

CHAPTER SIX

THE SHADOWS OF IDEAS
Paradiso 13

The *Purgatorio* calls attention to its shadows: the lone shadow cast by the pilgrim traveling with his body, and the darkness into which the earth falls when the sun goes behind its back. The *Paradiso* is instead pure radiance, where lights are distinguished from other lights by their relative effulgence, rather than by any darkness or shade. Dante often suggests that it is hard to see in Paradise precisely because of its luminosity, to which our vision is not accustomed. This chapter will focus on the long astronomical address to the reader in the heaven of the Sun where the stars function as fragments of light out of which the imagination might construct a dim approximation of an alleged splendor. This imaginative exercise, although doomed to failure, addresses the innate human desire for knowledge (in the heaven that celebrates knowers) and puts into operation the psychological faculties that constitute the image of God in man, thus connecting the seeker and what is sought in a logic of image and likeness.

The brightest natural light, the sun, is a symbol of pure knowledge, too brilliant to be contemplated directly; shadows are traces or means by which the brightness might be studied or known indirectly. In Michel Serres's reading, the story of Thales, who tracked the movements of the sun and determined the circumference of the earth by measuring shadows cast by the pyramids in Egypt, is about the disproportion between knowledge and opinion. Serres points out that whereas Thales measured and examined the differential between shadows, the true source of knowledge (the sun) was always on the other side of the pyramid. The study of shadows yields a proportion, or logos, but "the logos of shadows is still the shadow of the logos," Serres writes.[1]

This dichotomy between knowledge and opinion, between the sun and its shadows, informs the Platonic model of education. The freed prisoner in Plato's myth of the cave had to accustom his eyes first to shadows and reflections in water, then to the "light of the moon and the stars and the spangled heaven" before he could bear the light of the sun.[2] According to this model, wisdom is pursued by rejecting appearances, by turning away from shadows and toward the light. Serres has further suggested that the images of objects projected on the wall of Plato's cave ("vessels, statues and figures of animals") represent the signs formed by the constellations of the Zodiac passing continually over the surface of the sky.[3] Because celestial phenomena themselves are in this account mere phantasms—shadows projected by a source of light behind our backs, outside our range of vision—direct astronomical observations will have little to do with true wisdom. The world that Plato's myth describes, then, is one in which configurations of the stars, while appearing to be lights, are really just shadows—the shadows of ideas.

Dante's heaven of the Sun appears to be full of other suns (*ardenti soli*) compared to stars rotating around fixed poles (*come stelle vicine ai fermi poli*). So intense is the splendor of these star-souls that they are said to stand out against the body of the sun itself, owing to a difference not of shade but of brilliance (*non per color ma per lume parvente*).[4] This reverses the normal order of things, as in the natural world stars are obliterated in the vicinity of the sun and become perceptible only in its absence or obstruction—that is, in the shadow of something else. Like the stars in the natural world, however, these souls can be understood to shine not with their own light but with the borrowed light of the sun. In a later canto, Dante points out this assumption that the stars are in some sense images or reflections of the sun, re-emitting its absorbed light after sundown in scattered, dimmer fragments:[5]

> lo ciel, che sol di lui prima s'accende,
>   subitamente si rifà parvente
>   per molte luci, in che una resplende. (*Paradiso* 20.4–6)

[The sky, which was lit before only by him, suddenly makes itself visible again through many lights, in which one shines out.]

The luminous wise men appearing in this heaven are smaller and dimmer reflections, not of the planet (*questo sensibil*) that illuminates physical things and makes them visible, but of the supernatural sun that is the source of intelligibility (*sol degli angeli*).[6] Just as solar light is broken up and parceled out among the constellations, so God's light, or wisdom, is reflected in wise men, compared to the brightest stars. In either case, the dazzling light of the sun—virtually impossible to contemplate directly—can be more readily studied through its attendant constellations, which in the escalating brilliance of the *Paradiso* thereby serve the same function as shadows on earth.

The intensity of the Intelligible Sun is indicated by the fact that its "stars" already outstrip the imagination, even as the light of the sensible sun overpowers the eye. We are told that such things can never be imagined, that our fantasies are too low for such heights, for no eye ever penetrated beyond the sun.[7] These are constellations that can be admired solely by the intellect—the mind's eye (*l'occhio de la mente*).[8] Yet in canto 13, in one of the longest and most complex exordia of the *Commedia,* the poet makes a reiterated appeal to the imagination, that shadowy faculty of our soul, and directs us to compose a configuration of star-images in our own heads that will be a shadow of the true constellation he actually saw (*quasi l'ombra della vera costellazione*).

Canto 13 begins with the repeated command to "imagine" selected stars from the known heavens reshaped into a new configuration—two wheels circling one inside the other—in order to have an approximate shadow of the actual constellation of star-souls Dante claims to have seen in the heaven of the Sun. "Whoever longs to understand rightly" should first imagine the fifteen brightest stars in the sky that are scattered far and wide throughout its different zones:

> Imagini, chi bene intender cupe
>   quel ch'i' or vidi—e ritegna l'image,
>   mentre ch'io dico, come ferma rupe—,
> quindici stelle ch 'n diverse plage
>   lo cielo avvivan di tanto sereno
>   che soperchia de l'aere ogne compage. (*Paradiso* 13.1–6)

[Whoever desires to understand well that which I now saw, let her imagine, and hold the image like a firm rock while I speak, fifteen stars that in different zones vivify the sky with so much light that it overcomes all impurity of the air.]

One of Dante's probable astronomical sources, Alfraganus, says that
these fifteen first-magnitude stars range not only over the entire northern hemisphere (and thus can never be seen together on a single night),
but over the southern hemisphere as well (and thus will never be seen at
all by most readers).[9] The remaining nine stars we are asked to picture
are grouped all together; these arctic stars never set and are always visible circling the north pole. Seven are taken from the Big Dipper—Ursa
Major—also known as the chariot or Wain, here compared to a ship
whose tiller steers a circular course never veering beyond the "bosom" of
the northern sky:

> imagini quel carro a cu' il seno
>   basta del nostro cielo e notte e giorno,
>   sì ch'al volger del temo non vien meno . . . (*Paradiso* 13.7–9)

[Imagine that chariot for whom the bosom of our heaven suffices both night
and day, so that it doesn't disappear with the turning of the tiller.]

Two are from the mouth of the Little Dipper, Ursa Minor, or Septentrion, here compared to a horn stemming from Polaris, or the northern
pole star, which anchors one end of the axis of daily celestial rotation.

> imagini la bocca di quel corno
>   che si comincia in punta de lo stelo
>   a cui la prima rota va dintorno . . . (*Paradiso* 13.10–12)

[Imagine the mouth of that horn that begins in the point of the stem around
which the first movement circles.]

Once collected, these stars are to be pictured as having made of themselves "two signs in heaven" in the shape of Ariadne's garland, or the
Corona Borealis:

> aver fatto di sé due segni in cielo,
>   qual fece la figliuola di Minoi
>   allora che sentì di morte il gelo . . . (*Paradiso* 13.13–15)

[. . . to have made of themselves two signs in the sky like the one that Minos'
daughter made when she felt the chill of death.]

The two circles should be concentric:

> e l'un ne l'altro aver li raggi suoi . . .
>
> [. . . and one of them to have its radii inside the other . . .]

and they should rotate in somewhat diverse fashion, one *al prima* and the other *al poi*:

> e amendue girarsi per maniera
> che l'uno andasse al prima e l'altro al poi . . . (*Paradiso* 13.16–18)
>
> [. . . and both to turn in such a way that one goes according to the "first" and the other according to the "then."]

At best the result of this considerable mental exertion will be to produce the likeness of a shadow of what Dante claims he really saw—the two choruses of wise spirits dancing against the background of the sun:

> e avrà quasi l'ombra de la vera
>   costellazione e de la doppia danza
>   che circulava il punto dov' io era. (*Paradiso* 13.19–21)
>
> [And she (this person who desires to understand) will have a shadow, as it were, of the true constellation and the double dance that was circling the point where I was.]

This sort of imaginative failure is symptomatic of the *Paradiso,* which is all about places the intellect can go where neither imagination nor memory can follow. What is of particular concern to us is why the elaborate scheme engages our knowledge of the stars. The proposed image left to the reader's imaginative capabilities is astronomical, not only in its raw materials—bright stars collected from different regions of the sky—but also in its final configuration of two revolving concentric wheels. The "double dance" of the wise men is comparable to Aristotle's "double journey" of the sun, "dividing night from day by his rising and setting, and bringing the four seasons of the year as he moves forwards towards the North and backwards toward the South."[10] What the prescribed rotation (*che l'uno andasse al prima e l'altro al poi*) actually en-

tails is far from clear, although all agree it contains an echo of Aristotle's
definition of time, a quantity of movement according to before and after, which Dante translates in the *Convivio* as *numero di movimento secondo prima e poi*.[11] Because in that same context Dante explicitly identifies the movement defining time as celestial movement—*numero di
movimento celestiale*—we might well be justified in reducing the ambiguity of the wise men's rotation to the ambiguity of movement traditionally observed in the principal revolutions of the heavens. In the Middle Ages two possible explanations were given for the fact that some
planets seemed to overtake others: either some planets moved at a greater
speed in the same direction than others, or there was a motion proper to
each of them that was in the opposite direction of the daily rotation of
the fixed stars (as we will discuss in the next chapter).[12] The apparent
differential of movement between the motion of the planets and that of
the fixed stars is the "time lag" by which we distinguish among days,
months, and years. The expression *che l'uno al prima e l'altro al poi*, then,
identifies the star-circles constructed in the reader's imagination as an
image of the cosmic clock that measures time.[13]

The whole extent of Dante's instructions to the imagination in this
passage also owes much to Plato's cosmogonic myth, in which the two
great motions apparent in the heavens are reduced to the two great circles of Same and Different that the Demiurge is said to have formed at
the beginning of time. According to the *Timaeus*, the apparent daily motion of the heavens from east to west and the periodic motions of celestial bodies in the reverse direction are merely the sign, or the shadow,
of the perfect primordial intersection of the revolutions of Same and
Different in the World-Soul. The Demiurge takes the primeval con-
stituents of the World-Soul—Existence, Sameness, and Difference—
compounds them into certain mixtures, and divides the compound into
the proportions of musical harmony. He then constructs the two great
circles that comprehend the double motion of the heavens:

This whole fabric, then, he split lengthwise into two halves; and making the
two cross one another at their centres in the form of the letter *X*, he bent each
round into a circle and joined it up, making each meet itself and the other at
a point opposite to that where they had been brought into contact. He then

comprehended them in the motion that is carried round uniformly in the same place, and made the one the outer, the other the inner circle. The outer movement he named the movement of the Same; the inner, the movement of the Different. The movement of the Same he caused to revolve to the right by way of the side; the movement of the Different to the left by way of the diagonal.[14]

Guillaume de Conches called this act of divine artisanship described in the *Timaeus* the *excogitatio animae,* the "thinking out" of the World-Soul.[15] In the Christian adaptation of Plato's genesis myth, this ordering aspect of the creation—the harmonious arrangement of the cosmos—was attributed specifically to the second Person of the Trinity, also called *Sapientia,* which contains the exemplary forms Plato called "ideas."[16] The act of giving shape to all things is thus conceptually distinct from the creation "out of nothing." One bestows existence (*esse*), the other determines the different essence (*essentia*) of each different thing. Thomas Aquinas describes this essential distinction of creatures as follows: "This determination of forms must be brought back as in a first principle, into divine Wisdom, which thought out (*excogitavit*) the order of the universe which consists in the distinctions of things. And therefore we must say that the reasons (*rationes*) of all things, which we have also called 'ideas,' are in divine wisdom. That is to say, the exemplary forms existing in the divine mind."[17] The role of *Sapientia,* or the Logos, in the act of creation, then, has to do with the translation of eternal "ideas" into the vast and varied spectrum of extant species.

In the Book of Wisdom *Sapientia* is called the "emanation of God's brightness" (*emanatio . . . claritatis omnipotentis Dei*), "more beautiful than the sun" (*speciosior sole*), above the entire order of the stars (*super omnem stellarum dispositionem*), and the *artifex* of all things. It was Wisdom, the fashioner of all things, who taught Solomon everything he knew: "The disposition of the whole world, and the virtues of the elements, the beginning, and ending, and midst of the times, and alterations of their courses, and the changes of seasons, the revolutions of the year, and the dispositions of the stars, the natures of living creatures, and rage of wild beasts, the force of winds, and reasonings of men, the diversities of plants, and the virtues of roots, and all such things as are hid and not foreseen, I have learned, for wisdom, which is the worker of all things, taught me."[18]

Solomon's superlative wisdom, which Dante will have Thomas Aquinas define at length in the canto our passage introduces, is thus derived from divine Wisdom. What the wise man comes to know is what the Creator, by knowing, produced. Because creatures are images of their maker, God's act of creation can rightly be called an act of the imagination, a production of images tenuously analogous to the creative fantasies of human beings.[19] As Richard of St. Victor explains: "If you marvel how God the Maker of everything brought into actuality from nothing at the very beginning of the world so much and so many various species of things just as He willed, think (*cogita*) how easy it is for the human soul to fashion by means of the imagination any representation of things whatsoever at any hour and to form some unique creatures, as it were, as often as it wishes, without pre-existing material and from nothing, as it were. . . . God reserved the truth of things, which is the supreme truth, for Himself; but He conceded to His image the formation of images of things at whatever time."[20] The analogy of divine creation and human imagination is at least as old as the Old Testament itself, where the Hebrew word for creation is from the same root as the word for imagination—and which in Latin translations came to be rendered by *cogitatio*.[21] The reciprocal clichés of God as poet and poet as creator can also be traced as far forward as Coleridge's definition of the imagination as "the repetition in the finite mind of the eternal act of creation in the infinite I AM."[22]

The exhortation to the reader's imagination at the beginning of *Paradiso* 13, then, is an appeal to that human capacity that most resembles the creative act of divine *excogitatio*. The prescribed fabrication of two star-circles, one revolving inside the other, puts the person "who desires to understand" in the position of the Demiurge in the *Timaeus*. What the eternal *poietes* or *Sapientia* (in the Christian version of this myth) accomplished on a universal scale, human wisdom may aspire to approximate by means of images, either in the making of poetry or in meditating upon it.[23] Wisdom "thought out" the order of the cosmos in images; Dante's willing student who tries to "imagine" that cosmic order in his own mind will aspire to wisdom.

For Richard of St. Victor, who takes part in this dance as a superlative authority on such matters (*a considerar fu più che viro*), this active use of the rational imagination is the first stage of contemplation.[24] Out of the imagination comes thinking, or *cogitatio,* which Richard, following Paul, defines as grasping the quality of invisible things by means of similitudes of visible things.[25] In the *Benjamin Minor,* an allegory of contemplation in which all the members of Jacob's household take part, Richard describes how the pursuit of wisdom (*studium sapientiae*) begins with the rational imagination, allegorized as Bala, the handmaid of Rachel (reason). The rational imagination (as opposed to that kind we have in common with animals) comes into play when we compose imaginative fictions (*quando . . . aliquid imaginabiliter fingimus*). For example, we have seen gold and we have seen a house, and although we have never seen a golden house, we can nonetheless imagine such a thing if we like.[26] Bala has two sons, one of whom, Dan, is the imagination of future evils, and the other of whom, Naphtali, is the imagination of future goods, which "rises to the understanding of invisible things by means of the form of visible things." The difference between the two is that whereas the rhetorical descriptions of the torments of Hell are always literally meant, narrations of the splendors of Paradise must be metaphorical. They require interpretation, or the *cogitatio* of some other invisible reality: "None of the faithful who reads in holy Scripture about hell, the flames of Gehenna and the outer darkness believes that these things have been said figuratively, but he does not doubt that these things exist somewhere truly and bodily. . . . But when we read about a land flowing with milk and honey or heavenly Jerusalem having walls of precious stones, gates of pearl and streets of gold, what person of sane sense would wish to interpret these things according to the literal sense? Therefore immediately he has recourse to spiritual understanding, and he seeks what is contained there mystically."[27] Whereas the literal imagination of future evils represented by Dan well conforms to the realistic mimesis of Dante's *Inferno,* Richard's Naphtali (whose name means "comparison") well epitomizes the special poetic mode of the *Paradiso* as a whole, with its confessed dependence on provisional likenesses, and in particular the invocation to the imagination in canto 13.[28]

Like Dante's intimations of divine splendors, Richard's illustrations of this kind of *imaginatio* all involve examples of light. Richard writes: "For how great do you think that light will be, which will be in common with us and the angels, if this light that we have in common with the beasts is so great? . . . So he inquires what is this incorporeal light that the invisible and incorporeal nature of God inhabits, and he discovers that this light is the very wisdom of God because it is the true light."[29] The imaginative speculation on future goods retains nonetheless a "shadow of corporeality." Naphtali is thus compared to an animal that does not fly but springs off the ground: "Certainly it should be noted how rightly he may be compared not to a bird flying but to a hind running. For indeed a bird when flying is suspended far above the earth, while a hind when making a jump begins from the earth and is not separated very far from the earth in these jumps. So certainly Naphtali, when he seeks the nature of invisible things by means of the form of visible things, is accustomed to make a sort of leap, not however to gain strength for full flight, since to the degree that he raises himself to the heights he never entirely leaves the depths, carrying with him the shadow of corporeal things (*rerum corporearum secum umbram trahens*)."[30] Like Richard's paradisiac imagination, vaulting like a deer, Dante's exhortation to "imagine" also trails a corporeal shadow (*quasi l'ombra della vera costellazione*) and uses a metaphor of light to adumbrate wisdom, or true light. The conceptual sequence of shadow to image to "true constellation" might be reduced to the one proposed by Richard's teacher, Hugh of St. Victor, in which the wisdom of God is the "truth," of which rational creatures are the "image," of which the corporeal world is in turn a kind of "shadow."[31]

    In canto 13, the most splendid of corporeal creatures (the stars), which are already shadows (according to Hugh) of the image of divine wisdom, are remembered images to be dismembered, rearranged, and reconstituted. The sole laudable purpose in manipulating images (a hazardous occupation that can produce hallucinations and monstrous deceptions), either in rhetorical composition or in rumination upon one's reading, is to gain wisdom. Dante's elaborate address to the reader, in which the text provides instructions for its use, proposes a mental exercise of "cogitation," comparable to Richard of St. Victor's *ex imaginatione cogitatio*. In the ancient psychology, the *vis cogitativa* is usually defined as that power of the soul to compound and divide images and notions already retained in the mind. It is a power of creative composition, the ability to separate pieces of knowledge from their original context and combine them with others to make new ones—literally a power of re-collection. As Mary Carruthers puts it, "*Cogitatio* is basically the activity of putting images together in a consciously recollected, deliberative way." Dante's instructions to the reader in canto 13 are practically a textbook example in the medieval art of memory, cogitation, or "trained recollection."[32]

It is interesting to note that in his description of cogitation in *De Trinitate* as the capacity of the human will to combine and separate things taken from diverse places in the memory, Augustine also uses an astronomical example: "For I remember, no doubt, but one sun, because according to the fact I have seen but one; but if I please, I conceive of two, or three, or as many as I will (*duos cogito vel tres vel quotquot volo*); but the vision of my mind, when I conceive of many (*acies multos cogitantis*) is formed from the same memory by which I remember one."[33] In the famous discussion of thinking and memory in the *Confessions,* he defines *cogitatio* according to its etymological derivation from *cogo,* "to gather." Cogitation is literally the gathering together of things stored up in memory, both images of things we have seen, heard, and touched and imageless notions—among which is to be found the idea of God Himself:

From this we can conclude that learning these facts, which do not reach our minds as images by means of the senses but are recognized by us in our minds, without images, as they actually are, is simply a process of thought by which we gather together things which, although they are muddled and confused, are already contained in the memory. When we give them our attention, we see to it that these facts, which have been lying scattered and unheeded, are placed ready to hand, so that they are easily forthcoming once we have grown used to them. My memory holds a great number of facts of this sort, things which I have already discovered and, as I have said, placed ready to hand. This is what is meant by saying that we have learnt them and know them. If, for a short space of time, I cease to give them my attention, they sink back and recede again into the more remote cells of my memory, so that I have to think them out again, like a fresh set of facts, if I am to know them. I have to shepherd them out again from their old lairs, because there is no other place where they can have gone. In other words, once they have been dispersed, I have to collect them again, and this is the derivation of the word *cogitare*, which means *to think* or *to collect one's thoughts*. For in Latin the word *cogo*, meaning I *assemble* or *I collect*, is related to *cogito*, which means *I think*, in the same way as *ago* is related to *agito* or *facio* to *factito*. But the word *cogito* is restricted to the function of the mind. It is correctly used only of what is assembled in the mind, not what is assembled elsewhere.[34]

To think is to gather together or re-collect images or imageless notions dispersed throughout the expanses of memory. Whereas Aristotle taught that nothing is known except through sensory impressions, Augustine observes that "there can be an exercise of memory without any image of the thing remembered being presented by the imagination." We can, for example, "remember" eternity, which is not a thing of the past, nor conveyed through any figment of the imagination. Socrates thought that learning was a process of re-membering, or piecing back together dispersed fragments of a unified truth: "The things that we learn are not introduced to our minds as new, but brought back to memory by a process of recollection."[35]

Dante's poetic image in canto 13 instructs us to use images preserved in the memory—lights scattered throughout the *diverse plage* of heaven, some of which we have seen and some of which we will never see—to form a new image. The intent of the mnemonic procedure is, however, to give a trace to an imageless vision.[36] It is a selective retrieval of images closely parallel to Augustine's re-collection of notions dispersed throughout the "fields" of his memory, some of which he had perceived, some of which he had learned, and others which had been there all along. Dante's is thus a methodic manipulation of images that would be familiar to medieval students trained in the "art of memory."

In her pioneering study of the art of memory, Frances Yates showed how the mnemonic tools of ancient orators became in the Middle Ages detached from mere rhetoric and applied to ethics, contemplation, and even magic. Indeed, the star-circles Dante orders us to compose mentally at the start of the canto in which the wisdom of Solomon is discussed, have an unsettling resemblance to the star-wheels used in magical arts such as the *Ars Notoria,* designed to gain knowledge of all the sciences—many of which arts were attributed to Solomon himself.[37] A text bearing the title *Liber de umbris idearum,* which Cecco d'Ascoli cites as an authority on the stars, evidently "gave instructions on how to construct astronomical images in order to receive responses from demons." Giordano Bruno would later appropriate this title for his own hermetic art of memory, *De umbris idearum* (1582), a choice that Yates explains with the following remark: "Star-images *are* the 'shadows of ideas,' shadows of reality which are nearer to reality than the physical shadows in the lower world."[38]

With its instructions to divide, compound, and retain images, the exordium of canto 13 is an invitation to use memory actively. The raw material for Dante's constructed image comes from the constellations we are expected to remember, and the final product is to be held onto like a firm rock (*ritegna l'image . . . come ferma rupe*). It describes an exercise in "trained recollection," a mnemonic art whose goal is identical with the theme of these cantos of the *Paradiso:* wisdom. The mentally constructed wheels of stars no doubt recall the two great motions of the cosmos apparent in the heavens, the circuits of mind and providence, which Plato thought we were meant to imitate in our own minds.[39] It is an invitation to mimic the creative act of divine wisdom through a cogitative act.

In *Paradiso* 13, the active manipulation of images (*imagini*) is prescribed to the reader in order to feed her desire to understand (*intendere cupe*), which Aristotle in his *prima filosofia* says is common to all human beings.[40] The three verbs contained in the opening line of the canto, bound by a single subject—to imagine, to understand, and to desire— might be said to invoke those three faculties of the rational soul that according to Augustine constituted the image of the Trinity in human beings (*memoria, intelligentia, voluntas*).[41] *Imagini chi bene intendere cupe* refers to one mind that, desiring to understand, forms this image and "holds it like a rock." Augustine said that whenever memory and internal vision were bound together by the will, they form that trinity, and that gathering together is called thought (*cogitatio*). It is in the contemplation of the truth that the human mind becomes the image of God.[42]

The first line of the canto, and the mnemonic exercise it introduces, are thus an integral part of the trinitarian theme of the canto—beginning with the memory, intellect, and will of the individual reader and culminating in a hymn to *tre persone in divina natura*. Dante's twenty-four-line exordium represents an itinerary of the mind, sifting through images saved and modified in the memory, from the trinity in the individual soul to the Trinity celebrated in the song of the *spiriti sapienti*. Even if the reader cannot imagine what Dante now sees at this juncture in the poem, by her very effort to imagine this spectacle of wisdom she enlists memory in the desire to know and thereby engages the image of the Trinity that is her own mind. The two revolving signs fabricated out of remembered lights will bear a shadowy resemblance to the twin choruses of singing wise men already said to resemble stars orbiting around fixed poles.

The elaborate image, recognizing its own brilliance as a shadowy substitute, begins with the stars as its raw material because stars are themselves visual approximations, images or shadows of the underlying rationality of the universe. Angus Fletcher calls attention to a sixteenth-century correlation between the stars and representational language: "The use of an Allegorie serveth most aptly to ingrave the lively images of things, and to present them under deepe shadowes to the contemplation of the mind, wherein wit and judgement take pleasure, and the remembrance receiveth a long lasting impression, and there as a Metaphore may be compared to a starre in respect of beautie, brightnesse and direction: so may an Allegorie be truly likened to a figure compounded of many stars, which of the Grecians is called *Astron,* and of the Latines, *Sidus,* which we call a constellation, that is, a company or conjunction of many starres."[43]

Jacques Derrida compares metaphors to the sun, pointing out that metaphor both "illustrates" and obscures, just as the sun is "a presence disappearing in its own radiance."[44] All of philosophical discourse aims at grasping the sun of intelligibility, not through metaphors (of the sun, the line, the cave, and so forth), but by its proper name. The end of metaphor, then, would be *anamnesis,* the recollection of meaning, the total erasure or blanching of difference and shadow into the one true metaphor. Medieval Christians figured that this would happen at the end of time, when, as John Scotus Eriugena put it, "God will be all in all, and every creature, converted as it were into God, will become shadow, like stars at sunrise."[45] So, too, does Dante's imaginative spectacle of Paradise fade out as he nears its culmination, from vista to vista, until even the most beautiful is lost from view.

Chapter Seven

The Sufficient Example
Paradiso 28

The tension between a seductive surface beauty and a concealed rational order, germane to both poetry and astronomy, is Platonic in origin. Astronomy, like poetry, is notoriously condemned in Plato's *Republic,* because they both traffic in appearances, in images removed from the truth. The stars that decorate the sky are "the finest and most perfect of visible things," but remain comparable to ceiling ornaments or, at best, to "diagrams drawn and perfected with surpassing skill by Daedalus or some other artisan or draughtsman," which should be used as models (*paradeigmata*) for the sake of understanding something else. Just as the geometer never mistakes lines on the chalkboard, no matter how precisely they are drawn, for the intelligible proportions they represent, so the philosopher should not equate the erratic movements of the stars with the reality of the cosmos.[1]

The exemplary relation of celestial phenomena to the unseen rational construction of the universe is the thread of continuity between the aspersions cast on astronomy in the *Republic* and the extended astronomical hypothesis of the *Timaeus,* which teaches that the intelligible world is the *exemplum* of the sensible world (*mundus intelligibilis exemplum est mundi sensilis*).[2] This fundamental assumption of Platonic cosmology, that the physical cosmos is a representation of something else, remained intact even after the absorption of Aristotelian physics. In a standard thirteenth-century textbook on astronomy, John of Sacrobosco defends the spherical shape of the universe by asserting that "the sensible world is made in the likeness of the archetype, in which there is neither end nor beginning."[3]

As a mere image or exemplum of the unseen original on which it was modeled, the sensible world is congenitally flawed. At the same time, the logic of resemblance exalts the appearance of nature as a superior cognitive crutch, "a foothold from which to mount upwards to the perception of spiritual realities" or "a road leading to God," as the medieval commentators had understood Ptolemy to have said.[4] It is, however, a road fraught with uncertainty and differences of opinion, and one tragically dependent on sensible appearances. Already in the *Timaeus,* the fictional status of the cosmos, as an artifact imperfectly reflecting the idea of the artist, affects the level of certainty to which cosmological explanations can aspire. Plato has Timaeus excuse himself by acknowledging that "an account of what is made in the image of that other, but is only a likeness, will itself be but likely." The cosmology of the *Timaeus,* as Cornford concludes, is poetry, merely a beautiful hypothesis aimed at saving the appearances.[5] The science of astronomy is thus defined from the outset as a poetic endeavor.

The most general overall picture of the universe Dante offers in his *Commedia* appears only toward the end of the poem, in the visual emptiness of the *primum mobile,* just before we exit the physical cosmos altogether. Inside the unmarked crystalline sphere, Dante's traveler is presented with an image, simple and approximative, which he will identify as an exemplum. He sees nine concentric circles wheeling around a stable fixed point (Fig. 8). Although this geometrical configuration is im-

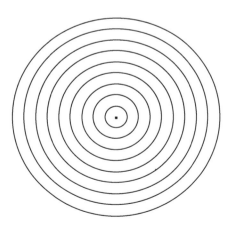

FIG. 8

mediately recognizable as a rendering of the homocentric Aristotelian universe, Dante will claim that it represents the nine orders of angels displayed around God. The paths of the planets are indeed a perceptible trace of their invisible and immaterial engines, the angels, because it is the angels who turn the spheres. It is fitting that it is in the sphere of the primum mobile, normally unblemished by any sensible signpost, that the pilgrim is privileged to view this invisible order directly. Yet he immediately mistakes it for the material cosmos with which he is more familiar.

Aristotle's cosmological model consisted of seven independently moving planetary spherical heavens contained and dragged along in daily rotation by the eighth sphere, or firmament, whose motion, he said, was uniform and circular.[6] Arab astronomers had added a starless ninth sphere to take over the role of the primum mobile after a very slight contrary movement, of which Aristotle had been blissfully unaware, had been detected in the sphere of the fixed stars. When Dante's traveler has reached this largest shell and casement of the world, he is thus actually standing inside an invention of post-Ptolemaic science, a pure astronomical hypothesis.

It is in this liminal space, the cusp of the physical world, itself confined only by the mind of God, that Dante perceives a series of nine concentric circles wheeling around a stable central point. Consistent with the medieval notion of the universe as image or reflection (*splendor di quella idea*), Dante first perceives the image he is about to describe as a reflection mirrored in Beatrice's eyes:

> come in lo specchio fiamma di doppiero
> > vede colui che se n'alluma retro,
> > prima che l'abbia in vista o in pensiero,
> e sé rivolge per veder se 'l vetro
> > li dice il vero, e vede ch'el s'accorda
> > con esso come nota con suo metro
> così la mia memoria si ricorda
> > ch'io feci riguardando ne' belli occhi. (*Paradiso* 28.4–11)

[As in a mirror he who lights a lamp behind himself before he has it in sight or thought, and turns around to see whether the glass tells him the truth, and sees that it agrees with it like a note to its measure, so my memory recalls that I did the same, looking into the beautiful eyes.]

Turning around, he sees the configuration in its unreflected form, claiming that it can seen by anyone who gazes on the invisible wheel of the primum mobile hard enough.[7] There he sees a point of light surrounded by circles of fire spinning at different rates, with the speediest closest to the hub and the slowest furthest from the center. Dante's protagonist immediately recognizes in the schematic configuration the basic form of the physical universe as Aristotle imagined it—a quiet center surrounded by circular revolutions—which is, moreover, described with constant reliance on astronomical examples.

The intense point of light is pictured as so minute that the smallest star visible in the night sky would look like a moon if placed beside it. The first wheel is compared in shape to the halo observed around luminous objects through a hazy medium, and in speed to the primum mobile itself in which Dante is presently being whirled along.[8] This spinning fiery circle is in turn surrounded by others, decreasing in velocity as they increase in size and distance from the center. Finally, Beatrice tells Dante that on that central point of light around which he sees the fiery wheels orbiting "depend the heavens and all of nature" (*da quel punto / depende il cielo e tutta la natura*). By invoking Aristotle's assertion that the heavens and the natural world depend on the principle of the First Mover, she gives further credence to the configuration as a cosmological representation.[9]

The sole fact that the geometrical arrangement is seen to move according to certain proportions makes it a proper subject of astronomy, the science of movement (see Chapter 1). Yet because we are told subsequently that the wheels are composed of angels, not planets and stars, this image is not usually numbered among the astronomical passages in the *Commedia*. Dante has thus chosen to represent the invisible movers by an arrangement that immediately calls to mind medieval representations of the things they move: the astronomical heavens. He represents the intelligible universe according to the pattern of the sensible universe, in keeping with the old formula of one being the exemplum of the other. What has changed is that Dante is now looking directly at the invisible pattern glimmering in the primum mobile and mistakes it for the mere copy, with which he is more familiar.

Dante's protagonist initially takes this vision for a somewhat inaccurate picture of the physical universe, a visible representation of an astronomical hypothesis, with which he humbly finds fault.[10] He says that what has been placed before him would have satisfied him entirely, were the world indeed organized in that order:

> E io a lei: "Se 'l mondo fosse posto
>   con l'ordine ch'io veggio in quelle rote,
>   sazio m'avrebbe ciò che m'è proposto. (*Paradiso* 28.46–48)

[And I to her, "If the universe were disposed in the order which I see in those wheels, I would find satisfactory that which is here proposed to me."]

Contrary to the image presented, in the sensible world he knows the planetary orbits to be faster, or more divine, the more distant they are from the earth:

> ma nel mondo sensibile si puote
>   veder le volte tanto più divine,
>   quant'elle son dal centro più remote
> Onde, se 'l mio disir dee aver fine
>   in questo miro e angelico templo
>   che solo amore e luce ha per confine,
> udir convienmi ancor come l'essemplo
>   e l'essemplare non vanno d'un modo,
>   ché io per me indarno a ciò contemplo. (*Paradiso* 28.49–57)

[But in the world of sense the revolutions may be seen so much the more divine as they are remote from the center. Wherefore, if my desire is to have its end in this wondrous and angelic temple, that has only light and love as its limit, I need still to know why the example and the exemplar do not go in the same way, for by myself I contemplate this in vain.]

Most commentators assume that Dante has already guessed the supernatural nature of what he is looking at when he refers to "this angelic temple," although there is some disagreement as to which is the *essemplo* and which the *essemplare*.[11] Yet it is equally possible and perhaps more likely, because no one ever before represented angels in this way, that the response of the poem's protagonist is that of an attentive student of astronomy. Indeed, the word *temple* might well have been suggested to Dante by Cicero's use of it in the *Dream of Scipio* to designate the whole system of the universe with the earth at its center. Macrobius says that Cicero calls the universe the temple of God "for the edification of those who think that there is no other god except the sky itself and the celestial bodies we are able to see. In order to show, therefore, that the omnipotence of the Supreme God can hardly ever be comprehended and never witnessed, he called whatever is visible to our eyes the temple of that God who is apprehended only in the mind, so that those who worship these visible objects as temples might still owe the greatest reverence to the Creator, and that whoever is inducted into the privileges of this temple might know that he has to live in the manner of a priest."[12] The Macrobian analogue suggests that by "temple" Dante means the physical universe; but it also underlines the provisional, representational, exemplary status of the material world.

The primum mobile and all the heavens contained within it can be accurately described as an angelic temple, because it is the locus of the angels' ministry insofar as they turn the spheres, thereby fulfilling the role of Aristotle's unmoved movers. Hypotheses of planetary motion are thus inevitably linked with speculations about these metaphysical beings, the separated substances that some people call angels. In the context of his discussion of separated substances, Albert the Great neatly summarized three leading explanations of the varying speeds of the different planetary orbits. The most ancient of all involves a theory of contrary movement: the planets and the stars move naturally from west to east against the general rotation of the celestial orb. In the exemplum he uses to illustrate this hypothesis, each planet is like an ant crawling around a wheel that is turning in the opposite direction. The second opinion, to which almost all the moderns subscribe, is that of Ptolemy, which is demonstrable not by a quaint image, Albert says, but by reliable equations. The opinion involves eccentrics and epicycles and posits a total of fifty separate motions in all. Yet it is the third opinion, which Albert attributes to Alpetragius, that Dante seems to have in mind:

The third opinion is derived from the ancients and has been recently renewed by the Spanish Arab, Alpetragius. He says that all the spheres move from east to west and that all are moved by one mover and thus have one movement. But since the *virtus* of this mover is stronger in the heaven immediate to it than in the one some distance away, the circuit is completed in the first heaven in the space of twenty-four hours. In the second heaven, that of Saturn, the circuit is not wholly completed [in the same time] but a little bit is left over. Every day the delay accumulates until after thirty years Saturn has fallen behind by a whole revolution. It therefore seems as if Saturn moves against the firmament, completing its revolution through all the signs of the Zodiac in thirty years. In the heaven of Jupiter, the *virtus* of the mover is even less, and therefore the delay increases, resulting in a full revolution every twelve years.[13]

Descending from Jupiter, Albert notes that the heaven of Mars seems to complete its revolution in two and a half years; the sun, Mercury, and Venus, in one. Being the lowest, the heaven of the moon receives so little of the motivating *virtus* that it completes the circle in less than a month. In similar fashion, Beatrice will go on to explain that the greater and lesser *virtù* of each angelic hierarchy corresponds to the corporeal size of each celestial body (*Li cerchi corporai sono ampi e arti / secondo il più e 'l men de la virtute*).[14]

Albert finds that he must reject Alpetragius' "figure of imagination," despite its aesthetic simplicity and adherence to Aristotelian physical principles, in favor of Ptolemy's explanation, because only the latter is consistent with all the observed motions. Oddly enough, Alpetragius himself used the same deprecation of "fictional" to describe the phenomena themselves, in order to preserve his beautifully simple solution. Perceived inconsistencies must be due, the Spanish philosopher explained, to an "error of the senses":

It is well known that the spheres are eight in number. The highest is the sphere of the fixed stars, and the lowest is the sphere of the moon. These eight spheres are perceived by the senses through the stars which lie on them. Modern astronomers have claimed that there are nine spheres, and this is correct as can be seen from their various motions and structure. Thus the highest (body) causes simple daily motion, and the sphere of the fixed stars succeeds it. It follows from our principle that the sphere of the fixed stars moves more swiftly than those below it; similarly the sphere of Saturn moves more swiftly than the rest, and so on, in the proper order. So the sphere of the fixed stars is simpler and swifter than those below it, and the next sphere is simpler than those further away. According to this principle, the sphere of the moon is the slowest and the most composite. However, the masters of this science and all my predecessors asserted the opposite because they took what they saw as a principle, paying attention to the motions of the stars which the senses force upon us but not taking into account what Reason forces upon us. They did not consider what their natures imply, despite the fact that they acknowledged that most of the planetary motions appear differently tó the senses than they are in truth. Moreover, the anomaly of some of these motions is only an appearance, whereas all the motions actually flow with uniform regularity in rotation, keeping to it without the defect of either increment or diminution. Our perception of these motions is the cause of error when we sense an anomaly in them. But since (scholars of this science) acknowledged that the senses contradict the truth which is the essence of the matter, how can sensory perception be the principle to be followed and built upon, considering the great distance between the observer and the (spheres)? The source of their opinion that these motions are fast or slow lies in an error of the senses.[15]

Alpetragius points out that according to the authority of the senses, the lower and smaller spheres move more quickly—just as they do in the configuration to which Dante objects. Dante's dissatisfaction with it as a representation of the sensible world is therefore based not on his senses, but on his reason, his studies in astronomy. The notion that the lower spheres are actually slower, and for this reason have difficulty keeping up with swiftest movement in the universe and are forever falling behind the pace of diurnal rotation, is counterintuitive. Anyone who watches the behavior of planets long enough can observe that they appear gradually to move in a direction opposite to the daily rotation of the whole heaven. It is easy to see that every day the sun rises a bit earlier, every evening the moon sets almost another hour later than the sun. Yet, contrary to what the pilgrim says, it is the lowest of the planets, the moon, that seems to travel the fastest, taking a mere twenty-eight days to travel through all the signs of the Zodiac, whereas the sun takes an entire year, and the most remote planet, Saturn, takes a good thirty years to complete the same circuit. To the uneducated eye, then, the figure placed before Dante's character would suffice. Only a student of astronomy familiar with the principles of the Aristotelian cosmos, in which the outermost revolution is believed to be the swiftest of all, would expect the opposite.[16]

Beatrice explains that in the material world, the bigger the body, the better: greater size corresponds to greater "virtue."

> Li cerchi corporai sono ampi e arti
>   secondo il più e 'l men de la virtute
>   che si distende per tutte lor parti. (*Paradiso* 28.64–66)

[The corporeal wheels are wide or narrow according to the degree of virtue that extends through them.]

In order to "save" the appearance of the configuration now set before him, she instructs her charge to ignore the *parvenza* or apparent physical size of the celestial wheels and to take stock instead of their relative "virtue" or, in other words, speed:

> per che, se tu a la virtù circonde
>   la tua misura, non a la parvenza
>   de le sustanze che t'appaion tonde,
> tu vederai mirabil consequenza
>   di maggio a più e di minore a meno,
>   in ciascun cielo, a süa intelligenza. (*Paradiso* 28.73–78)

[Wherefore, if you take measure of the virtue, not of the appearance, of the substances that seem round to you, you will see a marvelous correspondence of greater to more and smaller to less in each heaven with respect to its intelligence.]

Thus the heaven that spurs the rest of the universe along with it (the primum mobile) corresponds to the small but intensely spinning circle of angelic intelligences in the image he now sees:

> Dunque costui che tutto quanto rape
>   l'altro universo seco, corrisponde
>   al cerchio che più ama e che più sape. (*Paradiso* 28.70–72)

[Thus the one that sweeps the whole rest of the universe along with it corresponds to the circle that loves and knows the most.]

In Dante's ingenious representation of the interface between material and spiritual worlds, the familiar astronomical heavens are seen to invert the real order of their angelic movers. Thus the hierarchy of angels closest to God, the Seraphim, moves the celestial body furthest removed from the earth, the primum mobile. The next hierarchy of angels, the Cherubim, move the sphere of the fixed stars; the Thrones move Saturn, the Dominions move Jupiter, the Virtues Mars, the Powers the Sun, the Principalities Mercury, the Archangels Venus, and the Angels the moon.

Beatrice confirms the disposition of the angelic hierarchies as described by Dionysius in the *Celestial Hierarchy,* using an image based on the homocentric hypothesis of the astronomers. Dante says he saw the truth of her explanation "like a star in the sky" (*come stella in cielo il ver si vide*).[17] She furthermore states that Dionysius named them "even as I have done," thus transforming Dante's theological source into a follower of Beatrice. This audacious claim, like the natural science of the Platonists, also depends on a specular relationship, in which the "real" thing and its reflection might easily be interchanged: what looks like a copy is in fact the pristine original. The commentators' disagreement over the meaning of *essemplo* and *essemplare* is therefore very much to the point. It is an optical illusion in which the mismatch between reality and representation at first appears to be caused by an error in the sketch of the physical universe, but turns out to reflect accurately the metaphysical order of which the physical universe itself is an imperfect rendering.

Mistaking the real pattern for the physical copy is a conceit that marks the *Paradiso* from the beginning. In the encounter with the spirits in the moon, who look like watery reflections but are instead real substances, Dante says he fell into "an error contrary to the one that kindled love between the man and the fountain," referring to Narcissus' infatuation with his own reflection.[18] In fact the whole of the *Paradiso* is declared at the very outset to be nothing but an exemplum, when Dante abandons all pretense of being able to describe in words the experience he claims to have had beyond the earth:

> Trasumanar significar *per verba*
> non si poria; però l'essemplo basti
> a cui esperïenza grazia serba. (*Paradiso* 1.70–72)

[Because it would not be possible to signify transhumanization in words, let the example suffice for those to whom grace reserves the experience.]

In similar fashion he had warned at the start of his first book, the *Vita nuova,* that the words to follow were merely a reduced scribal copy (*le quali è mio intendimento d'assemplare*) of the book of his memory.[19] Like the semblance of the heavens, which Plato warned us against taking too literally, the text before our eyes is qualified from the start as a mere example, image, trace, and copy of the real experience that Dante asserts lies behind it. Yet like the stars, the text is all we have to go on.

CHAPTER EIGHT

PLANETS AND ANGELS
Paradiso 29

The relation of visible to invisible, of exemplum to exemplar, of astronomy to metaphysical reality, of planets to angels, is the theme of the vision of concentric wheels in canto 28. It is also, as this final chapter will show, the sense of the penultimate, grand astronomical exordium of the poem that introduces Beatrice's discourse on the angels in *Paradiso* 29. Like the difficult time-reference introduced by Tithonus' concubine back in *Purgatorio* 9, this simile requires the observer to supply a point of view; and like so many of Dante's invocations to look up at the stars, it places great stakes on the choice of perspective. With its simultaneous precision and ambiguity, its invocation of vast spaces and fleeting time, and its essential moral drama, this passage will serve as the focus of my concluding argument about what astronomy is meant to accomplish in the poetic structure of the *Commedia*.

We have no way of knowing whether the planetary configuration that opens *Paradiso* 29 describes dusk or dawn. On the one hand, the simile is unmitigatedly exact: it describes a single mathematical point, an instant of no duration. On the other hand, whether that instant occurs in the morning or the evening, in the spring or the fall, is perfectly undecidable. This seems odd, given that the sun and the moon are the "two great lights" made in the firmament of heaven precisely "to divide the day and the night" and to be "for signs and for seasons, and for days and years."[1] The verses describe an instant of balance, an equinoctial syzygy when the sun and the moon are diametrically opposed, one in Aries, the other in Libra, but we are not told which planet is in which sign:

> Quando ambedue li figli di Latona,
>   coperti del Montone e de la Libra,
>   fanno de l'orizzonte insieme zona,

quant' è dal punto che 'l cenìt inlibra
  infin che l'uno e l'altro da quel cinto,
  cambiando l'emisperio, si dilibra,
tanto, col volto di riso dipinto,
  si tacque Bëatrice, riguardando
  fiso nel punto che m'avëa vinto. (*Paradiso* 29.1–9)

[When both Latona's children, covered by the Ram and by the Scales, make
of the horizon a common belt, from the point that the zenith balances them
until the one and the other planet unbalance themselves from that belt as they
trade hemispheres—for so much was Beatrice silent, her face adorned with a
smile, as she gazed fixedly at the point that had overcome me.]

We know that if the sun is beneath the sign of the Ram, it is the time
of the vernal equinox; but if it is in the opposite sign of the Zodiac, Libra,
it is autumn. Whenever these two planets find themselves on opposite
sides of the earth, it is the moment of the full moon; and if all three bodies are perfectly aligned, it will also be a moment of total lunar eclipse.
When any celestial object is on the horizon, we can say that it is rising or
setting. If one of these objects happens to be the solar disk as it leaves one
hemisphere and enters the next, we must be experiencing either sunrise or
sunset. These two moments are so similar that they can in fact be said to
occur simultaneously, because it is, after all, always morning for the inhabitants of the antipodes when it is evening for us. On his first voyage to
South America, the anthropologist Claude Lévi-Strauss remarked on the
fact that for scientists dawn and dusk are a single phenomenon, as they
must have been for the Greeks who gave the same name to both; whereas
in reality, "nothing is more different than evening and morning."[2]

As Dante underlined repeatedly in the *Purgatorio,* in the distinction
between morning and evening everything depends on having a specific
point of reference, a determined point of view from which to judge the
scene—precisely what the prelude to canto 29 withholds. Its ambiguity
makes this an exordium in twilight, *crepusculum,* which means dubious
or uncertain light.[3] Knowing the difference between the crepusculum
that precedes the day and the crepusculum that precedes the night depends on knowing on which side you are. Once again the recourse to astronomy brings the imperative of choice to the fore.

The Book of Genesis recounts that the exordium of the universe itself consisted in just such a drama of choosing sides, narrated in terms of evening and morning, day and night. According to Augustine, the world was not created in the morning, but in a kind of twilight. The first day created had nothing to do with the sun, the moon, or the stars (which are not mentioned until the fourth day); indeed, *day* refers rather to the purely intellectual and immaterial creatures called angels. The first thing these spiritual beings did was to contemplate their own natures; it was only in a second act that they turned toward their Creator with thanks and praise, and knew all of creation in the Word of God Himself. This second action Augustine calls "morning knowledge" (*cognitio matutina*); the first he calls "twilight knowledge" (*cognitio vespertina*). This is the literal sense of the words "and there was evening and morning on the first day" (*factumque est vespere et mane dies unus*). The reason no intervening period of night is mentioned in these opening verses of Scripture is that the angels passed immediately from their twilight knowledge to the morning of their conversion. Yet it is well known that in the transition from evening to morning, some were lost. Those who "turned to themselves or took delight more in themselves than in Him in union with whom they are happy" fell, swollen with pride, and became night. Whether the twilight knowledge that all the angels shared in the first moment of their creation was the *crépuscule du soir* (evening) or the *crépuscule du matin* (morning) depended entirely on their first instantaneous and irrevocable choice. Those who remained with God were called day; those who turned away were made night (*facti sunt nox*). According to Augustine, this is the literal meaning of the words "God separated the light from the darkness, calling the light Day and the darkness Night."[4]

Perhaps one of the most troublesome Christian doctrines is that so momentous a decision in the fate of the universe had to happen so quickly. It was not a defective or even an inferior creature who made the choice for evil in a perfectly good world, but rather the best and the brightest: Lucifer. His very brilliance made it impossible for him to postpone his first exercise of free will, because there was nothing for him to learn, no doubts to make him hesitate, no weakness of willpower in making the decision stick. Yet if he sinned in the very first instant of his existence, his Creator might have to take responsibility for tragedy in the cosmos; and this is out of the question in any monotheistic worldview. The question of how long Lucifer lived "in peace and happiness with the other blessed angels" is, therefore, a formidable problem. It is a paradox in which the problem of evil—the hypothesis of creation and the undeniable phenomenon of iniquity—converges onto the extreme beginning of all things.

The first moment of canto 29, like the first moment of creation, takes place in an undecided twilight. The question that haunts both is how long that perfect equilibrium lasts. The sustained confusion over whether Dante's simile describes an instant or an interval is exactly parallel to the ongoing theological debate over when Lucifer sinned, that is, whether the fall of the angels was immediate or delayed. At first glance the difficulty in Dante's text appears somewhat more mundane. The elaborate planetary simile describes a single mathematical point, whereas its specified referent (Beatrice's smile) must take some space of time. It is the purpose of this chapter to demonstrate that the paradox of the opening planetary comparison in *Paradiso* 29 mimics the paradox of creation and sin that the canto addresses. Between the two disproportionate terms of Dante's simile, as between eternity and time's beginning, or between God and the evil observed in His creation, angels are the only supplement that will fill the gap. The astronomical exordium of canto 29 is thus a poetic representation of the enigmatic exordium of the universe.[5]

Dante's protagonist learns of the world's beginning when he arrives at its outermost limit in the primum mobile. Beatrice, gazing at the point where the crystalline sphere brushes up against eternity, pauses with a smile before speaking of that first instant when the angels, the heavens, and prime matter all came to be—out of nothing. The stunning astronomical exemplum, meant to express that pause, does not actually describe any period or duration, however fleeting, but rather a single, indivisible instant.

We are asked to imagine a moment when the sun and the moon (Apollo and Diana) in the diametrically opposed signs of Aries and Libra are both bisected by the plane of the same horizon. In the poetic image, the two planets are said to be "belted together," giving us the etymological force of the term *syzygy* ("to be yoked together": *syn*—together, *zygon*—yoke). In astronomy a syzygy refers to any conjunctional or oppositional alignment of sun, moon and earth, to make a full moon, a new moon, a solar eclipse, or a lunar eclipse. Dante's configuration corresponds to the equinoctial risings and settings that Ptolemy had described in his discussion of eclipses in his *Almagest* ("those rising and setting intersections made by the horizon crossing the head of Aries and of Libra, whose longitudes are always an equal quadrant from the meridian, we call rising and setting equalities").[6]

The two celestial bodies are also said to be "balanced" from the zenith (*il cenìt inlibra*). The location of the zenith depends entirely on one's location on earth, because it is defined as the point directly overhead. Evidently we are to think of the sun and moon hovering in space on either side of the earth, as if placed in the two dishes of a scales suspended from this imaginary point—the zenith—in the celestial vault. As the planets "change hemispheres" (*cambiando emisperio*)—for example, when more than a semicircle of the sun has risen above our horizon in the east, and when at the same time more than a half-disk of the moon has slipped below the western edge—they are said to be "unbalanced" (*si dilibra*) from that "belt." The distance measured between the first moment of equilibrium to the first moment of disequilibrium is the tenor of the simile. For so long, Dante says, Beatrice was silent—her face illumined with a smile as she looked fixedly at the point of light that had stupefied him. Figure 9 provides one possible mapping of the configuration. In this diagram, the placement of the sun rising in Aries and the moon setting in Libra is arbitrary; it might easily be the other way around. Furthermore, no attempt has been made to draw the planets, and their relative distances from each other and from the zenith, to scale. The essential features of the simile are nonetheless illustrated here: The line of the horizon is always perpendicular to the zenith; at the moment in question the horizon cuts all three planets through the middle, but whereas the earth and its horizon remain perfectly still, the planets are in constant motion.

The figure, like the simile, depicts Latona's two children in their moment of perfect balance, just before they head off in different directions, one going up, the other dropping down, with the unrelenting sweep of

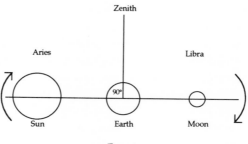

FIG. 9

heavenly rotation. As most of the commentators quickly perceived, the horizon will bisect the celestial bodies in just this way only at this exact moment. In the period before this instant and in the period immediately following, the horizontal belt will divide the spheres of the sun and the moon unequally. As Ptolemy remarked in the context of eclipses, in any such planetary alignment the angles of the various bodies and their shadows with respect to each other and to the horizon are constantly changing.[7] The amount of time measured from total equilibrium to the first point of unbalancing, as one planet rises and the other one sets, is therefore nil. Any moving body is located at any one geometrical point only at an instant, that is, for no time at all.

Clearly, Beatrice cannot be silent only for an instant. If the conclusion of her earlier discourse and the opening of her next are separated by no space of time whatever, then she never stops talking. Even the slightest aspiration between words would constitute a pause of some measurable length, but an instant has no duration. Such a "silence" could be only a logical point on a continuum of sound. What the simile seems to describe is not a pause at all but an extraordinary lack of interruption in the flow of Beatrice's voice. In the temporal world, whose duration is measured by the movement of celestial bodies, it takes time to be silent, to gaze fixedly at something, or to smile. This was the paradox that the Italian Dante scholar Manfredi Porena identified in 1930, which caused him to reject the traditional interpretation of an instant for the astronomical exordium of *Paradiso* 29.[8]

Against the majority opinion of the commentators, Porena declares that the simile does not describe a mathematical moment, or even a particularly brief time. He instead tries to demonstrate that a substantial delay of "somewhat more than a minute" is indicated. Porena focuses on the term *si dilibra,* which he interprets not as "to become unbalanced," but as a syncopation of *si dilibera,* which would mean "to become freed" or "to be released" from the belt of the horizon. In this case, from the moment the horizon cuts precisely through the center of each planet until the moment the disks of both planets pass entirely out of this plane, a significant measurable interval would indeed elapse. The distance between the first moment (of equilibrium) and the second (of release) is given by the time it takes the half disk of the apparently larger planet (the moon) to rise or set completely. For "a little more than a minute," then, Beatrice smiled. The need for this temporal break is didactic: to give Dante's mortal mind a rest. "This," Porena asserts, "is beautiful and it is dantesque."

In his criticism of the temporal paradox imposed by the mathematical instant, Porena is absolutely correct. Whereas less rigorous commentators had supposed that Dante wanted to indicate a second moment (of disequilibrium) separated from the first moment (of balance) by a single instant, any Aristotelian would immediately recognize that two moments can be separated only by an interval of time. An instant is not simply a very short period. Rather, it is either the beginning or end of some period, a mere boundary, and therefore has no size. It makes no sense to call such a moment a *brevissima pausa* or *brevissimo tempo* or "a flash of time . . . an infinitesimally small instant" or "one instant of intermediate stillness and suspense."[9] An instantaneous pause is a contradiction in terms. For Aristotle, an instant (or the "now," as he called it) is the temporal equivalent of a point on a line; yet time is no more made up of these "nows" than a line is composed of geometrical points. Between any two points there must be a line segment or a period of duration, however minute, in which there can be found an infinity of other points. A continuum, by definition, is infinitely divisible. Therefore, because no two "nows" can stand next to each other, in Dante's planetary puzzle we cannot find the first moment of disequilibrium immediately following a single instant of balance.[10] It would certainly be a contradiction to say that the planets become unbalanced at the same instant that they are perfectly balanced. They cannot become unbalanced at the very *next* instant, because instants are never contiguous any more than geometrical points on a line.[11] Nor can they become unbalanced "during" an instant, because an instant has no duration. Movement, rest, and change all require a space of time.

Porena also rightly pointed out that the planetary configuration, because of its alignment with the terrestrial horizon, is not just a syzygy, not just a full moon, but a lunar eclipse.[12] Because the moon is often inclined above or below the ecliptic (the sun's path through the Zodiac) by a range of about five degrees, eclipses do not occur with every new or full moon. In this case, however, the indication of the zenith and the horizon locates this syzygy in direct line with the earth. The horizon momentarily intersects the ecliptic; the earth blocks the light of the sun, and the moon has passed into the dark core of the earth's conical shadow (Fig. 10).[13] In a description reminiscent of Dante's image, Calcidius had said that an an eclipse occurs whenever the two orbs of the sun and moon are directly across from each other, such that a line drawn through the middle of both globes would mark, as it were, the spine of both planets; in other words, when the diameters of both bodies are one and the same line, "cutting" equally through both.[14] Despite its ostensible intent to describe the duration of Beatrice's gaze into the point of light that represents God, the planetary simile thus describes a moment of total obfuscation, not illumination.

Porena used the paradox of the indivisible instant and the seeming incongruence of the lunar eclipse to challenge the traditional interpretation of the simile. Yet these two problems are cause for confirming rather than rejecting this reading. The theme of eclipse, for example, is echoed later in the canto, once literally, when Beatrice deplores explanations of the darkening of the sun at the Crucifixion as a natural solar eclipse, and once metaphorically, when she says that angels need not remember because their vision is, as it were, uneclipsed. Since they first saw God "face to face," the good angels have never had their gaze interrupted; their light has never been blocked by a new object.[15] This continuous illumination is in contrast to the "impediment" to grace (as Thomas Aquinas would characterize it) quickly introduced by the fall of the bad angels. The sin of Satan and his followers is one of the issues

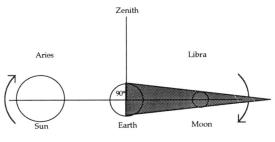

FIG. 10

discussed in the angelology of the canto. This first moral event of creation, which happened immediately, in a kind of eclipse, is exactly the conundrum that the opening astronomical simile attempts to illustrate.

The distinction between the two groups of angels—the haughty who "fell unripe" because they would not "wait for the light" and the modest who remained in heaven—occurred in a matter of moments. The perfect ambiguity of Dante's planetary image corresponds to the twilight knowledge of the angels in the first moment of creation when the light and the dark were as yet undecided. Just how long this crepuscular situation lasts depends on how we choose to understand the angels' relation to time caused by celestial motion. A temporal aporia of this sort is to be expected, not averted, now that we have arrived in the primum mobile, where time has its roots and eternity is just on the other side. In this place, Beatrice may well be able to smile "for an instant." She might indeed be "momentarily" silent so long as she is no longer in the realm of time measured by the movements of the planets—if she has entered, that is, the realm of the angels.

Angels are the subject of cantos 28 and 29 of the *Paradiso,* which are set in the outermost sphere of the material universe, the so-called watery heaven (over which the spirit of God moved on the first day of creation). The progress of the poem, in the reverse direction of a theological *summa,* is approaching its end in God through the increasingly metaphysical issues of angelic nature and the creation of the world. The discussion prefaced in canto 29 by the astronomical exordium and Beatrice's enigmatic pause has to do with when, where, and how the angels came to be. Beatrice explains that creation was both spontaneous and instantaneous. In the beginning, in the first *nunc* from which time began, three kinds of things were created all at once: angels, prime matter, and the physical heavens. The images she uses (three arrows from a three-stringed bow and the instantaneous penetration and reflection of a ray of light into three different materials) are all calculated to exclude an interval of time from the act of creation.[16] In this unique first instant, unlike any other along the continuum of time, coming to be and being happened simultaneously (as Aquinas says, *simul est fieri et factum*).[17] Nor was there any succession in the exordium (*essordire*) of these many things—the totality of unformed matter, all the different heavens, and the myriad of angelic species, were all created instantly, each in its own hierarchical degree. In the case of the angels, Dante chooses to believe that they came into being fully actualized (*puro atto*).[18] Their characterization as pure act also prohibits the notion of any delay between the creation of the angels and their operation (the turning of the celestial spheres).[19] Dante thus dismisses Jerome's supposition that the angels existed centuries before the other world was made, not only on the authority of Scripture ("He who lives in eternity created everything at once"), but also by reasoning that the mover-intelligences could not have had to wait so long for perfection.[20]

Even in Dante's account, however, another event must have taken place before the angels could begin their impetus of the celestial spheres: Lucifer had to fall. Scripture attests to the splendor of his primordial state: Ezekiel recalls that Lucifer was once in the joys of Paradise, adorned with every precious stone, and Isaiah exclaims, "How art thou fallen from heaven, O Lucifer, who didst rise in the morning?"[21] The story of the angels, which Beatrice is now relating, has two essential parts: their pristine creation and their subsequent division into good and evil. It is a point of consummate doctrinal importance that these two facts of angelic history did not occur simultaneously. If creation is instantaneous, and if the operation of the angelic will is also considered instantaneous, and if nothing—neither deliberation nor intellectual frailty—can account for an interval between their creation and their act, then these two distinct moments threaten to slide together into one and the same. To blur the separation between creation and choice is in effect to say that the angels were created in their ultimate bliss and, accordingly, that Satan was created fallen. Because it is unthinkable that God could produce evil (a conclusion that runs uncomfortably close to Manicheanism), most church thinkers posited a delay, however brief a *morula,* between the angels' coming into being and their division into good and evil.[22] Two notable exceptions to this tradition, however, were Augustine and Aquinas.

Dante's own opinion on this matter is the subject of some debate. His expression later in the canto that "you could not count to twenty before part of the angels disturbed the substrate of your elements" has often been interpreted as indisputable evidence that Dante was on the side of those who believed there was a *mora,* a delay, between creation and fall.[23] There is little question that Satan's actual precipitation from the summit of creation into its absolute nadir took some length of time. That is not the same as saying that he remained in peace and happiness with the other blessed angels for any interval, inexplicably postponing his first exercise of free will. Before addressing this point in full, however, I would like to present the arguments of those two influential thinkers, Augustine and Aquinas, which bear on the imagery of our astronomical simile.

Augustine, who continuously pondered the question of evil—*unde malum*—was compelled to assert that the devil sinned from the very beginning and never stood in the truth, as John in his gospel puts it: *ille homocida erat ab initio et in veritate non stetit.*[24] Lucifer cannot have been granted any time at all among the blessed angels, any postponement of his sin, because beatitude consists in the certainty and permanence of that beatitude, neither of which pre-lapsarian devils could have enjoyed.[25] At the same time, he cannot maintain that God created Satan in an evil state; indeed, the concept of his being "fallen" is incomprehensible without some point from which he could fall: "Nor did he fall, if he was made thus. But when he was made, he immediately turned away from the light of Truth, being swollen with pride and corrupted by delight in his own powers. It follows, then, that he did not taste the sweetness of the blessed life of the angels. . . . He fell not from what he had received but from what he would have received if he had chosen to obey God."[26] The distinction is subtle: the devil was not created fallen, yet, once created, he fell.

It has often been thought that Augustine puts forward two contradictory opinions on the time of Satan's fall, insisting on the immediacy of the sin in the *De Genesi*, and emphasizing the gap between creation and fall in the *De civitate Dei*. Yet Augustine certainly never talks about a delay or a sequence of moments between creation and fall. What is essential to both his accounts of this primordial event is that on the one hand the devil never shared the sweetness of the happy life, and on the other he was not created fallen. In the *De civitate Dei* the concept is put thus: the devil sins not from the beginning of his created existence, but from the beginning of his sin (*ab initio peccati*).[27] To say that the devil sinned from the start of his sin seems tautological, leaving the question of when he sinned still unanswered. It does not tell us how long the devils existed in a pre-lapsarian state but simply insists that such a state must have existed, at least logically. The peculiarity of the phrase "to sin from the beginning of sin" arises from the exigencies of Augustine's two premises: the devil was not created sinful, yet his sin was not deferred even for a split second. He makes the distinction that by nature the devil was good, by choice he became evil, so that the beginning of Lucifer's being and the beginning of his sin occurred at two separate moments.[28] Whether these are logical or chronological moments is not clear.

It was Augustine who first interpreted the evenings and mornings recounted in Genesis as different mental states of the angels, *cognitio vespertina* and *cognitio matutina*. There is no reason that (in Heaven) these "evenings" and "mornings" should not occur simultaneously. The point is illustrated by the observation that evening and morning in fact do occur simultaneously at different points on the earth:

But who cannot see, if he is willing to reflect on the matter, that the universe as a whole at one and the same time has day where the sun is, night where it is not, evening where the sun sets, and morning where it rises? We who dwell on this earth certainly cannot experience all this at one time. But we should not on that account consider the creatures of this world and the circular movement of material light, subject as it is to time and space, as the equal of the spiritual light of our home in heaven. In heaven there is always day in the contemplation of immutable truth, always evening in the knowledge of creatures in their own existence, always morning in the fact that this knowledge is referred to the praise of the Creator.[29]

But on the first day of creation, it is of some importance even to Augustine that these types of knowledge did not occur all together, because some of those creatures who experienced evening knowledge did not make it to morning. After the twilight, he says, "if the angelic mind chose to find delight rather in itself than in its Creator, there would be no morning, that is, the angelic mind would not rise up from its own knowledge to the praise of the Creator."[30]

What the Church father ends up suggesting in this passage of his interpretation of Genesis is the existence of simultaneous but ordered events—what some would call "logical" instants. As is typical, this concept is illustrated by the example of sunshine: when anything is lit up by the sun, we can only logically distinguish an origin and a destination, a cause and an effect, a beginning and an end; these events are not, however, chronologically separated (since illumination was thought to be instantaneous). Although there is no lapse of time to mark what is before and what is after, there must nevertheless be a kind of sequence of events when our gaze reaches over land, sea, and sky to observe the rising sun. Or, as another example, when we close our eyes and then open them suddenly, we instantly perceive the sun, though it be incalculably distant. This must be the speed, supposes Augustine, with which, as Paul suggested, we will rise from the dead—"in the twinkling of an eye."[31]

Augustine's examples of vision, sunlight, evenings, and mornings are an attempt to describe what angelic apprehension, free from chronology, might be like. Yet presumably it would not do to say that the devils ever experienced morning knowledge, whether before, after, or together with their initial twilight. Angelic operations of intellect and will in Heaven might be understood as "quasi-changes" where temporal sequence or simultaneity matters little, but the rebellious act that precipitated the bad angels out of Heaven and into Hell was a change of cosmic proportions.[32] The difference between Lucifer "who rose in the morning" (as the prophet Isaiah put it) and the arrogant reprobate who pierces the earth like a worm (as Dante says) is literally the difference between day and night. If the good angels' illumination is comparable to the instantaneous diffusion of the sun's light, then those who did not receive that light must have somehow blocked it immediately. The fall of the bad angels, then, must have been something like an eclipse. This is the conclusion that Thomas Aquinas came to many centuries later.

Like Augustine, Aquinas thinks it perfectly reasonable that two separate events, such as creation and angelic action, should occur simultaneously. He too uses the example of solar, as well as lunar, illumination to anaylze instantaneous changes in which "the termini of the first and second changes can happen at the same time and in the same instant, just as in the same instant that the moon is lit up by the sun, the air is lit up by the moon."[33] These two changes are logically successive, because the illumination of the night air is absolutely contingent on the sun's illumination of the moon, even though both effects were thought to occur simultaneously. The simple fact that the devils first had to be created before they could sin does not therefore necessitate the passage of time between the one event and the other. They would have been immediately confirmed in the good, Aquinas says, had they not placed an obstacle to their happiness (*nisi statim impedimentum beatitudinis praestitisset*).[34] In other words, sin blocked the light. In his disputed question on evil, Aquinas writes that even the bad angels, as created by God, originally had a whole and perfect nature, which they immediately "impeded" of their own free will, "just as when a ray of the sun is hindered it will not light up the air even as the sun rises."[35]

The opinion of the Angelic Doctor on this controversial point was as original as it was influential. The consensus among other scholastics was that the devils simply hesitated before they fell. The necessity of sequentially distinguishing creation from fall persuaded most theologians after Augustine to argue that there was some kind of delay, however brief, between the two events. Yet in the thirteenth century, the notion of the devil's sin as simultaneous with his creation was evidently entertained frequently enough to invite the official condemnation of the Parisian doctors.[36] Augustine's perceived ambivalence was exploited by both sides, as can be seen from the testimony of Peter Lombard. The statements about the devil sinning from the beginning (*ab initio*) served those who inferred that the bad angels not only fell without delay and from the very exordium of their creation (*sine mora in ipso creationis exordio ceciderint*), but that they were in fact created evil by God.[37]

Although all these discussions depend on various statements of Augustine, the conclusion that the bad angels were created evil is not his; nor is the conclusion of the opposing view, which Peter Lombard and all his followers considered the more probable, that there was a delay of some extent between creation and fall: "And in that brief period of time all were good, not by the exercise of their free will, but because of the goodness of creation."[38] Yet whereas Augustine simply said they must have fallen *after* creation (*post creationem*) or immediately after the beginning of time (*statim post initium temporis apostatavit*), this was assumed to entail a little delay (*interposita aliqua morula . . . licet brevissima*).[39]

The scholastics who defended this opinion in the thirteenth century were left with the task of justifying this hesitation, of explaining exactly why this brief interval might have been "impeccable." The recent conflation of Aristotle's immaterial mover-intelligences with the angels of the Bible made this task somewhat difficult (*etsi difficile,* as Aquinas says). If angels understand everything immediately, there is no reason why they cannot make up their minds in a single moment, without the period of deliberation most of us require.[40] As Aquinas points out, even humans, as soon as they have figured out their options through consideration, deliberation, or consultation, decide instantly (*sicut et homo in ipso instanti quo certificatur per consilium, eligit quid est faciendum*).[41] Against those who said that sin must be excluded from the first moment to save the perfection of creation, the Angelic Doctor denied that the sin of a free creature taints the goodness of creation in any way, even if it occurs immediately.[42] He makes the point with a planetary example we have already noted: if a ray of the rising sun does not light up the air because it is impeded, the darkness is not the fault of the sun, but of the obstacle that blocks the light.

In his discussion of this problem in the *De malo,* Aquinas begins his explanation with an analysis of celestial motion and its relation to time; that is, the displacement of the primum mobile and all the apparent stars and planets as they are swept along with that motion. The difference between sidereal movement and the movements of sublunar, animated things (although both are measured by time) is that if heavenly motion were to stop, so would time; whereas an animated thing can stay put and time continues to flow. "Before" and "after" in celestial motion are identical with the "before" and "after" of time itself, as Aristotle said.[43] Although angels are not, like us, subject to time, Aquinas argues that in their various thoughts and affections there is also certain temporal succession (*quaedam temporalis successio*), which is not defined by the movement of the primum mobile.[44] An angel, however bright it may be, can understand more or fewer things in a single glance, depending on its rank in the hierarchies. As the angel considers one thing and then another, which it does not see in one species alone, there must be succession—but this is not a succession measured by celestial motion, which is far beneath the angels. Instead it is *angelic* time, differentiated only by the angel's own mental movements: "In those things therefore which an angel cannot apprehend in a single glance, then, it must be that it moves through different instants of its own time (*sui temporis*)."[45] An analogy between angelic time and celestial time can still be made: "before" and "after" in the angels' thoughts and affections are identical with the "before" and "after" of their own angelic time, just as "before" and "after" in planetary motion are identical with the "before" and "after" of time itself.

Aquinas points out that if an angel, no matter how smart it is, cannot even see all things of nature in one aspect, far less can it comprehend both natural and supernatural things at the same instant. Therefore, for all angels without exception there had to be a succession from the first moment they naturally considered creation by looking into their own essences to the moment they advanced to a knowledge that is above nature and belongs to grace. Aquinas thus reduces the famous *morula* to two separate moments. In the first instant, the instant of creation, all angels were naturally good; they were neither just nor unjust, neither sinners nor saints: "In the first instant of its creation the angel was neither blessed through perfect conversion to God, nor a sinner through any aversion from God."[46] This undecided state, according to Aquinas, is what Augustine meant by the evening of the first day. In the second instant, the instant of choice, the angels were divided, some turning toward their Creator in morning knowledge, some turning away or remaining in themselves, swollen with pride, to become night. This is the explanation given in the *Summa Theologica:* "Thus in the angels the first instant is understood as the operation of the angelic mind, by which it turned toward itself in twilight knowledge; since evening, but not morning is recorded on the first day. And in all angels this operation was good. But from this act some were converted through morning knowledge to the praise of the Word; whereas others, remaining in themselves, were made night, swollen with pride, as Augustine says. Thus the first act was shared by all; but in the second they were divided. And therefore in the first instant all were good; but in the second the good were distinguished from the evil."[47] What Aquinas is suggesting here is in regular, celestially governed time simply impossible, as we have already shown in the example of Dante's moving planets. One instant of time cannot immediately follow another. The fourth objection to this article in the *Summa* points out the contradiction. Two different moments cannot be consecutive or contiguous without any interval to separate them. After the first moment of the devil's existence and before the first moment of his sin there must therefore have been some delay.[48]

The response to this objection entails a new analysis of the nature of time. Despite Aristotle's long efforts to prove that time is and can only be a continuum, Aquinas now demonstrates that time is only accidentally continuous, because our temporal existence depends on celestial motion, which happens to be continuous. Yet it is possible to imagine another kind of time, based on noncontinuous events, that would not be an infinitely divisible continuum, but a succession of indivisible instants. Angelic time, constituted only by their own intellective or affective actions, would be atomic.[49] The objection raised in the *Summa* is based on an Aristotelian notion of time, which ignores the possibility of other modes of existence. Hence Aquinas responds as follows: "To the fourth objection, it should be said that it is true that 'between any two instants there is time intervening' insofar as time is continuous, as is demonstrated in the sixth book of the *Physics*. But in angels, who are not subject to celestial motion (which is first measured by continuous time), 'time' is understood as the very succession of their operations of intellect or will."[50]

The continuity or discontinuity of different kinds of time depends on the motion or succession on which that time is based. It has been suggested that Aquinas invented the mode of existence called the *aevum* expressly to accommodate the angels, although the concept of a third mode, intermediate to time and eternity, was not new. The aevum was previously thought to apply to anything that had a beginning but no ending, such as prime matter, the corporeal heavens, the angels, and each and every individually created human soul. Time begins and ends; aeviternity begins but does not end; eternity neither begins nor ends.[51] Aquinas makes a further, more precise distinction among these three: Time has a "before" and "after"; the aevum has neither "before" nor "after," but both can be connected with it; eternity has neither "before" nor "after," nor can they be connected with it. The angels are involved in not one but all three of these modes of existence: as regards their vision of glory, they participate in eternity; as regards their natural being, they are measured by the aevum; but as regards their affections and intellections, in which there is succession, they are measured by time. Boethius had defined time as a fleeting instant, eternity as an instant that persists. Angelic time, which is noncontinuous, would seem to be made up of a sequence of discrete moments constituted by the succession of their own actions.[52] The real innovation Aquinas makes in order to accommodate the separated substances is this new concept of a different kind of instant, which defies Aristotle's analysis of time.[53]

To conclude, then, Aquinas understood the phrase "the devil sinned from the beginning (*ab initio*)," as did most other theologians, as meaning "immediately after the beginning (*statim post initium*)."[54] Unlike all the others, however, by *statim post* Aquinas means a matter of two consecutive instants, not an interval of delay. All the angels were created in grace, all were naturally good in the first instant of their existence, and none could be considered either a sinner or a saint. Because angels have an inflexible will after making a choice, the devils must have placed an impediment to their happiness immediately after this first instant of their creation; otherwise, they too would have been confirmed in the good.[55] This primordial drama consisted in but two discrete, consecutive instants: one (of twilight) in which all were good, and another (of either morning or night) when there were suddenly good and evil: "And therefore in the first instant all were good, but in the second the good were distinguished from the evil."[56]

In this debate over the immediacy or deferral of Lucifer's fall, it has been argued that Dante himself envisioned a significant delay between the angels' creation and their choice. In the *Convivio* he had said that perhaps a tenth of the angelic orders fell as soon as (*tosto che*) they were created—an easy equivalent of *statim post*.[57] Yet in canto 29 he seems to imply that there was an interval of some twenty seconds between the creation and the fall, when he has Beatrice say:

> Nè giugneriesi, numerando, al venti
>   sì tosto, come de li angeli parte
>   turbò il suggetto d'i vostri alimenti. (*Paradiso* 29.49–51)

[Nor, counting, would you get to twenty, before a part of the angels disturbed the substrate of your elements.]

On the basis of these lines, Bruno Nardi denied (against the Thomists) that Dante's twenty counts are anything like the two discrete instants with which Aquinas describes the events of creation and fall. Yet in order to maintain his view, Nardi is forced to imagine a peculiar sequence of events in the moments after creation: in the second instant the modest angels had their vision increased, but "on the other hand, the rebellious angels were not so quick about it."[58] This implies that the good angels made their choice right away, but the bad ones got to deliberate for a while longer. While Lucifer "lost time" trying to convince the remaining neutral angels to follow him, the confirmed good angels fashioned the four elements and pulled the earth up out of the water in preparation for his fall. Not only does Nardi need to posit an interval of indecision, deliberation, and consultation; he is also obliged to assume that the angels had already been radically divided even before the fall, because the good ones acted in a matter of moments, whereas the bad ones were detained.[59]

Dante's "twenty counts" might be meant to describe the interval not between creation and choice, but between creation and Satan's fall into matter.[60] In that case, there is no disagreement that this calamity, starting in Heaven and ending in Hell, occurred over time. Yet one of Dante's earliest commentators understood the lines as referring to the actual moment of sin. Benvenuto da Imola evidently read "you could not even count to twenty" as a form of hyperbolic denial, expressing the immediacy of the sin, not its deferral: "that is to say, you could not count to twenty—not even to two—because they sinned in the instant of their creation."[61]

Even if by this expression Dante did in fact mean to allude to a short delay between creation and fall, it seems arbitrary that he should choose twenty as the exact number of seconds that pause would have lasted, unless that particular figure had some symbolic force. Albert the Great, for example, saw no reason to understand the tradition that the devil fell "on the second day" as a literal reference to a measure of time. He instead exploits the symbolic value of the number two, saying that two is the first number to recede from one, just as the angels departed from God's unity.[62] Dante avails himself of similar numerological symbolism in the *Convivio* when he says that two stands for local motion, because any movement necessarily goes from one point to another. Twenty instead signifies the movement of change, the perfect alteration of the number ten added to itself.[63] If twenty is the number of alteration, it is for that reason alone suitable to describe the first cosmic change in the universe precipitated by the fall of the rebellious angels.[64]

Yet what is most intriguing about the time-reference in the canto describing the fall is its similarity to the time-reference of the canto's exordium. For example, Nardi understands that the planetary configuration describes a mathematical instant but nonetheless feels free to refer somewhat rhapsodically to that moment as a brief pause, the hush before the start of a symphony. As for the twenty counts between the creation and fall, he calls them *pochi istanti* ("a few instants") or a *rapida successione d'istanti* ("a rapid succession of instants").[65] In both cases the difference between an interval and an instant becomes somewhat blurred, even to the point of equating Aquinas' two instants themselves with a *morula*.[66] Giorgio Petrocchi, who follows Nardi, noticed that the measure of time in the "twenty counts" is not much different from the one used to *cronometrare* Beatrice's silence at the start of the canto.[67] If an instant can be called a *brevissima durata* and the duration of twenty counts can be called *pochi istanti,* then the two time-references begin to look all the more interchangeable. Beatrice begins to speak and the angels begin their decided existence immediately after a first enigmatic moment; yet no one seems to have been able to decide whether this *statim post* entails a single instant or a brief delay. The similarity of the problem confirms our thesis: the astronomical exordium introduces and anticipates one of the canto's topics of discussion. That the poetic prelude should allude specifically to the temporal aspect of this debated point of angelology is not surprising, now that we have come to the primum mobile, the root of time itself.

We might now be able to give a full interpretation of the astronomical periphrasis that opens *Paradiso* 29. Just as the angels were created at an impeccable moment at which they were neither saints nor sinners (*neque beatus . . . neque peccator*), the astronomical image focuses on a moment of ambiguity, when neither planet is higher than the other, and when those of us without a point of view must remain ignorant as to which of the planets is about to rise and which is about to set. As any two planets pass through the horizon in a mathematical line of equilibrium, what actually happens is that first, for an extended period of time, the two bodies are in a state of imbalance in which planet *A* is closer to the zenith than is planet *B,* up to the instant at which they fall precisely into line. Immediately after that point, they become out of balance once again, but in the reverse sense, with planet *B* rising above, closer to the zenith, and planet *A* slipping below. The moment of balance is nothing more than the dividing line between two periods of disequilibrium and the limit of both, at which neither body is higher or lower than the other.[68] What makes Dante's expression of this simple fact in his simile so uncanny, however, is that it pretends to measure the temporal distance between the point of equilibrium to the first point of subsequent imbalance (*dal punto che 'l cenìt inlibra . . . infin che l'uno e l'altro . . . si dilibra*) as if these were two consecutive instants. Insofar as the prior temporal states of the planets preceding the moment at which their paths intersect do not enter into its verses, the simile presents an exordium from the instant of balance comparable to the *nunc* of creation from which time began.[69] One must come to the same conclusion about Dante's planets as Aquinas did about the angels. Although, like the angels, the planets are in their neither/nor position of equilibrium for no period or interval at all, as expressed in the simile they nevertheless began there.

This kind of one-to-one correspondence between planets and angels in Dante's poetry might appear excessively subtle or ingenious were it not perfectly familiar to scholastic disputation of the Middle Ages. We know from Aquinas that sidereal time, caused by the displacement of the primum mobile, and angelic time, caused by the succession of their own actions, are not the same. One is continuous, the other discontinuous. Yet planets and angels are nonetheless comparable in that they both regulate their own kinds of time and insofar as they are both measured by the aevum. In his discussion of the different modes of existence, the Angelic Doctor makes this parallel between the planets and their movers explicit: "Thus it appears that celestial bodies, whose substantial being is unchangeable, nonetheless have unchangeable being combined with changeability with respect to place (*secundum locum*). Similarly, it appears that the angels also have unchangeable being combined with changeability as regards their choice (*secundum electionem*)."[70]

Both these creatures are immutable—the incorruptible physical substance of the heavens and the unchanging separated substance of the angels—but are also mutable, the planets with regard to movement in space, the angels with regard to the movement of the will. This passage demonstrates that the measures of planets and of angels are comparable precisely on the grounds that Dante's simile compares them: change in place in the planets is equivalent to choice in the angels. Thus the analogy I have established throughout this chapter between Dante's moving planets (at the very outset of the canto) and the question of the angels' duration before the fall (addressed explicitly in the body of the canto) is, I submit, neither far-fetched nor excessively ingenious, but standard.

I have already remarked that the peculiar ambiguity of Dante's astronomical exordium, which could describe either dawn or dusk, portrays the momentary balance of planets in a kind of twilight. Yet if we assume the sun to be rising in Aries, as do most commentators, probably because of the tradition of the world's having begun at the vernal equinox, the season is spring and the twilight becomes dawn. At the same time, the full moon on the opposite side of the earth would have to be setting in the west in the sign that Dante calls "nocturnal Aries"— Libra, the sign of the autumnal equinox. The angelic relevance of these two astrological signs is readily available as near as canto 28, not many verses before the simile itself. There Dante compares the blessed state of the angels to a *primavera sempiterna / che notturno Arïete non dispoglia* (eternal spring that nocturnal Aries does not despoil).[71]

The astronomical exordium can indeed be seen as a representation of the first instant of creation, but of the angels rather than of the planets.[72] The balance of the first instant corresponds to the momentary neither/ nor in which the angels were created equal, undecided, in imperfect grace, and in an ambiguous half-light. Yet the twilight and dawn immediately distinguish themselves as one entity rises into a spring morning, and the other, under an autumnal sign, drops beneath the earth to night. The same simple movement yields two opposite results. In addition, the celestial zenith from which depend the two lights of heaven, as we are asked to imagine them, can then correspond to the point *"là 've s'appunta ogne* ubi *e ogne* quando"* (where every *where* and *when* comes to a point) on which Beatrice fixes her gaze.[73] The universe has thus been imbalanced ever since it was released from the zenith of eternity and ubiquity—*statim post.*

Just as Augustine rendered the evenings and mornings of the first lines of Genesis comprehensible by suggesting that the exaltation of angelic knowledge is their literal meaning, the significance of the opening image of *Paradiso* 29 requires the same metaphysical link. Dante's choice of the sun and the moon to evoke the temporal aporia of the world's beginning reflects the correlation of time with celestial movement that has persisted since antiquity. The immediate admittance of evil into the pristine work of a perfect Creator is represented by the various effects of those same celestial bodies: twilight, morning, night. In a universe whose mechanics are never morally indifferent, the moment described by Dante's moving planets is at once a chronological "now" like any other along the continuum of time, and a primordial *kairos,* or decisive moment, of conversion after which time became irreversible and the world forever changed.

CONCLUSION

The depiction of the first free choice in the universe as a moving astronomical configuration in *Paradiso* 29 is the epitome of what I have argued is the essential function of celestial patterns throughout the poem. Even what we might call objective reality or observed phenomena are, for Dante, texts open to differing interpretations. Different readings may make little or no difference as regards these remote and immutable bodies, their position, and their movement. But they do make all the difference as regards the attitude, position, or experience of their observer. The sphericity of the earth makes their effects felt differently according to where we happen to be, and the whole drama of time in which we live turns out to be a highly contingent affair.

The opening image of *Paradiso* 30, and the last astronomical exordium of the poem, can be seen as a sequel to the difficult beginning of canto 29 glossed in the last chapter:

> Forse semilia milia di lontano
>   ci ferve l'ora sesta, e questo mondo
>   china già l'ombra quasi al letto piano
> quando 'l mezzo del cielo, a noi profondo,
>   comincia a farsi tal, ch'alcuna stella
>   perde il parere infino a questo fondo;
> e come vien la chiarissima ancella
>   del sol più oltre, così 'l ciel si chiude
>   di vista in vista infino a la più bella. (*Paradiso* 30.1–9)

[Perhaps six thousand miles away the sixth hour is burning, and this world is already inclining its shadow to a level bed, when the middle of the sky, which looks deep to us, begins to lighten so that stars up to that point are lost from view; and as the most bright handmaid of the sun advances further, so does the sky shut off its vistas, one by one, until even the most beautiful one is gone.]

Now the ambiguity is no longer between dusk and dawn, night and day, as it was at the start of the previous canto, but rather between dawn and noon, between the imminent return of light and its maximum splendor. The darkest hour may be just before the dawn, but the reader of Dante's cosmology is reminded that somewhere else, say six thousand miles away, the noon hour could be burning. In this final, grand vision of the earth orbited by lights great and small, the shadows of Hell, of Purgatory, and even of *Paradiso,* as it passes over our heads like the shadow of the Argo over the astonished sea god (*Paradiso* 33.96), are being laid to rest, or leveled (*quasi al letto piano*). There is an aura of millennial imminence and hence urgency to this photograph of the world as it gently tilts toward the horizontal, suggesting that the expected dawn or noon might not be that far off at all. The comparison of terrestrial time zones so prominent in the *Purgatorio* prepares in the last canticle the more essential comparison between what may be going on here and now in our own souls with what is happening all the time in the brilliant afternoon of Heaven.

For Dante, as the foregoing chapters have demonstrated, stars are lures toward virtue, as well as to higher understanding; like superlatively beautiful ladies, they enamor and exalt the mind. They are thus effective, as well as significant. In their few dim appearances in the *Inferno,* the stars appear as guides in agriculture, navigation, time-keeping, and literary pursuits; elsewhere they are recognized as causes and portents of momentous events and, in all cases, are ignored or misread at one's peril. Heavenly bodies are, moreover, rhetorical; they are part of the God's eloquence in the sacramental commemoration of the central event of history according to the Christians (the Passion and Resurrection), to which Dante has yoked his journey and his poem. Their varying appearance according to different locations on the globe calls attention to a multiplicity of perspectives, and to the advantage of maintaining a double vantage point. Removed from the context of the earth, Dante's astronomy loses its application as chronometer to become a tool of a different sort, a measure of resemblance and difference, a mirror and a shadow, a paradigm for primordial and proximate change.

In his examination on love in the heaven of the fixed stars, itself a metaphor for the written authorities from which one can derive knowledge (*da molte stelle mi vien questa luce*), Dante makes explicit the equation of creation with writing.[1] The alpha and omega of all "scripture" is God, the good that makes the saints happy in Heaven. As I interpret these lines (which can, significantly, be read at least two ways), creation is a text, a *scrittura* that reads or spells out "Love," sometimes vaguely and sometimes powerfully:

> Lo ben che fa contenta questa corte,
>> Alfa e O è di quanta scrittura
>> mi legge Amore o lievemente o forte. (*Paradiso* 26.16–18)

[The good that contents this court is the Alpha and O of all the writing that reads Love to me [alternately: that Love reads to me], either lightly or strongly.]

In canto 26 of the *Paradiso,* the student at the examination is expounding on what he has learned during his long journey. The new understanding is perhaps not that love is the message of the book, because even Francesca, who blamed her adulterous passion on a book back in *Inferno* 5, made that much of her reading, but that all the loves signified in the writing of the universe point back to the ultimate source and object of love, toward which Dante's educated soul, unlike poor Francesca's, is now wholly pointed (*ove s'appunta / l'anima tua*).[2] Love is the meaning not only of sacred Scripture and of vernacular literature, of which Francesca and Dante are both avid consumers, but also of profane science, epitomized by Aristotle who "demonstrates the first love" (*colui che mi dimostra il primo amore*).[3] In a striking incorporation of scientific theory into received religion, Dante puts Aristotle's erotic cosmological engine into his profession of faith: "I believe in one God, alone and eternal, who, unmoved, moves the whole heaven by means of love and desire" (*Io credo in uno Dio / solo ed etterno, che tutto 'l ciel move, / non moto, con amore e con disio*).[4] Unlike any before or since, Dante's consistent use of the stars as paragons or models for reading thus produces a synthesis of science and faith, learning and love, or, to invoke the twin goals of Ulysses, Dante's condemned alter ego, "knowledge and virtue."

NOTES

Citations of Dante's texts are from the following editions:

"La commedia" secondo l'antica vulgata, ed. Giorgio Petrocchi, 4 vols. (Milan: Mondadori, 1966–1967).
Convivio, ed. Franca Brambilla Ageno (Florence: Casa Editrice Le Lettere, 1995).
De vulgari eloquentia, ed. Vincenzo Mengaldo, in Dante Alighieri, *Opere minori,* vol. 3, part 1 (Milan: Ricciardi, 1996).
Epistole, ed. Arsenio Frugoni and Giorgio Brugnoli, in Dante Alighieri, *Opere minori,* vol. 3, part 2 (Milan: Ricciardi, 1996).
Rime, ed. Gianfranco Contini, in Dante Alighiere, *Opere minori,* vol. 1, part 1 (Milan: Ricciardi, 1984).
Vita nuova, ed. Fredi Chiappelli (Milan: Mursia, 1965).

References to the Latin Bible are from *Biblia Sacra, iuxta vulgatam versionem,* ed. B. Fischer, J. Gribmont, H. F. D. Sparks, W. Thiele, and R. Weber (Stuttgart: Deutsche Bibelgesellschaft, 1963). English translations are from the Rheims-Douay version of *The Holy Bible* (New York: Douay Bible House, 1944).

The following abbreviations are used in the notes:

ED   *Enciclopedia Dantesca,* 6 vols. (Rome: Istituto dell'Enciclopedia Italiana, 1970–1978).
ST   Thomas Aquinas, *Summa Theologiae,* Blackfriars edition, 61 vols. (New York: McGraw-Hill; London: Eyre and Spottiswoode, 1964–1981).
PL   *Patrologiae cursus completus . . . Series latina,* 221 vols., ed. Jean-Paul Migne (Paris: Garnier, 1844–1904)

English translations are mine unless otherwise specified.

INTRODUCTION

1. *Convivio* 2.13.30: "[L'Astrologia] è altissima di tutte l'altre; però che, sì come dice Aristotile nel cominciamento dell'Anima, la scienza è alta di nobilitade per la nobilitade del suo subietto e per la sua certezza; e questa più che alcuna delle sopra dette è nobile e alta per nobile e alto subietto, ch'è dello movimento del cielo; e alta e nobile per la sua certezza, la quale è sanza ogni difetto, sì come quella che da perfettissimo e regolatissimo principio viene."

2. Cassiodorus, *Institutiones divinarum et humanarum rectionum* 2, conclusio 1, ed. R. A. B. Mynors (Oxford: Clarendon Press, 1937), p. 158: "Consideremus ordo iste disciplinarum cur fuerit usque ad astra perductus; scilicet ut animos vel saeculari sapientiae deditos disciplinarum exercitatione defecatos a terrenis rebus abduceret, et in superna fabrica laudabiliter collocaret."

3. Lynn Thorndike, *The "Sphere" of Sacrobosco and Its Commentators* (Chicago: University of Chicago Press, 1949), p. 199; Latin text, p. 143: "Et per cognitionem passionum et proprietatum illorum corporum admiratur anima rationalis de mirabili opere creatoris, propter quam causam multum disponitur ipse homo ut deveniat ad cognitionem creatoris. Et ideo dicit Ptholomeus in principio Almagesti quod ista scientia est quasi semita ducens ad deum."

4. *Epistola* 12.4: "Quidni? nonne solis astrorumque specula ubique conspiciam? nonne dulcissimas veritates potero speculari ubique sub celo, ni prius inglorium, ymo ignominiosum populo Florentino, civitati me reddam? Quippe nec panis deficiet."

5. For the category of astronomical periphrasis, see Ernst Robert Curtius, *European Literature and the Latin Middle Ages* (Princeton: Princeton University Press, 1953), p. 276, where he cites as exemplary Gervase of Melkey's remark that "perfecto versificatori non hyemet, non estuet, non noctescat, non diescat sine astronomia."

6. Pier Giorgio Ricci, "Manetti, Antonio," in *ED* 3, p. 801. Girolamo Benivieni, "Dialogo di A. Manetti, cittadino fiorentino circa al sito, forma et misura dello inferno di Dante Alighieri," in *Studi sulla "Divina Commedia" di Galileo Galilei, Vincenzo Borghini ed altri,* ed. Ottavio Gigli (Florence, 1855), pp. 35–132.

7. Pierfrancesco Giambullari, *De'l sito, forma, et misura dello Inferno di*

Dante (Florence, 1544). In his 1481 commentary, Landino included a section entitled "Sito, forma, et misura dello 'nferno et statura de' giganti et di Lucifero." Vellutello's contrasting analysis can be found together with Landino's in *Dante con l'espositione di Christoforo Landino, et di Alessandro Vellutello, etc.* (Venice, 1564). Galileo's lecture to the Florentine Academy was first published by Ottavio Gigli in *Studi sulla "Divina Commedia."* For an overview, see Aldo Vallone, *L'interpretazione di Dante nel cinquecento* (Florence: Olschki, 1969).

8. Filippo Angelitti, "Sulla data del viaggio dantesco," *Atti dell'accademia Pontaniana* (1897): 1−100; "Sulle principali apparenze del pianeta venere durante dodici sue rivoluzioni sinodiche dal 1290 al 1309; E sugli accenni ad esse nelle Opere di Dante," *Reale accademia di scienze, lettere e belle arti di Palermo* (1901): 1−24; "Dante e l'astronomia," in *Dante e l'Italia* (Rome: Fondazione Marco Besso, 1921).

9. Edward Moore, "The Astronomy of Dante," *Studies in Dante*, 3rd ser. (1903; New York: Haskell House, 1968), pp. 1−108; M. A. Orr, *Dante and the Early Astronomers* (London: Gall and Inglis, 1913).

10. Chauncey Wood, *Chaucer and the Country of the Stars* (Princeton: Princeton University Press, 1970), p. ix.

11. Benedetto Croce, *La poesia di Dante* (Bari: Laterza, 1921), p. 67−68: "Ma chi ha occhio e orecchio per la poesia discerne sempre, nel corso del poema, ciò che è strutturale e ciò che è poetico." Giorgio Stabile provides a critique of Croce specifically in relation to Dante's cosmology, in *Cosmologia e teologia nella Commedia: La caduta di Lucifero,* Letture Classensi 12 (Ravenna, Italy: Longo, 1983), pp. 139−173.

12. Croce, *Poesia di Dante*, p. 174: "Il modo acconcio di commentarlo è dare breve e chiara notizia delle cose, fatti e persone che egli memora, spiegare i suoi sentimenti, 'entrando nello spirito di ciò che ha voluto dire,' per intendere la bellezza del suo parlare poetico, e 'tralasciare ogni morale e molto più altra scienziata cognizione.'" See Giambattista Vico, "Discoverta del vero Dante ovvero nuovi principi di critica dantesca," in *Opere,* vol. 1, ed. R. Parenti (Naples: Fulvio Rossi, 1972), p. 421.

13. Giovanni Buti and Renzo Bertagni, *Commento astronomico della "Divina Commedia"* (Florence: Remo Sandron, 1966), p. 233. Other useful Italian handbooks are Ideale Capasso, *L'astronomia nella Divina Commedia* (Pisa: Domus Galilaeana, 1967); and Corrado Gizzi, *L'astronomia nel po-*

ema sacro, 2 vols. (Naples: Loffredo Editore, 1974). The scientific imprecision of many of the standard interpretations has been challenged by Paolo Pecoraro, *Le stelle di Dante: Saggio di interpretazione di riferimenti astronomici e cosmografici della Divina Commedia* (Rome: Bulzoni, 1987).

14. Ilvano Caliaro, "Per una poetica dell'astronomia dantesca," *Atti dell'Istituto Veneto di Scienze, Lettere ed Arti* 137 (1978–1979): 181–188; and Caliaro, *Poesia, astronomia, poesia dell'astronomia in Dante* (Venice: Istituto Veneto di Scienze, Lettere, ed Arti, 1985). See also James Dauphiné, *Le cosmos de Dante* (Paris: Les Belles Lettres, 1984).

15. *De vulgari eloquentia* 2.4.2: "Si poesim recte consideremus: quae nichil aliud est quam fictio rethorica musicaque poita." *Convivio* 2.11.9: "Ponete mente la sua bellezza, che è grande sì per [la] construzione, la quale si pertiene alli gramatici, sì per l'ordine del sermone, che sì pertiene alli rettorici, sì per lo numero delle sue parti, che si pertiene alli musici."

16. This is Dante's analysis of his *congedo,* or farewell, to his canzone, in *Convivio* 2.11.8–9: "Se per aventura incontra che tu vadi là dove persone sieno che dubitare ti paiano nella tua ragione, non ti smarrire, ma dì loro: Poi che non vedete la mia bontade, ponete mente almeno la mia bellezza." He remarks on the untranslated Homer and the ruptured poetry of the Psalms in *Convivio* 1.7.14–15: "Nulla cosa per legame musaico armonizzata si può della sua loquela in altra transmutare sanza rompere tutta sua dolcezza ed armonia. E questa è la cagione per che Omero non si mutò di greco in latino, come l'altre scritture che avemo da loro. E questa è la cagione per che i versi del Salterio sono sanza dolcezza di musica e d'armonia."

17. *Convivio* 2.1.4: "una veritade ascosa sotto bella menzogna." *Vita nuova* 25.10: "Grande vergogna sarebbe a colui che rimasse cose sotto vesta di figura o di colore rettorico, e poscia, domandato, non sapesse denudare le sue parole da cotale vesta, in guisa che avessero verace intendimento. E questo mio primo amico e io ne sapemo bene di quelli che così rimano stoltamente."

18. Augustine, Epistle 55.1.21, *PL* 33.214: "Ista omnia pertinent quae nobis figurate insinuantur; plus enim movunt et accendunt amorem, quam si nuda sine ullis sacramentorum similitudinibus ponerentur. . . . aliquid per allegoricam significationem intimatum plus moveat, plus delectet, plus honoretur, quam si verbis propriis diceretur apertissime." Roland

Barthes also uses the analogy of stages of undress in his meditations on the pleasure of the text; see *Le plaisir du texte* (Paris: Editions du Seuil, 1973), p. 19. For a sensitive discussion of the erotics, as well as the risks, of medieval reading, see Catherine Brown, *Contrary Things: Exegesis, Dialectic, and the Poetics of Didacticism* (Stanford: Stanford University Press, 1998), esp. pp. 15–35.

19. M.-D. Chenu, "The Symbolist Mentality," in *Nature, Man, and Society in the Twelfth Century,* ed. and trans. J. Taylor and L. Little (Chicago: Chicago University Press, 1968), p. 100.

20. *De vulgari eloquentia* 2.1.8: "Optimis conceptionibus optima loquela conveniet. Sed optimae conceptiones non possunt esse nisi ubi scientia et ingenium est: ergo optima loquela non convenit nisi illis in quibus ingenium et scientia est. Et sic non omnibus versificantibus optima loquela conveniet, cum plerique sine scientia et ingenio versificentur, et per consequens nec optimum vulgare."

21. Francesco De Sanctis, "Francesca da Rimini" (1869), in *Lezioni e saggi su Dante,* ed. S. Romagnoli (Turin: Einaudi, 1967), pp. 640–641: "Confondendo poesia e scienza, immaginava che dove fosse maggiore virtú e verità e perfezione, ivi fosse maggiore poesia, e la cosa è tutta al rovescio, perché la scienza poggia verso l'astratto, l'idea come idea, e l'arte ha per obbiettivo il concreto, la forma, l'idea celata e dimenticata nell'immagine."

22. The Latin jingle, "all creatures of the world are like a book and a picture to us," is by Alan of Lille, *PL* 210.579. For the audacity of Dante's likening of his poem to the universe, see John Ahern, "Dante's Last Word: The *Comedy* as a *liber coelestis,*" *Dante Studies* 102 (1984): 1–14. On the topos of the universe as book more generally, see Tullio Gregory, "L'idea di natura nella filosofia medievale prima dell'ingresso della fisica di Aristotele: Il secolo XII," in *Filosofia della natura nel medioevo* (Milan: Società Editrice Vita e Pensiero, 1966); Andrea Battistini, "'L'universo che si squaderna': Cosmo e simbologia del libro," *Letture classensi* 15 (1986): 61–78; M.-D. Chenu, "Symbolist Mentality"; Eugenio Garin, "La nuova scienza e il simbolo del libro," *La cultura filosofica del rinascimento italiano* (Florence: Sansoni, 1961), pp. 1–14; Ernst Robert Curtius, "The Book as Symbol," in *European Literature,* pp. 302–326. Jesse M. Gellrich, *The Idea of the Book in the Middle Ages: Language Theory, Mythology, and*

Fiction (Ithaca: Cornell University Press, 1985), p. 143, dissents from the traditional view that Dante's text imitates the Book of Creation, arguing that the "language of the poem is itself an interpretation."

23. On Dante's ways of establishing his own authority, see especially Albert Ascoli, "The Vowels of Authority (Dante's *Convivio* IV.vi.3–4)," in *Discourses of Authority in Medieval and Renaissance Literature,* ed. Kevin Brownlee and Walter Stephens (Hanover, N.H.: University Press of New England, 1989), pp. 23–46; and "Dante's Rhetoric of Authority in *Convivio* and *De vulgari eloquentia,*" in *The Cambridge Companion to Dante,* ed. R. Jacoff (Cambridge: Cambridge University Press, 1993).

24. John Freccero sees the stars punctuating the poem primarily as a cognitive goal in "The Dance of the Stars: *Paradiso* X," in *Dante: The Poetics of Conversion* (Cambridge: Harvard University Press, 1986), p. 226: "So in Dante's poem, the stars represent the goal of the itinerary of the mind: a goal barely glimpsed at the end of the *Inferno,* within reach by the end of the *Purgatorio,* and achieved at the journey's end."

25. The addresses to the reader were the subject of a celebrated debate between Erich Auerbach ("Dante's Addresses to the Reader," *Romance Philology* 7 [1954]: 268–278) and Leo Spitzer ("The Addresses to the Reader in the *Commedia,*" *Italica* 32 [1955]: 143–165. More recent discussions can be found in Giuliana Carugati, *Dalla menzogna al silenzio e la scrittura mistica della "Commedia" di Dante* (Bologna: Il Mulino, 1991), chap. 3; Teodolinda Barolini, *The Undivine Comedy* (Princeton: Princeton University Press, 1992), p. 14; and William Franke, *Dante's Interpretive Journey* (Chicago: University of Chicago Press, 1995).

26. Judson Boyce Allen, *The Ethical Poetic of the Later Middle Ages: A Decorum of Convenient Distinction* (Toronto: University of Toronto Press, 1982), p. 15.

27. *Epistola* 13.16: "Genus vero phylosophie sub quo hic in toto et parte proceditur, est morale negotium, sive ethica; quia non ad speculandum, sed ad opus inventum est totum et pars. Nam si in aliquo loco vel passu pertractatur ad modum speculativi negoti, hoc non est gratia speculativi negoti, sed gratia operis; quia, ut ait Phylosophus in secundo Metaphysicorum, 'ad aliud et nunc speculantur practici aliquando.'"

28. John Dagenais, *The Ethics of Reading in Manuscript Culture: Glossing the "Libro de buen amor"* (Princeton: Princeton University Press, 1994), p. xvii.

29. Augustine, *De doctrina Christiana* 1.36 (40), ed. J. Martin, in *Corpus christianorum series latina,* vol. 32 (Turnhout, Belgium: Brepols, 1962), p. 29: "Quisquis uero talem inde sententiam duxerit, ut huic aedificandae caritati sit utilis, nec tamen hoc dixerit, quod ille quem legit eo loco sensisse probabitur, non perniciose fallitur nec omnino mentitur." Cf. 3.10.15. English translation from *On Christian Doctrine,* trans. D. W. Robertson (New York: Liberal Arts Press, 1958), p. 30. For relatively recent studies and bibliography on this fundamental text, see *De doctrina Christiana: A Classic of Western Culture,* ed. Duane W. H. Arnold and Pamela Bright (Notre Dame: University of Notre Dame Press, 1995); and *Reading and Wisdom: The "De doctrina Christiana" of Augustine in the Middle Ages,* ed. Edward D. English (Notre Dame: University of Notre Dame Press, 1995). On the reduction of Scripture's lesson to charity, see D. W. Robertson, "The Doctrine of Charity in Medieval Literary Gardens: A Topical Approach Through Symbolism and Allegory," in *Essays in Medieval Culture* (Princeton: Princeton University Press, 1980); and on its complications, see Brown, *Contrary Things.*

30. Paul de Man, *Allegories of Reading: Figural Language in Rousseau, Nietzsche, Rilke, and Proust* (New Haven: Yale University Press, 1995).

31. J. Hillis Miller, *The Ethics of Reading: Kant, de Man, Eliot, Trollope, James, and Benjamin* (New York: Columbia University Press, 1987), p. 43.

32. Ross Chambers, *Room for Maneuver: Reading (the) Oppositional (in) Narrative* (Chicago: University of Chicago Press, 1991), p. xii. See Andrew Bennett, ed., *Readers and Reading* (London: Longman, 1995).

33. Lee Patterson, *Negotiating the Past: The Historical Understanding of Medieval Literature* (Madison: University of Wisconsin Press, 1987). For the ambiguity of language as a central preoccupation in Dante, see Giuseppe Mazzotta, *Dante: Poet of the Desert* (Princeton: Princeton University Press, 1979), especially the chapter titled "Rhetoric and History."

34. A good example of this is the pretense maintained throughout the *Commedia* that the spring equinox still occurs in the first point of Aries. See Chapter 2 of this book, "The Date of the Journey."

35. For an excellent overview of the assumptions of the medieval cosmos in general, see C. S. Lewis, *The Discarded Image: An Introduction to Medieval and Renaissance Literature* (Cambridge: Cambridge University Press, 1964). For Dante's cosmos in particular, see Patrick Boyde, *Dante,*

Philomythes and Philosopher: Man in the Cosmos (Cambridge: Cambridge University Press, 1981).

36. *Convivio* 2.4.13: "La circulazione del cielo, che è del mondo governo; lo quale è quasi una ordinata civilitade."

37. Richard Kay, *Dante's Christian Astrology* (Philadelphia: University of Pennsylvania Press, 1994).

38. Boethius, *Philosophiae consolationis libri quinque,* ed. Rudolfus Peiper (Leipzig, Germany: Teubner, 1871), 1.4: "Cum tecum naturae secreta rimarer, cum mihi siderum vias radio describeres, cum mores nostros totiusque vitae rationem ad caelestis ordinis exempla formares." Translation from Boethius, *The Consolation of Philosophy,* trans. Richard Green (Indianapolis: Bobbs-Merrill, 1962), p. 10.

39. Bonaventure, *Itinerarium mentis in deum, Opera omnia* vol. 5 (Quaracchi, 1891), pp. 298-299: "mutabilia et incorruptibilia, ut caelestia."

40. Claudius Ptolemy, *Almagestum* (Venice: 1515), p. 2: "Quapropter dico quod duo relique genera divisionis theorice sola estimatione cognoscuntur: et non scientie veritate comprehenduntur. Theologicum vere quod nunquam videtur necque comprehenditur; naturale vero propter motionem materie, et levitatem sui cursus: et velocitatem sue alterationis, et parvitatem sue more. Quare convenientia sapientum numquam in eis expectatur."

41. Ibid.: "Preterea in actionibus quoque et honestatibus morum laudabilium non est eius necessitas parva. Imo nihil est magis adiuvans ad acuendos oculos mentis nostre et intellectus: ad considerandum ea que operibus similantur divinis: propter bonitatem moderaminis et equalitatis: et parvitatem arrogantie."

42. Ibid.: "Et quoniam ipsa facit eum qui perseveranter eam inquirit: hanc celestem pulchritudinem diligere: et ducit eum ad perseverantiam divini studii: et coniungit eum ipsi quod anime simile est propter bonitatem forme: et assimilat eum creatori suo."

43. *Purgatorio* 30.1–7: "Quando il settentrïon del primo cielo, / che né occaso mai seppe né orto / né d'altra nebbia che di colpa velo, / e che faceva lì ciascuno accorto / di suo dover, come 'l più basso face / qual temon gira per venire a porto / fermo s'affisse."

44. Barolini, *Undivine,* p. 21, describes Dante's ambition to make "a text in which we make choices within a simulacrum of reality."

45. Isidore, *Etymologiae* 3.39-41, ed. W. M. Lindsay (Oxford: Clarendon Press, 1911): "Sed nonnulli siderum pulcritudine et claritate perlecti, in lapsus stellarum caecatis mentibus corruerunt, ita ut per subputationes noxias, quae mathesis dicitur, eventus rerum praescire posse conentur; . . . Ordo autem iste septem saecularium disciplinarum ideo a Philosophis usque ad astra perductus est, scilicet ut animos saeculari sapientia implicatos a terrenis rebus abducerent, et in superna contemplatione conlocarent."

CHAPTER ONE: THE ALLURE OF THE STARS

Parts of this chapter appeared in an article, "Beatrice and the Astronomical Heavens," in *Lectura Dantis* 18–19 (Spring–Fall 1996): 20–29.

1. So concludes the *Vita nuova* 41.10: "Oltre la spera che più larga gira."
2. *Vita nuova* 2.1: "Nove fiate già appresso lo mio nascimento era tornato lo cielo de la luce quasi a uno medesimo punto, quanto a la sua propria girazione, quando a li miei occhi apparve prima la gloriosa donna de la mia mente." On the *Vita nuova* generally, see Guglielmo Gorni, "Saggio di lettura," in Dante Alighieri, *Vita nuova,* ed. G. Gorni (Turin: Einaudi, 1996); Charles Singleton, *Essay on the "Vita Nuova"* (Cambridge: Harvard University Press, 1949); Domenico De Robertis, *Il libro della Vita nuova* (Florence: Sansoni, 1970); Mark Musa, *Dante's "Vita Nuova"* (Bloomington: Indiana University Press, 1973); Michelangelo Picone, *Vita nuova e tradizione romanza* (Padua: Liviana, 1979); Giuseppe Mazzotta, "The Language of Poetry in the *Vita nuova,"* *Rivista di studi italiani* 1 (1983): 3–14; Robert Harrison, *The Body of Beatrice* (Baltimore: Johns Hopkins University Press, 1988); J. F. Took, *Dante, Lyric Poet and Philosopher: An Introduction to the Minor Works* (Oxford: Clarendon Press, 1990).
3. *Vita nuova* 23.5: "Pareami vedere lo sole oscurare, sì che le stelle si mostravano di colore ch'elle mi faceano giudicare che piangessero."
4. *Vita nuova* 29.1: "Io dico che, secondo l'usanza d'Arabia, l'anima sua nobilissima si partio ne la prima ora del nono giorno del mese; e secondo l'usanza di Siria, ella si partio nel nono mese . . . e secondo l'usanza nostra, ella si partio in quello anno de la nostra indizione, cioè de li anni Domini, in cui lo perfetto numero nove volte era compiuto in quello centinaio in quale in questo mondo ella fue posta." For a rich background to Dante's use of the number nine, see Carlo Vecce, "Ella era uno nove (*V.N.*

XXIX.3)," *La gloriosa donna della mia mente: A Commentary on the "Vita nuova,"* ed. Vincent Moleta (Florence: Olschki, 1994), pp. 161–179.

5. *Vita nuova* 3.1, 3.9, 23.2, 29.1, 6.2.

6. *Vita nuova* 29.2: "Perché questo numero fosse in tanto amico di lei, questa potrebbe essere una ragione: con ciò sia cosa che, secondo Tolomeo e secondo la cristiana veritade, nove siano li cieli che si muovono, e, secondo comune oppinione astrologa, li detti cieli adoperino qua giuso secondo la loro abitudine insieme, questo numero fue amico di lei per dare intendere che ne la sua generazione tutti e nove li mobili cieli perfettissimamente s'aveano insieme."

7. *Convivio* 4.5.7: "Poi che esso cielo cominciò a girare, in migliore disposizione non fu che allora quando di là su discese Colui che l'ha fatto e che 'l governa; sì come ancora per virtù di loro arti li matematici possono ritrovare."

8. *Vita nuova* 29.3.

9. The phrase "science of movements" was introduced to the West through John of Seville's 1133 translation of Albumasar's *Introductorium Maius*. See Richard Lemay, "The True Place of Astrology in Medieval Science and Philosophy: Towards a Definition," in *Astrology, Science, and Society,* ed. Patrick Curry (Woodbridge, Suffolk: Boydell, 1987), p. 67.

10. *Didascalicon, PL* 176.757: "Immobilem magnitudinem geometriae attribuimus, et mobilem astronomiae. . . . Geometria enim non considerat motum, sed spatium. Quod autem astronomia speculatur mobile sit, id est, cursus astrorum et intervalla temporum. Sicque universaliter dicemus immobilem magnitudinem geometriae esse subjectam: mobilem astronomiae; quia, licet ambae de eadem re agant, una tamen contemplatur id quod permanet, altera id quod transit speculatur." English translation from Hugh of St. Victor, *Didascalicon* 2.14, trans. Jerome Taylor (New York: Columbia University Press, 1981), p. 70.

11. Albertus Magnus, *Metaphysica* 11.2.10, *Opera Omnia,* vol. 16, pt. 2, ed. Bernhard Geyer (Münster, Germany: Aschendorff, 1964), p. 496.

12. *Vita nuova* 24.5: "E chi volesse sottilmente considerare, quella Beatrice chiamerebbe Amore, per molta simiglianza che ha meco."

13. Albertus Magnus, *Metaphysica* 11.2.6, p. 489.

14. Aristotle, *Physica* 265a13. Latin text in Albertus Magnus, *Physica* 8.3.9, *Opera omnia,* vol. 4, pt. 2, ed. Paul Hossfeld (Münster, Germany: Aschen-

dorff, 1993), p. 638: "Quod autem motuum circularis primus sit, mani-
festum est."

15. *Paradiso* 1.74, 76–77.

16. *Paradiso* 24.130–132.

17. *Paradiso* 8.127–128: "La circular natura, ch'è suggello / a la cera mortal,
fa ben sua arte." Aristotle, *Physica* 260a20, p. 618: "Tribus autem existen-
tibus motibus, alio quidem secundum magnitudinem et alio secundum
passionem et quodam secundum locum, quem vocamus loci mutationem, hunc necessarium est esse primum."

18. Thomas Aquinas, *ST* 2.26.1 resp.

19. Dante reviews the doctrine of love and natural place in *Convivio* 3.3.2–
14. Cf. Albertus Magnus, *Metaphysica* 11.2.6, p. 490: "Ipsa igitur est
maxime amata et desiderata ab omnibus, et omne quod movetur,
desiderat ipsam . . . desiderium autem est causa motus omnis."

20. *Purgatorio* 17.91–92.

21. Aristotle, *Metaphysica* 1072a26: "Movet autem sicut appetibile et intelli-
gibile. Haec enim sola movent non mota." Latin text in Thomas Aquinas,
In duodecim libros Metaphysicorum Aristotelis Expositio, ed. R. M. Spiazzi
(Turin: Marietti, 1950), p. 590. English translation in Thomas Aquinas,
Commentary on the Metaphysics of Aristotle, vol. 2, book 12, lesson 7, trans.
John P. Rown (Chicago: Henry Regnery, 1961), p. 886.

22. *Aristotelis Stagiritae Metaphysicorum Libri XIII cum Averrois Cordubensis
in eodem commentariis* (Venice: Giunta, 1552), fol. 149v: "Iste motor
moveat, quemadmodum desyderatum et affectatum movent nos, quare
actio videtur esse bonum."

23. Ibid.

24. Dante insists that in his love for Beatrice, the god who ruled him always
kept reason as a steady counselor. *Vita nuova* 2.9: "Nulla volta sofferse che
Amore mi reggesse sanza la fedele consiglio de la ragione."

25. *Paradiso* 28.72: "che più ama e che più sape."

26. See Stephen Bemrose, *Dante's Angelic Intelligences: Their Importance
in the Cosmos and in Pre-Christian Religion* (Rome: Bulzoni, 1983),
pp. 45–55.

27. Albertus Magnus, *Metaphysica* 11.2.9, p. 494: "Movet autem istud bonum
quasi desideratum et per motum desiderantium ipsum movet omnia alia,
ita quod bonitas eius per universum esse rerum causatarum distenditur.

Et sic omnia descendunt ab ipso, ita quidem quod intelligentiae intellectualiter capiunt ipsum, et quaelibet intelligentia bonum, quod sibi influitur, per motum sui orbis exsequitur et explicat. Et id quod intelligentia per motum explicat, materiae generabilium et corruptibilium infunditur, et sic semper tota impletur naturae capacitas. Et quod intelligentia recipit intellectualiter, explicatur a caelesti circulo corporaliter, et materialiter recipitur a materia activorum et passivorum."

28. "Al cor gentil," lines 47–50. Italian text from *The Poetry of Guido Guinizelli,* ed. and trans. Robert Edwards (New York: Garland, 1987), p. 22. Translation mine.

29. *Oboedit* is the word Albert uses to describe the way celestial spheres conform to the will of their movers. *Metaphysica* 11.2.10, p. 495: "[Caelestis circulus] oboedit ei, sicut materia corporis oboedit animae."

30. Kenelm Foster and Patrick Boyde, *Dante's Lyric Poetry,* vol. 2 (Cambridge: Cambridge University Press, 1967), p. 107. See also the discussion of Robert Durling and Ronald Martinez in their *Time and the Crystal* (Berkeley: University of California Press, 1990), pp. 35f.

31. *Vita nuova* 21.5–6: "Questa donna riduce questa potenzia in atto secondo la nobilissima parte de li suoi occhi; e ne la terza dico questo medesimo secondo la nobilissima parte de la sua bocca . . . si come virtuosamente fae gentile tutto ciò che vede, e questo è tanto a dire quanto inducere Amore in potenzia là ove non è." For a political interpretation of Philosophy's "eyes" and "mouth," see Mario Trovato, "The True Donna Gentile as Opposed to the Apocalyptic Whore," *Dante Studies* 112 (1994): 177–227.

32. *Vita nuova* 26.2; *Convivio,* "Voi che 'ntendendo," line 29.

33. Albertus Magnus, *Metaphysica* 11.2.26, p. 516: "Sicut enim intelligentia agens, quae est in nobis, per spiritus invehit manibus et instrumentis formam, quam inducere vult in materiam, ita intelligentia agens, quae movet orbem et stellam vel stellas, luminari invehit formam, et per lumen luminaris traducit eam in materiam, quam movet, et hoc sic tangens materiam educit eam de potentia ad actum."

34. "Tanto gentile," *Vita nuova* 26.5.

35. The pivotal role of these two canzoni is confirmed by their citation in the *Commedia:* "Donne che avete" in *Purgatorio* 24.51; "Voi che 'ntendendo" in *Paradiso* 8.37.

36. *Convivio* 2.14.21–2.15.1: "Per lo terzo cielo io intendo la Rettorica . . . ché sono di quella movitori, sì come Boezio e Tulio . . . colli raggi della stella loro, la quale è la scrittura di quella: onde in ciascuna scienza la scrittura è stella piena di luce."

37. *Convivio* 3.9.13–14: "quasi a guisa che fa la nostra lettera in sulla carta umida."

38. *Convivio* 3.7.16: "Questa donna sia una cosa visibilemente miraculosa, della quale li occhi delli uomini cotidianamente possono esperienza avere;" 3.8.3: "Nel suo corpo, per bontade dell'anima, sensibile bellezza appare."

39. *Convivio* 3.8.9: "Li quali due luoghi, per bella similitudine, si possono appellare balconi della donna che nel dificio del corpo abita, cioè l'anima."

40. *Convivio* 2.15.4: "Li occhi di questa donna sono le sue dimostrazioni, le quali, dritte nelli occhi dello 'ntelletto, innamorano l'anima liberata nelle [sue] condizioni. O dolcissimi e ineffabili sembianti, e rubatori subitani della mente umana, che nelle dimostrazioni, [cioè] nelli occhi della Filosofia apparite, quando essa colli suoi drudi ragiona!"

41. *Convivio* 3.15.2: "Li occhi de la Sapienza sono le sue dimostrazioni, colle quali si vede la veritade certissimamente; e lo suo riso sono le sue persuasioni, nelle quali si dimostra la luce interiore della Sapienza sotto alcuno velamento: e in queste due cose si sente quel piacere altissimo di beatitudine lo quale è massimo bene in Paradiso."

42. *Convivio* 3.15.11: "Dove è da sapere che la moralitade è bellezza della filosofia: ché così come la bellezza del corpo resulta dalle membra in quanto sono debitamente ordinate, così la bellezza della sapienza, che è corpo di Filosofia come detto è, resulta dall'ordine delle vertudi morali, che fanno quella piacere sensibilmente."

43. *Convivio* 3.7.13, 3.13.11: "Per che aviene che li altri miseri che ciò mirano, ripensando lo loro difetto, dopo lo desiderio della perfezione caggiono in fatica di sospiri."

44. J. A. Mazzeo, *Medieval Cultural Tradition in Dante's Comedy* (Westport, Conn.: Greenwood Press, 1968), pp. 106–107: "The physical light of the stars proceeds directly or indirectly from the immaterial qualities of the moving intellect, for 'the mingled virtue shines through the body.' The gleam of the heavenly bodies is a reflection of God's joy in His creation, as joy in humans is evidenced by light spreading through the pupil of the

eye. . . . The sensible beauty and light of the heavens is the 'translation' of the immaterial light and beauty which is God. In human beings this translation of the internal into the external light was most manifest in the eyes and the smile. The stars are, metaphorically, the eyes of God: they most reveal His beauty and His joy, they gleam with a kind of rejoicing."

45. *Convivio* 2.15.11: "Poi quando dice: *tu vedrai / di sì alti miracoli adornezza,* annunzia che per lei si vedranno li addornamenti delli miracoli: e vero dice, ché li addornamenti delle maraviglie è vedere le cagioni di quelle; le quali ella dimostra, sì come nel principio della Metafisica pare sentire lo Filosofo, dicendo che per questi addornamenti vedere, cominciaro li uomini ad innamorare di questa donna."

46. Aristotle, *Metaphysica* 982b12–15; Latin text of Aristotle in Aquinas, *In duodecim libros,* p. 17: "Nam propter admirari homines nunc et primum incoeperunt philosophari: a principio quidem pauciora dubitabilium mirantes, deinde paulatim procedentes, et de maioribus dubitantes, ut de lunae passionibus, et de his quae circa solem et astra, etiam de universi generatione." For a discussion of this passage in relation to Dante, see Patrick Boyde, *Dante: Philomythes and Philosopher* (Cambridge: Cambridge University Press, 1981), pp. 49–51.

47. Albertus Magnus, *Metaphysica* 1.2.6, *Opera omnia,* vol. 16, pt. 1, p. 23: "*Sicut de passionibus lunae* secundum mansiones, accessiones et eclipses, et de his *quae sunt circa solem et astra,* sicut quod sol declinat ad utramque partem aequinoctialis, quod quartus circuli signorum transit temporibus inaequalibus, quod eclipsatur, quod aequat tempus generationis et corruptionis terrae nascentium et huiusmodi, et quod astra moventur a locis suis et non a figura imaginum, quod motum proprium habent super polos circuli signorum et motum diurnum super polos mundi et huiusmodi, quae ignorans scientiam astrorum admiratur."

48. *Purgatorio* 31.52–54: "E se 'l sommo piacer sì ti fallio / per la mia morte, qual cosa mortale / dovea poi trarre te nel suo disio?"

49. *Petri Allegherii super Dantis Ipsius Genitoris Comoediam Commentarium,* ed. V. Nannucci (Florence, 1845), pp. 620–621. See also John Freccero, "The Dance of the Stars: *Paradiso* X," in *Dante: The Poetics of Conversion* (Cambridge: Harvard University Press, 1986); and Kenelm Foster, "The Celebration of Order: *Paradiso* X." in *The Two Dantes and Other Studies* (Berkeley: University of California Press, 1977), pp. 120–125.

50. *Paradiso* 10.22–23: "Or ti riman, lettor, sovra 'l tuo banco, / dietro pensando a ciò che si preliba."

51. *Paradiso* 10.4–6: "Quanto per mente e per loco si gira / con tant' ordine fé, ch'esser non puote / sanza gustar di lui chi ciò rimira." *Convivio* 3.12.13: "Quasi come druda della quale nullo amadore prende compiuta gioia, ma nel suo aspetto [mirando] contenta[se]ne la loro vaghezza."

52. *Paradiso* 31.32–33: "Che ciascun giorno d'Elice si cuopra, / rotante col suo figlio ond'ella è vaga"; *Paradiso* 8.11–12: "La stella / che 'l sol vagheggia or da coppa or da ciglio." See also Lucan, *Pharsalia* 9.12, in *Lucan,* trans. J. Duff (London: Heinemann, 1962), p. 504: "stellasque vagas." See also Boethius, *Consolatio* I, meter 2, line 10, in *Philosophiae consolatio,* ed. E. Rapisarda (Catania, Italy: Centro di Studi sull'Antico Cristianesimo, 1961), p. 6: "Et quaecumque vagos stella recursus."

53. Plato, *Timeaus* 47A–B; Francis M. Cornford, *Plato's Cosmology: The "Timaeus" of Plato* (London: Routledge and K. Paul, 1952), p. 158.

54. On the last lines of the poem, see Bruno Nardi, "'Sì come rota ch'igualmente è mossa'" in *Nel mondo di Dante* (Rome: Edizioni di Storia e Letteratura, 1944), pp. 337–50; John Freccero, "The Final Image," in *Dante: The Poetics of Conversion* (Cambridge: Harvard University Press, 1986); and Lino Pertile, "Poesia e scienza nell'ultima immagine del *Paradiso,"* in *Dante e la scienza,* ed. P. Boyde and V. Russo (Ravenna: Longo, 1995).

CHAPTER TWO: THE DATE OF THE JOURNEY

1. On the range of medieval notions of time, see Anne Higgins, "Medieval Notions of the Structure of Time," *Journal of Medieval and Renaissance Studies* 19.2 (1989): 227–250.

2. Psalm 89:10: "Dies annorum nostrorum in ipsis septuaginta anni." See Boccaccio, *Esposizioni sopra la comedia* I.1.3, ed. G. Padoan (Milan: Mondadori, 1965), p. 19.

3. *Convivio* 4.23.11: "Onde si può comprendere per quello 'quasi' che al trentacinquesimo anno di Cristo era lo colmo della sua etade." Dante also explains that the course of a man's life is similar to the arc that celestial bodies (which are the proximate cause of our physical existence) make as they revolve over the earth, from their rising to their setting (*Convivio* 4.23.6).

4. Leonardo Bruni, *Le vite di Dante e del Petrarca,* ed. A. Lanza (Rome:

Archivio Guido Izzi, 1987), p. 36. "Tutti i mali e l'inconvenienti miei dalli infausti comizi del mio priorato ebbono cagione e principio; del quale priorato, benché per prudenzia io non fusse degno, niente di meno per fede e per età non ne era indegno." For an elaboration of Dante's personal reasons for choosing the coincidence of Easter and the Florentine New Year, see Peter Armour, *The Door of Purgatory: A Study of Multiple Symbolism in Dante's Purgatorio* (Oxford: Clarendon Press, 1983), pp. 174–175.

5. Giovanni Villani, *Nuova cronica,* vol. 2, book 9, ed. G. Porta (Parma, Italy: Ugo Guando, 1991), p. 58: "Ma considerando che la nostra città di Firenze, figliuola e fattura di Roma, era nel suo montare e a seguire grandi cose, sì come Roma nel suo calare, mi parve convenevole di recare in questo volume e nuova cronica tutti i fatti e cominciamenti della città di Firenze."

6. *Paradiso* 9.37–42. For the 1300 Jubilee, see Paolo Brezzi, *Storia degli anni santi* (Milan: Mursia, 1975). Villani, *Nuova cronica,* p. 36, uses a similar phrase: "Negli anni di Cristo MCCC, secondo la Nativitade di Cristo, con ciò fosse cosa che si dicesse per molti che per adietro ogni centesimo d'anni della Natività di Cristo il papa ch'era in quei tempi facie grande indulgenza."

7. Filippo Angelitti (*Rassegna di letteratura italiana* 2 [1897]: 193–207, p. 194) uses the word *terrore,* and D'Ovidio ("L'anno della visione dantesca," ibid., pp. 283–284), declares that *dantisti* will be *sbigottiti* ("dismayed") by Angelitti's findings. See also Demetrio Marzi, *Bulletino della società dantesca* 5, nos. 6–7 (1898): 82–96; and Armour, *Door,* pp. 174–175. Walter and Teresa Parri (*Anno del Viaggio e Giorno Iniziale della Commedia* [Florence: Olschki, 1956], p. 10) protest the importance of determining the correct date: "Per chi invece tenta di far rivivere quanto fu la passione di Dante e come prese forma nella Commedia, la definizione di anno non è una ridicola precisazione anagrafica, non è la gloriuzza del computista che, razzolando tra le carte, scova un vecchio errore di cifra."

8. Pierfrancesco Giambullari, *De'l sito, forma, et misure, del Inferno di Dante* (Florence, 1544), p. 25: "Ma perché in tutto questo viaggio, descrive egli molto particolarmente tutto il Corso della Luna; Bisogna diligentemente avvertire, che avvegna che secondo le Tavole, la véra opposizione della Luna, fusse stata al Meridiano di Firenze il Lunedi santo e cio è il Giorno

quarto di Aprile circa ore XV dopo mezzo dì, essendo il Sole ne' gradi XXII dello Ariete, et la Luna ne XXII della Libra: il Poeta nientedimeno per servirsene forse al senso mistico, dice che ella fu tonda la notte, che si ritrovò nella Selva, la quale come appresso fia manifesto, fu la notte che è tra il Giovedì et il Venerdì santo. La onde se non vogliamo scordar dal testo, bisogna che poniamo la luna tonda et tutta piena, non il lunedì, ma il Giovedì notte, cóme egli stesso ce la descrive nel Canto XX, dello Inferno."

9. Dante Alighieri, *La Divina Commedia di Dante Alighieri . . . ridotta a miglior lezione degli accademici della Crusca* (Florence, 1595). The "Opinione intorno al tempo del viaggio di D" in that volume states that, according to the "tavole Pruteniche," the sun was "ne' gra. 22.m.55. d'Ariete" and that Venus was "29.m.29 d'Ariete." Lagging behind the sun by some 7 degrees, Venus would therefore be an evening star, setting after the sun and rising invisibly well after dawn.

10. Filippo Angelitti, "Sulla data del viaggio dantesco," *Atti dell'Accademia Pontaniana* (1897): 1–100. Allegiance to Angelitti's date of 1301 has been maintained in recent times by Ideale Capasso, *L'astronomia nella Divina Commedia* (Pisa: Domus Galilaeana, 1967).

11. In his response to D'Ovidio in *Rassegna di letteratura italiana* 2 (1897): 193–207, Angelitti declared that his science "è di una sicurezza assoluta ed imprescindibile"; and that "le verità scientifiche, e specialmente le astronomiche, in generale si possano manomettere meno delle storiche." In further defense of his 1301 thesis, Angelitti systematically reinterprets all Dante's references to historical dates in "Sull'anno della visione dantesca: Nuove considerazioni," *Atti dell'Accademia Pontaniana* 28.17 (1898): 1–38.

12. Edward Moore, "The Astronomy of Dante," *Studies in Dante,* 3rd ser. (1903; reprint, New York: Haskell House, 1968), p. 2. In another context, however, he says that it would never occur to Dante to alter or distort the plainest facts "for the sake of poetic effect, least of all in any description intended . . . to give a datum of time" (p. 58). See also Moore's essay "The Date Assumed by Dante for the Vision of the *Divina Commedia*," in the same volume, pp. 144–177.

13. M. A. Orr, *Dante and the Early Astronomers* (1913; reprint, London: Gall and Inglis, 1956), p. 420. Orr's source is Profacio, Jacob ben Machir ben

Tibbon (b. 1236), *Almanach Dantis Aligherii*, ed. G. Boffitto and C. Melzi d'Eril (Florence, 1908).

14. Patrick Boyde, *Dante Philomythes and Philosopher: Man in the Cosmos* (Cambridge: Cambridge University Press, 1981), pp. 163–164. Similarly, Armour, in *Door*, pp. 174–176, asserts that Dante is likely to "blur" personal experiences to "render them indeterminate, and so to capture their symbolic and universal essence," and refers to his astronomy as "ideal." In less flexible interpretations, theology as well as science can produce strident arguments regarding the exact date of the journey, as can be seen in Antonio Mastrobuono's discussion in *Dante's Journey of Sanctification* (Washington, D.C.: Regnery Gateway, 1990), pp. 131–166.

15. Charles S. Singleton, *Commedia: Elements of Structure* (1954; reprint, Baltimore: Johns Hopkins University Press, 1977), p. 62. For recent reassessments of the tension between prophetic truth and literary fiction, see Teodolinda Barolini, *The Undivine Comedy: Detheologizing Dante* (Princeton: Princeton University Press, 1992), esp. pp. 1–20; and John Freccero, "Introduction to the *Inferno*," in *The Cambridge Companion to Dante*, ed. R. Jacoff (Cambridge: Cambridge University Press, 1993).

16. The atomic clocks do have to be adjusted periodically by the intercalation of so-called leap seconds. K. P. Moesgaard, "Basic Units in Chronology and Chronometry," in *The Gregorian Reform of the Calendar*, ed. G. V. Coyne, M. A. Hoskin, and O. Pedersen (Vatican City: Specola Vaticana, 1983), pp. 3–14.

17. J. D. North, "The Western Calendar," in *The Universal Frame* (Ronceverte, W.V.: Hambledon Press, 1989), pp. 39–77.

18. Roger Bacon, *Compotus*, in *Opera hactenus inedita*, ed. Robert Steele, vol. 6 (Oxford: Clarendon Press, 1926), p. 2: "Sciencia de tempore est sciencia distinccionis et numeracionis temporum, exteriorum corporum motibus et ex humanis legibus nascencium. Et hec vocata est compotus ab autoribus, quasi compotus a computando dictus, eo quod docet tempora computare per partes ejus, quarum divisio et annotacio tripliciter invenitur; quedam enim a natura, quedam auctoritate, quedam solo usu et voluntate in compotis auctorum designantur." Cf. Robert Grosseteste, *Compotus*, also in Bacon, *Opera*, vol. 6, p. 213: "Compotus est scientia numerationis et divisionis temporum. Numerantur enim tempora et signantur et dividuntur per signationes et differentias quas dant eius motus

celestium corporum, et iterum per signationes et differentias quas dant eis cultus regionum." Translation of Bacon taken from Arno Borst, *The Ordering of Time,* trans. A. Winnard (Cambridge: Polity Press, 1993), p. 79.

19. *Vita nuova,* 2.2: "Ella era in questa vita già stata tanto, che ne lo suo tempo lo cielo stellato era mosso verso la parte d'oriente de le dodici parti l'una d'un grado, sì che quasi dal principio del suo anno nono apparve a me." See Boyde's discussion of Dante's "cosmic clock" in *Dante Philomythes,* p. 165f.

20. In *Convivio* 2.14.10−12, Dante calls it "lo movimento quasi insensibile che fa da occidente in oriente per uno grado in cento anni."

21. Macrobio, *Commento al "Somnium Scipionis"* 2.11.9, ed. M. Regali (Pisa: Giardini, 1990), p. 76: "Stellae omnes et sidera quae infixa caelo videntur, quorum proprium motum numquam visus humanus sentire vel deprehendere potest, moventur tamen, et praeter caeli volubilitatem, qua semper trahuntur, suo quoque accessu tam sero promovent ut nullius hominum vita tam longa sit quae observatione continua factam de loco permutationem, in quo eas primum viderat, deprehendat."

22. "Voi che 'ntendendo" is usually dated to 1294. For bibliography on the question, see Cesare Vasoli's note in Dante Alighieri, *Convivio, Opere minori,* vol. 2 (Milan: Ricciardi, 1995), p. 120. "Io son venuto" can be dated to 1296. See Robert Durling and Ronald Martinez, *Time and the Crystal: Studies in Dante's Rime Petrose* (Berkeley: University of California Press, 1990), p. 80; and F. Angelitti, "Sulle principali apparenze del Pianeta Venere . . . dal 1290 al 1309," *Atti del Reale Accademia di Scienze, Lettere, e Belle Arti di Palermo* 6 (1901): 3−24.

23. *Paradiso* 16.34−39: "Dissemi: 'Da quel dí che fu detto "Ave" / al parto in che mia madre, ch'è or santa, / s'alleviò di me, ond'era grave, / al suo Leon cinquecento cinquanta / e trentra fïate venne questo foco / a rinfiammarsi sotto la sua pianta.'"

24. *Paradiso* 27.142−148: "Ma prima che gennaio tutto si sverni / per la centesma ch'è la giú negletta, / raggeran sí questi cerchi superni / che la fortuna che tanto s'aspetta, / le poppe volgerà u' son le prore, / sì che la classe correrà diretta; / e vero frutto verrà dopo 'l fiore."

25. On the error in the Julian calendar, see Boyde, *Dante Philomythes,* p. 163 and note; Moore, "Astronomy," pp. 95−97; and Beniamino Andriano, "La centesma negletta," *Studi danteschi* 48 (1971): 83−103.

26. *Vita nuova* 29.1: "Io dico che, secondo l'usanza d'Arabia, l'anima sua nobilissima si partio ne la prima ora del nono giorno del mese; e secondo
l'usanza di Siria, ella si partio nel nono mese de l'anno, però che lo primo
mese è ivi Tisirin primo, lo quale a noi è Ottobre; e secondo l'usanza nostra, ella si partio in quello anno de la nostra indizione, cioè de li anni Domini, in cui lo perfetto numero nove volte era compiuto in quello centinaio nel quale in questo mondo ella fue posta, ed ella fue de li cristiani del
terzodecimo centinaio." It is generally thought that all this adds up to
June 8, 1290. An "indiction" is a fifteen-year cycle of time-reckoning. The
De aggregationibus stellarum of Alfraganus, one of Dante's likely astronomical handbooks, begins with just such a brief exposition of various
semitic calendars. See Alfragano, *Il "Libro dell'aggregazione delle stelle,"*
ed. Romeo Campani (Florence, 1910), chap. 19.

27. Herodotus, the founder of historiography, had no universal standard of
dating, and yet one of his primary tasks, indeed the very definition of the
historical task, seems to be to relate disparate events in temporal relation
to each other, as in "this happened three years after that." In the 1250s Vincent of Beauvais still preferred using the names of rulers as chronological
reference points, rather than relying on the problematic methods of calculating past dates. See Borst, *Ordering of Time*. Livy, the most prestigious
of all classical historians, makes the moment of Rome's foundation the title and guiding principle of his monumental work *Ab urbe condita*.

28. See I. W. Raymond's introduction to Orosius' *Seven Books Against the Pagans* (New York: Columbia University Press, 1936), pp. 16–18, for the
chronological structure of the work and methods of time-reckoning. I
disagree with Donald J. Wilcox ("The Sense of Time in Western Historical Narratives from Eusebius to Machiavelli," in *Classical Rhetoric and
Medieval Historiography,* ed. E. Breisache [Kalamazoo: Medieval Institute, 1985], pp. 167–237), who says that "Orosius' concern to narrate history as a series of disasters overcame his search for meaning in the linear
pattern of historical events" (p. 178).

29. Orosius, *Seven Books,* p. 74. Paul Orose, *Histoires (contre les païens),* vol.
I, ed. and trans. M.-P. Arnaud-Lindet (Paris: Les Belles Lettres, 1991),
pp. 87–88: "Siquidem sub una eademque convenientia temporum illa cecidit, ista surrexit; illa tunc primum alienigenarum perpessa dominatum,
haec tunc primum etiam suorum aspernata fastidium; illa tunc quasi

moriens dimisit hereditatem, haec vero pubescens tunc se agnovit here-
dem; tunc Orientis occidit et ortum est Occidentis imperium."

30. Orosius, *Seven Books,* p. 321. According to Orosius, Rome was privileged
to survive the coming of Christ with her empire unbroken, although he
carefully notes some minor calamities that she suffered around the 750-
year mark. Cf. Dante, *Convivio* 3.11.3: "Quasi dal principio della costi-
tuzione di Rome—che fu se[tte]cento cinquanta anni [innanzi, o] poco
dal più al meno, che 'l Salvatore venisse, secondo che scrive Paulo Oro-
sio."

31. Orosius, *Seven Books,* p. 317; *Histoires* 6.22.8, vol. 2, p. 236: "Nec dubium
quoniam omnium cognitioni fidei inspectionique pateat quia Dominus
noster Iesus Christus hanc urbem nutu suo auctam defensamque in hunc
rerum apicem prouexerit, cuius potissime uoluit esse cum uenit, dicen-
dus utique ciuis Romanus census professione Romani."

32. *Convivio* 4.5.4: "Nella sua venuta lo mondo, non solamente lo cielo ma
la terra, convenia essere in ottima disposizione; e la ottima disposizione
della terra sia quando ella è monarchia, cioè tutta ad uno principe."

33. *Convivio* 4.5.6: "E tutto questo fu in uno temporale, che David nacque e
nacque Roma, cioè che Enea venne di Troia in Italia, che fu origine della
cittade romana, sì come testimoniano le scritture. Per che assai è manifesto la divina elezione del romano imperio, per lo nascimento della santa
cittade che fu contemporaneo alla radice della progenie di Maria."

34. *Convivio* 4.5.7: "E incidentemente è da toccare che, poi che esso cielo
cominciò a girare, in migliore disposizione non fu che allora quando di
là su discese Colui che l'ha fatto e che 'l governa; sì come ancora per virtù
di loro arti li matematici possono ritrovare."

35. *Vita nuova* 29.2: "Questo numero fue amico di lei per dare ad intendere
che ne la sua generazione tutti e nove li mobili cieli perfettissimamente
s'aveano insieme." See Chapter 1 of this book.

36. *Paradiso* 1.40—41.

37. *Inferno* 1.37—43.

38. See Grosseteste's explanation, *Compotus,* p. 216; S. Stambursky, *The Physical World of the Greeks* (Princeton: Princeton University Press, 1956),
p. 58; Moore, "Astronomy," pp. 8—12.

39. In order to save Dante from such a gross error, Angelitti claims that he
was following a more obscure tradition that set the *exordium mundi* in

winter, although even he admits that Dante creates "a little confusion" between signs and constellations ("Sulla data," p. 41). See Moore, "Astronomy," pp. 64 and 72; and Boyde, *Dante Philomythes,* p. 163. Paolo Pecoraro's book *Le stelle di Dante* (Rome: Bulzoni, 1987) is devoted to a vigorous argument that Dante never confuses signs with constellations.

40. Dante himself in *Convivio* 3.5.13 refers to the sun crossing the equator "nel principio dell'Ariete e nel principio della Libra." Moore, "Astronomy," p. 54n, uses the example of Gower's *Confessio "Amantis."* See also Lynn Thorndike, *The Sphere of Sacrobosco* (Chicago: University of Chicago Press, 1949), p. 123: "The equinoctial is a circle dividing the sphere into two equal parts and equidistant at its every point from either pole. And it is called 'equinoctial' because, when the sun crosses it, which happens twice a year, namely, in the beginning of Aries and in the beginning of Libra, there is equinox the world over. Wherefore it is termed the 'equator of day and night,' because it makes the artificial day equal to the night. And 'tis called the 'belt of the first movement.'" Ristoro d'Arezzo's account paraphrases that of Sacrobosco in *La composizione del mondo,* ed. E. Narducci (Rome: 1859), p. 176: "Et troviamo un altro cierchio mirabile lo quale e ampio e tutto istoriato di fighure e e chiamato zodiacho lo quale segha lequatore per mezo en due punti oppositi. Luno e chiamato lo primo punto dariete laltro e chiamato lo primo punto de libra. . . . E quando lo sole passa per questi punti e iguale lo di colla notte en tutto lo mondo."

41. "Tractatus in Exodus" 1, in *Sancti Gaudentii Episcopi Brixiensis Tractatus,* ed. A. Glueck, *Corpus Scriptorum Ecclesiasticorum Latinorum,* vol. 68 (Vienna: Hoelder-Pichler, 1936), p. 19: "Filius ergo dei, per quem facta sunt omnia, eodem die eodemque tempore pro stratum mundum propria resurrectione resuscitat, quo eum prius ipse crearat ex nihilo, ut omnia reformarentur in Christo quae in caelis sunt et quae in terra sunt."

42. Philo of Alexandria, *Special Laws* 2, trans. F. H. Colson (Cambridge: Harvard University Press, 1958), p. 399.

43. Nicetas of Remesiana, *De ratione paschae,* in A. E. Burn, *Nicetas of Remesiana: His Life and Works* (Cambridge: Cambridge University Press, 1905), p. 98: "Resurrexit enim Christus in aequinoctio veris, luna plena, die dominica: quae in mundi convenire principium Genesis relatione cognoscimus."

44. Attributed to Anatolius of Alexandria, *Canon Paschalis,* in *Patrologia Graeca* 10.215: "Et ideo in hac concordantione solis et lunae Pascha non est immolandum, quia quandiu in hoc cursu deprehenduntur, tenebrarum potestas non est victa; et quandiu aequalitas inter lucem et tenebras perdurat, nec a luce diminuta, Pascha non esse immolandum ostenditur."

45. Exodus 12:18: "Primo mense quartadecima die mensis ad vesperam comedetis azyma usque ad diem vicesimam primam eiusdem mensis ad vesperam."

46. Philo of Alexandria, *Special Laws* 2, p. 401.

47. Text in *Patrologia Graeca* 46.621; English translation from Anscar Chupungco, *The Cosmic Elements of Christian Passover* (Rome: Editrice Anselmiana, 1977), p. 69.

48. Epistle 55, to Januarius, chap. 9.16. English translation from Philip Schaff, ed., *A Select Library of the Nicene and Post-Nicene Fathers of the Church,* vol. 1 (New York: Christian Literature Company, 1886), p. 308.

49. Chupungco, *Cosmic Elements,* pp. 63–68.

50. Nicetas, *De ratione,* p. 105: "Sane quia rursus frequenter cum dominica die lunae plenitudo non convenit, extendi lunam in septem dies maluerunt, dummodo diem dominicam in resurrectionis memoriam retineret."

51. Chupungco, *Cosmic Elements,* p. 69.

52. Ibid., pp. 86–90.

53. Ibid., pp. 67–68.

54. Epistle 55.4.9.

55. Epistle 55.7.13.

56. Augustine, *Tractatus in evangelium Iohannis* 55, ed. R. Willem, *Corpus Christianorum Series Latina* 36 (Turnhout, Belgium: Brepols, 1954), pp. 463–464. Translation adapted from Raniero Cantamalessa, *La Pasqua nella chiesa antica* (Turin: Società Editrice Internazionale, 1978), p. 127. Cf. Augustine, Epistle 55.1.2.

57. Epistle 55.4, 55.9.14.

58. Augustine, *De civitate Dei* 16.32, in *Opera, Corpus Christianorum Series Latina,* vol. 48, pt. 14.2, ed. B. Dombart and A. Kalb (Turnhout, Belgium: Brepols, 1955), p. 537: "Quis erat ille aries, quo immolato impletum est significatiuo sanguine sacrificium? Nempe quando eum uidit Abraham,

cornibus in frutice tenebatur. Quis ergo illo figurabatur, nisi Iesus, antequam immolaretur, spinis Iudaicis coronatus?"

59. *Inferno* 20.127—129: "E già iernotte fu la luna tonda: / ben ten de' ricordar, ché non ti nocque / alcuna volta per la selva fonda." *Purgatorio* 10.14—15: "Tanto che pria lo scemo della luna / rigiunse al letto suo per ricorcarsi." *Purgatorio* 18.76—79: "La luna, quasi a mezza notte tarda, / facea le stelle a noi parer piú rade / fatta com' un secchion che tuttor arda." *Purgatorio* 23.119—121: "L'altr'ier, quando tonda / vi si mostrò la suora di colui / (e il sol mostrai)." On error in the ecclesiastical moon, see Grosseteste, *Compotus,* p. 258f.

60. Angelitti, "Sull'anno della visione," p. 3: "Né capisco come e perchè i calcoli astronomici, per reggersi, abbiano bisogno della cronologia e del calendario ecclesiastico!" Interestingly, Angelitti also discovered in the course of his research that none of the traditional dates for the Crucifixion coincide with a full moon either; response to D'Ovidio, p. 21. Edward Moore ("Astronomy," pp. 86, 166) argued that the date of the calendar moon would have been more easily checked after the fact by the average person than the lunar phases charted in astronomical tables would have been; see also Moore, *The Time References in the Divine Comedy* (London: De Nutt, 1887).

61. John Chrysostom, *Adversus Judaeos Orationes,* in *Patrologia Graeca* 48.867: "Pascha vero ter in hebdomada, nonnumquam etiam quater, vel potius quotiescumque volumus."

62. "Pascha qui celebrant, nisi qui a morte peccatorum suorum transeunt ad vitam iustorum?" Augustine, "Sermo habitus in festivitate Paschali," in Germain Morin, *Miscellanea Augustiniana,* vol. 1 (Rome: Tipografia Poliglotta Vaticana, 1930), p. 32. Morin doubts its authenticity. Also in Raniero Cantalamessa, *La Pasqua nella chiesa antica* (Turin: Società Editrice Internazionale, 1978), p. 204.

63. E.g., Virgil, *Eclogue* 8.17; Ovid, *Metamorphoses,* 15.148; Lucan, *Pharsalia* 10.434; Statius, *Thebaid* 2.134.

64. *Missale Gothicum,* ed. L. C. Mohlberg (Rome: Herder, 1961): "Flammas ejus lucifer matutinus inveniat, ille quam, lucifer, qui nescit occasum. Ille, qui regressus ab inferis, humano generi serenus illuxit." Attributed to Ambrose by Bernard Capelle, "L'exultet: Oeuvre de Saint Ambroise," *Miscellanea Giovanni Mercati,* vol. 1 (Vatican City: Biblioteca Apostolica

Vaticana, 1946), pp. 219–246. The expression *nescit occasum* is perhaps resonated in *Purgatorio* 30.2: "Che né occaso mai seppe né orto."

65. Rhabanus Maurus, "De Lucifero," in *De universo* 9.15, *PL* III.274: "Luciferum ergo se Christus innotuit, quia diluculo a morte resurrexit, et fulgore sui luminis mortalitatis nostrae caliginem pressit. Cui bene per Joannem dicitur: 'Stella splendida et matutina' (Apoc. xxii). Vivus quippe apparendo post mortem matutina nobis stella factus est; quia dum in semetipso exemplum nobis resurrectionis praebuit, quae lux sequator indicavit."

66. Pseudo-Strabo, *Glossa ordinaria, Apoc. Joannis* 20.16, *PL* 114.751: "Clara stella, id est, magna charitas annuntians diem, id est futuram beatitudinem, per meam resurrectionem in mane factam." Cf. Prudentius' poem on Easter eve, "Illa nocte sacer qua rediit deus / Stagnis ad superos ex Acheronticis, / Non sicut tenebras de face fulgida / Surgens Oceano lucifer imbuit, / Sed terris Domini de cruce tristibus / Maior Sole novum restituens diem," in Hugo Rahner, *Greek Myths and Christian Mystery* (London: Burns and Oats, 1963), p. 122.

67. Augustine, Sermo 220, *PL* 38.1089: "Semel Christum mortuum esse pro nobis. . . . Hoc semel factum esse, optime nostis. Et tamen solemnitas tanquam saepius fiat, revolutis temporibus iterat, quod veritas semel factum tot Scripturarum vocabis clamat. Nec tamen contraria sunt veritas et solemnitas, ut ista mentiatur, illa verum dicat. Quod enim semel factum in rebus veritas indicat, hoc saepius celebrandum in cordibus piis solemnitas renovat." Chupungco, *Cosmic Elements,* p. 98.

68. *On Christian Doctrine,* book 2, chap. 35, trans. D. W. Robertson (New York: Liberal Arts Press, 1958), p. 70.

69. Pseudo-Chrysostome, "Sur la Pâque de 387," in *Homélies Pascales,* ed. F. Floëri and P. Nautin (Paris: Editions du Cerf, 1957), p. 148: "In our imitation (*mimesis*) of the true Easter, we try to combine as best as we can the imitation of these times [the equinox, Sunday, and the full moon] with this subject, leaving the exact manipulation of them to the Savior's prototypical Easter." My translation is from the French.

70. Ibid, pp. 168–170.

71. Maximus Taurinensis, *Sermones* 54.1, ed. A. Mutzenbecher, *Corpus Christianorum Series Latina,* vol. 23 (Turnhout, Belgium: Brepols, 1962), p. 218: "Dum enim ille ab inferis transit ad superos, nos de morte transire fecit

ad uitam. Pascha enim hebraeice latine transitus dicitur uel profectus, scilicet quia per hoc mysterium de peioribus ad meliora transitur. Bonus igitur transitus est transire de peccatis ad iustitiam de uitiis ad uirtutem ad infantiam de senectute."

72. See Thomas P. Roche, "The Calendrical Structure of Petrarch's *Canzoniere*," *Studies in Philology* 7 (1974): 152–172; Carlo Calcaterra, "Feria sexta Aprilis," *Nella selve di Petrarca* (Bologna: Cappelli, 1942), pp. 209–245.

CHAPTER THREE: THE HARVEST OF READING

1. John Webster Spargo, *Virgil the Necromancer* (Cambridge: Harvard University Press, 1934); Domenico Comparetti, *Vergil in the Middle Ages* (London: S. Sonnenschein, 1895).

2. "Hoc ergo, o lector, quod tibi proponimus: hic campus tui laboris vomere bene sulcatus, multiplicem tibi fructum referet." Hugh of St. Victor, *Didascalicon* 6.3, *PL* 176.801; cf. 808. English translation from Hugh of St. Victor, *Didascalicon,* trans. Jerome Taylor (New York: Columbia University Press, 1981), p. 138. Augustine also uses agricultural metaphor in his interpretation of the literal sense of Genesis, suggesting that to stick to the meaning of the author and never deviate from the rule of piety is to have fruit from one's reading. Augustine, *De Genesi* 1.21, *PL* 34.262: "Aliud est enim quid potissimum scriptor senserit non dignoscere, aliud autem a regula pietatis errare. Si utrumque vitetur, perfecte se habet fructus legentis."

3. Virgil, *Georgics* 1.1–2, 1.5–6, 1.204–207, 1.252–258, 1.302–304. Text and translation from Virgil, *Eclogues. Georgics. Aeneid, 1–6,* trans. H. R. Fairclough (Cambridge: Harvard University Press, 1916).

4. Michael Putnam, *Virgil's Poem of the Earth: Studies in the Georgics* (Princeton: Princeton University Press: 1979), p. 24.

5. Cassiodorus, *Institutiones* 2.4, ed. R. Mynors (Oxford: Clarendon Press, 1963), p. 156: "Est alia quoque de talibus non despicienda commoditas, si oportunitatem navigationis, si tempus arantium, si aestatis caniculam, si autumni suspectos imbres inde discamus." English translation adapted from Cassiodorus Senator, *An Introduction to Divine and Human Readings,* trans. L. W. Jones (New York: Columbia University Press, 1946), p. 156.

6. Dominicus Gundissalinus, in *De divisione philosophiae,* ed. L. Baur, in *Beiträge zur Geschichte der Philosophie des Mittelalters,* vol. 4 (Münster, Germany: Aschendorff, 1903), pp. 119–120, expressed the difference this way: "Alfarabius dicit, quod astronomia est sciencia de significacione stellarum, quid scilicet stelle significent de eo, quod futurum est, et de pluribus presentibus et de pluribus preteris." See Cesare Vasoli's commentary to *Convivio* 2.13.28, in Dante, *Opere minori,* vol. 1, part 2, ed. C. Vasoli and D. De Robertis (Milan: Ricciardi, 1985), p. 241. See also Richard Kay, "Astronomy and Astrology," in *The "Divine Comedy" and the Encyclopedia of Arts and Sciences,* ed. G. Di Scipio and A. Scaglione (Amsterdam: John Benjamins, 1988), pp. 147–162; Richard Kay, *Dante's Christian Astrology* (Philadelphia: University of Pennsylvania Press, 1994), esp. pp. 1–9; Richard Lemay, "The True Place of Astrology in Medieval Science and Philosophy: Towards a Definition," in *Astrology, Science, and Society,* ed. Patrick Curry (Woodbridge, England: Boydell, 1987); Bruno Nardi, "Dante e Pietro d'Abano," in *Saggi di filosofia dantesca* (Florence: La Nuova Italia, 1967), pp. 60–62; I. Capasso and G. Tabarroni, "Astrologia," in *ED,* vol. 1, pp. 427–431; J. D. North, "Celestial Influence—The Major Premiss of Astrology," in *"Astrologi hallucinati": Stars and the End of the World in Luther's Time,* ed. Paola Zambelli (Berlin: Walter de Gruyter, 1986); Edward Grant, "Medieval and Renaissance Scholastic Conceptions of the Influence of the Celestial Region on the Terrestrial," *Journal of Medieval and Renaissance Studies* 17.1 (Spring 1987): 1–23; Paola Zambelli, *The Speculum Astronomiae and Its Enigma: Astrology, Theology and Science in Albertus Magnus and His Contemporaries* (Dordrecht: Kluwer Academic, 1992).

7. *ST* 1.115.4 ad 3, vol. 15 (New York: McGraw-Hill, 1970), p. 106: "Plures hominum sequuntur passiones, quae sunt motus sensitivi appetitus, ad quas cooperari possunt corpora caelesti." For an analysis of Aquinas' view on astrology, see Thomas Litt, *Les corps célestes dans l'univers de saint Thomas d'Aquin,* chaps. 6, 7, and 8 (Louvain: Publications Universitaires, 1963).

8. *Convivio* 4.2.7: "E così la nostra mente in quanto ella è fondata sopra la complessione del corpo, che [ha] a seguitare la circulazione del cielo, altrimenti è disposta in un tempo e altrimenti un altro"; 4.21.7: "E però che . . . la disposizione del Cielo a questo effetto puote essere buona, migliore

e ottima (la quale si varia [per] le constellazioni, che continuamente si transmutano), incontra che dell'umano seme e di queste vertudi più pura [e men pura] anima si produce; e secondo la sua puritade, discende in essa la vertude intellettuale possibile." In *Convivio* 2.14.16–17, he lists all the things that would not exist without the movement of the crystalline heaven.

9. *Convivio* 4.23.6: "Onde, con ciò sia cosa che la nostra vita, sì come detto è, ed ancora d'ogni vivente qua giù, sia causata dal cielo e lo cielo a tutti questi cotali effetti, non per cerchio compiuto ma per parte di quello a loro si scuopra; e così conviene che 'l suo movimento sia sopra essi come uno arco quasi, [e] tutte le terrene vite (e dico terrene, sì delli [uomini] come delli altri viventi), montando e volgendo, convengono essere quasi ad imagine d'arco asimiglianti."

10. Such seems to be the sense of the opening lines of *Paradiso* 8: "Solea creder lo mondo in suo periclo / che la bella Ciprigna il folle amore / raggiasse, volta nel terzo epiciclo." That it is not an indictment of belief in celestial influence is easily proved by Cunizza's happily confessing that she was conquered by the light of this planet ("perché mi vinse il lume d'esta stella" [*Paradiso* 9.33]) and by a similar admission by the Provençal poet Folquet de Marseilles ("questo cielo / di me s'imprenta, com'io fe' di lui" [*Paradiso* 9.95–96]). Cf. *Convivio* 2.5.15: "E perché li antichi s'accorsero che quello cielo era qua giù cagione d'amore, dissero Amore essere figlio di Venere"; and 2.6.5: "L'operazione vostra, cioè la vostra circulazione, è quella che m'ha tratto nella presente condizione."

11. *Inferno* 15.55; *Inferno* 26.23–24; *Paradiso* 22.112–115.

12. *Convivio* 4.5.7: "Poi che esso cielo cominciò a girare, in migliore disposizione non fu che allora quando di là su discese Colui che l'ha fatto e che 'l governa: sì come ancora per virtù di loro arti li matematici possono ritrovare. Né 'l mondo mai non fu né sarà sì perfettamente disposto come allora."

13. "Poscia ch'Amor," lines 58–60; "Tre donne," lines 66–67.

14. *Epistole* 6.4: "Et si presaga mens mea non fallitur, sic signis veridicis sicut inexpugnabilibus argumentis instructa prenuntians;" *Epistole* 5.8: "Et si ex notioribus nobis innotiora; si simpliciter interest humane apprehensioni ut per motum celi Motorem intelligamus et eius velle; facile predestinatio hec etiam leviter intuentibus innotescet." In *Monarchia* 3.15,

Dante also argued that only God, who had a full and total view of the disposition of heaven, on which the disposition of earth depends, could be qualified to elect a world governor: "Cumque dispositio mundi huius dispositionem inherentem celorum circulationi sequator, necesse est ad hoc ut utilia documenta libertatis et pacis commode locis et temporibus applicentur, de curatore isto dispensari ab Illo qui totalem celorum dispositionem presentialiter intuetur."

15. *Inferno* 1.100–102; *Purgatorio* 33.41–45. Francesco da Buti interpreted Virgil's prophecy of the *veltro* as referring to "una influenzia di corpi celesti, che in processo di tempo verrà secondo il movimento de' cieli, che tutto il mondo si disporrà a sapienzia, virtù e amore . . . e questo era noto all'autore secondo la ragione dell'astrologo, et in ciò si manifesta ch'elli fosse astrologo." *Commento di Francesco da Buti sopra la Divina comedia di Dante Alighieri*, ed. C. Giannini (Pisa: Nistri, 1858), p. 46. Pietro, the poet's son, in the earlier drafts of his own commentary, believed that his father predicted that the longed-for political change would come about in the great conjunction due to occur in 1345. See Kennerly M. Woody, "Dante and the Doctrine of the Great Conjunctions," *Dante Studies* 95 (1977): 119–134; Leo Olschki, *The Myth of Felt* (Berkeley: University of California Press, 1949); Bruno Nardi, "Influenze celesti sugli avvenimenti di storia umana," in *Saggi,* pp. 55–61; Lemay, "The True Place," p. 22.

16. Kay, "Astrology and Astronomy," p. 158; "The Spare Ribs of Michael Scot," *Dante Studies* 103 (1985): 1–14; and "Dante's Double Damnation of Manto," in *Res publica litterarum* 1 (1978): 113–128.

17. Teodolinda Barolini ("True and False See-ers in Inferno XX," *Lectura Dantis* 4 [1989]: 42–54) declares that this canto "deals with the validity and legitimacy of the acts of writing and reading" because "prophecy is in fact a textual issue . . . essentially a matter of correct and incorrect reading." Zygmunt Barański, "The Poetics of Meter: Terza Rima, 'Canto,' 'Canzon,' 'Cantica,'" in *Dante Now,* ed. Theodore Cachey (Notre Dame: University of Notre Dame Press, 1995), p. 17: "As is now widely recognized, the *canto* of the soothsayers stands as one of Dante's major statements on classical literature."

18. This is the argument of Robert Hollander, "The Tragedy of Divination in *Inferno* XX," in *Studies in Dante* (Ravenna, Italy: Longo, 1980), pp. 131–218.

19. Lucan, *Pharsalia* 1.639. Cicero provides the classical definitions of the various arts of divination in his *De Divinatione*. See "Divination" in *Oxford Classical Dictionary,* ed. N. Hammond and H. Scullard (Oxford: Clarendon Press, 1970), pp. 356–357.

20. Lucan, *Pharsalia* 2.584–587: "Haec propter placuit Tuscos de more vetusto / acciri vates. Quorum qui maximus aevo / Arruns incoluit desertae moenia Lucae, / fibrarum et monitus errantis in aere pinnae." Latin text of the *Pharsalia* from *Lucan* (Cambridge: Harvard University Press, 1957). Translation by P. F. Widdows, ed., *Lucan's "Civil War"* (Bloomington: Indiana University Press, 1988).

21. Cassiodorus, *Institutiones* 2.7.4: "Est alia quoque de talibus non despicienda commoditas, si oportunitatem navigationis, si tempus arantium, si aestatis caniculam, si autumni suspectos imbres inde discamus. Dedit enim Dominus unicuique creaturae suae aliquam virtutem, [quam] tamen innoxie de propria qualitate [noscamus]. Cetera vero quae se ad cognitionem siderum coniungunt, id est ad notitiam fatorum, et fidei nostrae sine dubitatione contraria sunt, sic ignorari [debent], ut nec scripta esse videantur."

22. *Ioannis Saresberiensis episcopi Carnotensis Policratici* 2.1 and 2.2, ed. C. Webb (New York: Arno, 1979), pp. 65, 68: "Rusticanum et forte Offelli proverbium est: Qui sompniis et auguriis credit, numquam fore securum"; "Futuras itaque tempestates aut serenitates signa quaedam antecedentia praeloquuntur, ut homo, qui ad laborem natus est, ex his possit exercitia sua temperare. Hinc agricolae hinc nautae familiaribus quibusdam experimentis." Translation from John of Salisbury, *Frivolities of Courtiers and Footprints of Philosophers,* trans. Joseph B. Pike (Minneapolis: University of Minnesota Press, 1938), pp. 55–56.

23. Ibid.: "Ad laborem natus est, ex his possit exercitia sua temperare. Hinc agricolae hinc naturae familiaribus quibusdam experimentis quid quo tempore geri oporteat colligunt, qualitatem temporis futuri ex eo quod praeteriit metientes."

24. Augustine, *De doctrina christiana* 2.46, *PL* 34.57: "Sicut autem plurimis notus est lunae cursus, qui etiam ad passionem Domini anniversarie celebrandam solemniter adhibetur; sic paucissimis caeterorum quoque siderum vel ortus, vel occasus, vel alia quaelibet momenta sine ullo sunt errore notissima. Que per seipsam cognitio, quanquam superstitione non

alliget, non multum tamen ac prope nihil adjuvat tractationem divinarum Scripturarum, et infructuosa intentione plus impedit; et qui fa-
miliaris est perniciosissimo errori fatua fata cantantium, commodius
honestiusque contemnitur." English translation from Augustine, *On
Christian Doctrine,* trans. D. W. Robertson (New York: Liberal Arts,
1958), p. 65.

25. Augustine, Epistle 55.8.15; *PL* 33.211: "Sed quantum intersit inter siderum
observationes ad aerias qualitates accomodatas, sicut agricolae vel nautae
observant; aut ad notandas partes mundi cursumque aliquo et alicunde
dirigendum, quod gubernatores navium faciunt, et ii qui per solitudines
arenosas in interiora Austri nulla semita certa vel recta gradiuntur; aut
cum ad aliquid in doctrina utili figurate significandum, fit nonnullorum
siderum aliqua commemoratio; quantum ergo intersit inter has utilitates,
et vanitates hominum ob hoc observantium sidera, ut nec aeris qualitates,
nec regionum vias, nec solos temporum numeros, nec spiritualium simil-
itudines, sed quasi fatalia rerum jam eventa perquirant, quis non intelli-
gat?" On the skills of prognostication and prophecy necessary to peasants
and herdsmen, see also Piero Camporesi, *The Anatomy of the Senses: Natural Symbols in Medieval and Early Modern Italy,* trans. Allan Cameron
(Cambridge: Polity Press, 1994), pp. 186–196.

26. Anonimo Fiorentino, *Commento alla Divina commedia,* vol. 1, ed. P. Fan-
fani (Bologna: Romagnoli, 1866), p. 446.

27. Francesco D'Ovidio, "Dante e la Magia," *Nuova antologia* (1892): 213f.;
and "Esposizione del canto XX dell' *Inferno,*" in *Nuovo volume di studi danteschi* (Caserta, Italy: A. P. E., 1926); Comparetti, *Vergil in the Middle Ages.*

28. Barolini, "True and False See-ers," p. 50.

29. Hollander, "The Tragedy of Divination." Aristide Marigo ("Le 'Geor-
giche' di Virgilio fonte di Dante," *Giornale dantesco* 17 [1909]: 31–44) suggested *Georgics* 2.159 as a source: "Teque / Fluctibus et fremitu assurgens,
Benace, marino." Edward Moore (*Studies in Dante,* 1st ser. [Oxford:
Clarendon Press, 1896], p. 178) thought that Dante knew the *Georgics*
only through passages found in florilegia, such as the episode of Orpheus'
head rolling down the river and calling the name of Eurydice (*Georgics*
4.523). But Marigo notes that virtually all Virgilian codices, including
those of the thirteenth and fourteenth centuries, contain the *Bucolics* and
the *Georgics* in addition to the *Aeneid.*

30. *Inferno* 20.61–81: "Suso in Italia bella giace un laco, / a piè de l'Alpe che serra Lamagna / sovra Tiralli, c'ha nome Benaco. / Per mille fonti, credo, e piú si bagna / tra Garda e Val Camonica, Apennino / de l'acqua che nel detto laco stagna . . . / Ivi convien che tutto quanto caschi / ciò che 'n grembo a Benaco star non può, / e fassi fiume giú per verdi paschi. / Tosto che l'acqua a correr mette co, / non piú Benaco, ma Mencio si chiama / fino a Governol, dove cade in Po. / Non molto ha corso, ch'el trova una lama, / ne la qual si distende e la 'mpaluda; / e suol di state talor esser grama."

31. *Inferno* 20.97–102: "'Però t'assenno che, se tu mai odi / originar la mia terra altrimenti, / la verità nulla menzogna frodi.' / E io: 'Maestro, i tuoi ragionamenti / mi son sì certi e prendon sì mia fede, / che li altri mi sarien carboni spenti.'"

32. Hollander notes Dante's "watery" sense of Virgil in "Tragedy," p. 192. David Quint ("The Virgilian Source," in *Origin and Originality in Renaissance Literature* [New Haven: Yale University Press, 1983], pp. 32–42), has identified the episode at the end of Virgil's own *Georgics* involving a visit to the source of all rivers as an allegorical topos of poetic originality and inspiration, much copied in the Renaissance.

33. Augustine, *Confessions* 13.19: "Lucete supra omnen terram, et dies sole candens eructet diei verbum sapientiae, et nox, luna lucens, annuntiet nocti verbus scientiae. Luna et stellae nocti lucent, sed nox non obscurat eas, quoniam ipsae inluminant eam pro modulo eius." Text and translation from *St. Augustine's Confessions,* trans. William Watts (Cambridge: Harvard University Press, 1912). This observation was made by Albert E. Wingell, in "Dante, St. Augustine, and Astronomy," *Quaderni d'italianistica* 2, no. 2 (1981): 123–142.

34. Virgil, *Georgics* 3.304. Robert Hollander, "Dante's 'Georgic' (*Inferno* XXIV, 1–18)," *Dante Studies* 102 (1984): 111–121. He credits Pietro di Dante (1340) with having first pointed out this Virgilian echo. Also noting the presence of the *Georgics* is David Baker, "The Winter Simile in *Inferno* XXIV," *Dante Studies* 92 (1974): 77–91.

35. This line can be interpreted to mean either that the nights are headed toward becoming half the length of the days or that "night," as the point directly opposite the sun, is now headed toward the south (*mezzogiorno*) just as the sun is headed north.

36. Margherita Frankel ("Dante's Anti-Virgilian *Villanello*," *Dante Studies* 102 [1984]: 81–109) notes that the *rime equivoche* "raise the contrast of their dynamic differentiation" and participate in the whole issue of appearance versus reality. See also Richard Lansing, *From Image to Idea: A Study of the Simile in Dante's "Commedia"* (Ravenna, Italy: Longo, 1977), p. 75: "The equivocal rhymes point up the problem of perception."

37. *Inferno* 23.145–146: "Appresso il duca a gran passi sen gì, / turbato un poco d'ira nel sembiante."

38. *Inferno* 4.42. Robert Durling and Ronald Martinez call attention to the affinities between this simile and the *rime petrose* and to its hopeful tendency, against those who would see it as a "paralyzed poetics." Robert M. Durling and Ronald L. Martinez, *Time and the Crystal* (Berkeley: University of California Press, 1990), p. 215.

39. See Frankel, "Dante's Anti-Virgilian *Villanello*," and Robert J. Ellrich, "Envy, Identity, and Creativity: *Inferno* XXIV–XXV," *Dante Studies* 102 (1984): 61–79, in which Ellrich notes the simile's christological meaning, as "caring for the flock" relates the scene to the image of Christ as Good Shepherd. See also Warren Ginsberg, "Dante, Ovid, and the Transformation of Metamorphosis," *Traditio* 46 (1991); Peter Hawkins, "Virtuosity and Virtue: Poetic Self-Reflection in the *Commedia*," *Dante Studies* 98 (1980): 1–18; Lawrence Baldassaro, "Metamorphosis as Punishment and Redemption in *Inferno* XXIV," *Dante Studies* 99 (1981): 89–112.

40. Durling and Martinez also link the summer pastoral simile of *Inferno* 26 to the hibernal one of two cantos earlier. *Time and the Crystal*, p. 217.

41. *Inferno* 26.125.

42. James 3:2–7: "Si quis in verbo non offendit hic perfectus est vir. Potens etiam freno circumducere totum corpus. Si autem equorum frenos in ora mittimus ad consentiendum nobis et omne corpus illorum circumferimus. Ecce et naves, cum magnae sint, et a ventis validis minentur, circumferuntur a modico gubernaculo ubi impetus dirigentis voluerit. Ita et lingua modicum quidem membrum est, et magna exaltat. Ecce quantus ignis quam magnam silvam incendit. Et lingua ignis est, universitas iniquitatis. Lingua constituitur in membris nostris, quae maculat totum corpus, et inflammat rotam nativitatis nostrae inflammata a gehenna." See Alison Cornish, "The Epistle of James in *Inferno* 26," *Traditio* 45 (1989–1990): 367–379; Richard Bates and Thomas Rendall, "Dante's

Ulysses and the Epistle of James," *Dante Studies* 107 (1989): 33–44; and Maria Corti, "On the Metaphors of Sailing, Flight, and Tongues of Fire in the Episode of Ulysses (Inferno 26)," *Stanford Italian Review* 9, nos. 1–2 (1990): 33–47.

43. *Paradiso* 25.76–77: "Tu mi stillasti, con lo stillar suo, / ne la pistola poi; sì ch'io son pieno."

44. *Convivio* 4.2.10. James 5:7: "Ecce agricola expectat pretiosum fructum terrae, patienter ferens donec accipiat temporivum et serotinum." In his discussion of the fruits of the Virgin's womb in *Sermones de B. V. M.* 3.3, in *Opera omnia*, vol. 9 (Quaracchi, 1882–1902), p. 670, of the *fructus spei*, Bonaventure writes: "'Debet in spe qui arat arare; et qui triturat, in spe fructus percipiendi' [Cor 9.10] Ista autem spes non permittit hominem fatigari, secundum illud Iacobi ultimo: 'Ecce, agricola...'" [James 5.7]. See Cornish, "The Epistle," pp. 378–379.

45. For the definition of hope as the sure expectation of the glory to come, see *Paradiso* 25.67–68: "'Spene,' diss'io, 'è uno attender certo / de la gloria futura.'" Teodolinda Barolini has reconciled the debate over Ulysses' fate, which has fueled a vast bibliography, by suggesting that the Greek hero so closely represents the poet's own ambitions that he is damned "for Dante's sins." Barolini, "Dante's Ulysses: Narrative and Transgression," in *Dante: Contemporary Perspectives*, ed. Amilcare Iannucci (Toronto: University of Toronto Press, 1997), p. 132.

46. Lucan, *Pharsalia* 8.172–176: "Signifero quaecumque fluunt labentia caelo, / numquam stante polo miseros fallentia nautas, / sidera non sequimur; sed qui non mergitur undis / axis inocciduus gemina clarissimus arcto, / ille regit puppes."

47. Lucan, *Pharsalia* 8.159–161: "Iam pelago medios Titan demissus ad ignes / nec quibus abscondit nec si quibus exerit orbem / totus erat."

48. Ovid, *Metamorphoses* 8.217–220: "Hos aliquis tremula dum captat harundine pisces, / aut pastor baculo stivave innixus arator / vidit et obstipuit, quique aethera carpere possent, / credidit esse deos."

49. *Inferno* 26.21–22: "E più lo 'ngegno affreno ch'i' non soglio, / perché non corra che virtù nol guidi."

50. Virgil, *Georgics* 2.467.

51. Virgil, *Georgics* 2.475–478, 575–579: "Me vero primum dulces ante omnia Musae, / quarum sacra fero ingenti percussus amore, / accipiant

caelique vias et sidera monstrent, / defectus solis varios lunaeque la-
bores;" lines 481–82 are repeated in *Aeneid* 1.745. Philip Hardie, *Virgil's
"Aeneid": Cosmos and Imperium* (Oxford: Clarendon Press, 1986), p. 37:
"On the surface this is an appeal for the communication of information
on matters astronomical, but, given the underlying tendency in this
whole passage to identify the landscape of the poet with that of his sub-
ject-matter, it is easy to read this as a request for directions on literal 'paths
to the sky' (rather than 'the paths of heavenly bodies')."

52. Virgil, *Georgics* 1.493–497: "Scilicet et tempus veniet, cum finibus illis /
agricola incurvo terram molitus aratro / exesa inveniet scabra robigine
pila, / aut gravibus rastris galeas pulsabit inanis, / grandiaque effossis
mirabitur ossa sepulcris."

53. Virgil, *Georgics* 1.511–513: "Saevit toto Mars impius orbe: / ut cum
carceribus sese effudere quadrigae, / addunt in spatia, et frustra reti-
nacula tendens / fertur equis auriga neque audit currus habenas." English translation from Gary B. Miles, *Virgil's "Georgics": A New Interpretation* (Berkeley: University of California Press, 1988), p. 108. On this
passage in the *Georgics,* see Putnam, *Virgil's Poem of the Earth,* p. 79. See
also David O. Ross, *Virgil's Elements: Physics and Poetry in the "Georgics"* (Princeton: Princeton University Press, 1987); and Giuseppe Mazzotta, *Worlds of Petrarch* (Durham, N.C.: Duke University Press, 1993),
p. 276. Dante's depiction of Phaeton abandoning the reins is in *Inferno*
17.107.

54. Virgil, *Georgics* 2.458–460: "O fortunatos nimium, sua si bona norint, /
agricolas! quibus ipsa, procul discordibus armis, / fundit humo facilem
victum iustissima tellus"; 2.473–475: "Extrema per illos / Iustitia exce-
dens terris vestigia fecit."

CHAPTER FOUR: ORIENTATION

1. This is the definition of Miriam Eliav-Feldon, *Realistic Utopias: The Ideal
Imaginary Societies of the Renaissance, 1516–1630* (Oxford: Clarendon
Press, 1982), p. 1. Giuseppe Mazzotta defines Ulysses' desire to reach that
other hemisphere, the unnamed world he presumed to be unpeopled, as
the "tragic history of utopia" in *Dante: Poet of the Desert* (Princeton:
Princeton University Press, 1979), p. 90; and more recently Mazzotta has
declared that "the simultaneity of history and utopia is the heart of

Dante's exilic poetry," in *Dante's Vision and the Circle of Knowledge* (Princeton: Princeton University Press, 1993), p. 217.

2. Augustine, *De Genesi* 1.10.21, *PL* 34.253: "Eo tempore quo nox apud nos est, eas partes mundi praesentia lucis illustret, per quas sol non ab occasu in ortum redit; ac per hoc omnibus viginti quator horis non deesse per circuitum gyri totius, alibi diem, alibi noctem." English translation from *The Literal Meaning of Genesis*, vol. 1, trans. J. H. Taylor (New York: Newman Press, 1982), pp. 30–31. On the reciprocal illumination of the antipodes, see Brunetto Latini, *Li livres dou Tresor* 112, ed. F. J. Carmody (Berkeley: University of California Press, 1948): "Et pour ce dois tu bien croire k'il est toute fois jour et nuit; car quant li solaus est desous nous, et il alume ci u nous somes, il ne puet pas alumer de l'autre part la terre. Et quant il alume deça, il ne puet pas alumer dela, por la terre ki est entre nous et eus, ki ne laisse passer s'esplendour . . . car jour ne est autre chose que solei sour terre, ki sormonte totes lumieres."

3. For the early Christian symbolism of the sun's movements, see Hugo Rahner, *Greek Myths and Christian Mystery* (New York: Biblo and Tannen, 1971), pp. 114–116.

4. A. C. Charity, *Events and Their Afterlife* (Cambridge: Cambridge University Press, 1966), p. 179.

5. Cf. Charles Singleton, *Dante Studies*, vol. 1: *Commedia, Elements of Structure* (Cambridge: Harvard University Press, 1957), p. 10, apropos of *Inferno* 1: "The journey to the scene of which we may say 'then' and 'there' and 'his' will leave behind it another of which we may speak in terms of 'here' and 'now' and 'our,' leave it and yet not lose touch with it."

6. *Purgatorio* 1.22–24: "I' mi volsi a man destra, e puosi mente / a l'altro polo, e vidi quattro stelle / non viste mai fuor ch'a la prima gente." *Purgatorio* 1.30: "Là onde il Carro già era sparito."

7. Virgil, *Georgics* 1.246. Macrobius, *Commentary on the Dream of Scipio* 1.16, trans. W. H. Stahl (New York: Columbia University Press), p. 153.

8. For these and other opinions, see Bruno Nardi, "Il mito d'Eden," *Saggi di filosofia dantesca* (Florence: La Nuova Italia, 1967), pp. 311–340; and Alison Morgan, *Dante and Medieval Other Worlds* (Cambridge: Cambridge University Press, 1990), pp. 144–165.

9. *Purgatorio* 4.52–54.

10. *Purgatorio* 4.56–60. Lucan, *Pharsalia* 3.247–248: "Ignotum vobis,

Arabes, venistis in orbem / Umbras mirati nemorum non ire sinistras." Latin text of the *Pharsalia* from *Lucan* (Cambridge: Harvard University Press, 1957).

11. *Purgatorio* 4.67–71: "Come ciò sia, se 'l vuoi poter pensare, / dentro raccolto, imagina Sïon / con questo monte in su la terra stare / sì, ch'amendue hanno un solo orizzòn / e diversi emisperi."

12. *Purgatorio* 4.71–75: "Onde la strada / che mal non seppe carreggiar Fetòn, / vedrai come a costui convien che vada / da l'un, quando a colui da l'altro fianco, / se lo 'ntelletto tuo ben chiaro bada."

13. *Purgatorio* 4.76–84: "'Certo, maestro mio,' diss' io, 'unquanco / non vid' io chiaro sì com' io discerno / là dove mio ingegno parea manco, / che 'l mezzo cerchio del moto superno, / che si chiama Equatore in alcun' arte, / e che sempre riman tra 'l sole e 'l verno, / per la ragion che di', quinci si parte / verso settentrïon, quanto li Ebrei / vedevan lui verso la calda parte.'"

14. See Charles Singleton, "In exitu Israel de Aegypto," in *Dante: A Collection of Critical Essays*, ed. John Freccero (Englewood Cliffs, N.J.: Prentice-Hall, 1965), pp. 102–121.

15. Jacques Le Goff, *The Birth of Purgatory*, trans. A. Goldhammer (Chicago: University of Chicago Press, 1984), pp. 229–230, 290–295, 352–354.

16. In his commentary on *Purgatorio* in Dante, *La Divina Commedia* (Florence: Sansoni, 1957), p. 330, A. Momigliano remarks on the "nostalgia insieme terrena e celeste, che unisce in una medesima malinconia le anime che aspirano alla patria celeste e il pellegrino che ha in cuore la lontana patria terrena."

17. *Purgatorio* 1.22–27: "I' mi volsi a man destra, e puosi mente / a l'altro polo, e vidi quattro stelle / non viste mai fuor ch'a la prima gente. / Goder pareva 'l ciel di lor fiammelle: / oh settentrïonal vedovo sito, / poi che privato se' di mirar quelle!" Charles Singleton, "A Lament for Eden," in *Journey to Beatrice* (Baltimore: Johns Hopkins University Press, 1977), pp. 141–158.

18. This fact was duly noted by Edward Moore, *The Time-References in the "Divina Commedia"* (London: D. Nutt, 1887).

19. *Purgatorio* 16.26–27: "E di noi parli pur come se tue / partissi ancor lo tempo per calendi?" Emphasis on the body as shadow-maker can be found in several passages. *Purgatorio* 3.16–18: "Il sol, che dietro fiameg-

giava roggio, / rotto m'era dinanzi a la figura, / ch'avëa in me de' suoi raggi l'appoggio." *Purgatorio* 3.25–26: "Vespero è già colà dov' è sepolto / lo corpo dentro al quale io facea ombra." *Purgatorio* 6.55–57: "Prima che sie là su, tornar vedrai / colui che già si cuopre de la costa / sí che 'suoi raggi tu romper non fai."

20. As noted by Jeffrey Schnapp, "Introduction to the *Purgatorio*" in *The Cambridge Companion to Dante,* ed. R. Jacoff (Cambridge: Cambridge University Press, 1993).

21. Peter Burke, *The Renaissance Sense of the Past* (New York: St. Martin's Press, 1969), pp. 1–20.

22. The expression "elimination of time" was originally used by G. Raynaud de Lage apropos of Alain de Lille; see Henri de Lubac, *Exégèse médiévale: Les quatre sens de l'écriture,* part 2.1 (Paris: Aubier, 1964), p. 418.

23. H. Savon, "Le temps de l'exégèse allégorique dans la catéchèse d'Ambroise de Milan," in *Le temps chrétien de la fin de l'antiquité au moyen age, IIIe–XIIIe siècles* (Paris: Centre Nationale de la Recherche Scientifique, 1984), pp. 345–361. See also H. de Lubac, "'Typologie' et 'allégorisme,'" *Recherches de science réligieuse* 34 (1947): 180–226.

24. Peter Damon, "Dante's Canzoni and the 'Allegory of the Poets,'" in *Modes of Analogy in Ancient and Medieval Verse* (Berkeley: University of California Press, 1961), pp. 329–334; Singleton, *Dante Studies* I; Robert Hollander, *Allegory in Dante's "Commedia"* (Princeton: Princeton University Press, 1969); Singleton, *Dante's Epistle to Cangrande* (Ann Arbor: University of Michigan Press, 1993); Jean Pépin, *Dante et la tradition de l'allégorie* (Paris: J. Vrin, 1970); *Le forme dell'allegoresi,* ed. Michelangelo Picone (Ravenna: Longo, 1987); Zygmunt Bara Nski, "*Comedìa:* Notes on Dante, the Epistle to Cangrande, and Medieval Comedy," *Lectura dantis* 8 (1991): 26–55.

25. Dante, *Epistola* 13.8: "Est ergo subiectum totius operis, litteraliter tantum accepti, status animarum post mortem simpliciter sumptus."

26. *Convivio* 2.1.6: "Lo terzo senso si chiama morale, e questo è quello che li lettori deono intentamente andare apostando per le scritture ad utilitade di loro e di loro discenti."

27. John Freccero, "Introduction to the Inferno," in *The Cambridge Companion to the Divine Comedy,* ed. R. Jacoff (Cambridge: Cambridge University Press, 1993), pp. 182–183. See also his "Ironia e mimesi: Il disdegno

di Guido," in *Dante e la Bibbia,* ed. G. Barblan (Florence: Olschki, 1988), p. 54; and "Ancora sul disdegno di Guido," in *Letture classensi* 18, ed. A. Oldcorn (Ravenna: Longo, 1989), p. 81. Freccero has perceived this temporal, allegorical structure as integral even to the poem's meter and rhyme. The "significance of terza rima" lies in its similarity to the medieval allegorical interpretation of Christian history as *recapitulatio.* Freccero, "The Significance of Terza Rima," in *The Poetics of Conversion* (Cambridge: Harvard University Press, 1986), pp. 258–271.

28. Charity, *Events,* p. 179.
29. Oscar Cullman, *Christ and Time: The Primitive Christian Conception of Time and History,* rev. ed., trans. F. Filson (Philadelphia: Westminster Press, 1964), p. 219 (emphasis in original). Cf. Charity, *Events,* p. 117.
30. On the form of the alba, see Jonathan Saville, *The Medieval Erotic Alba: Structure as Meaning* (New York: Columbia University Press, 1972); Arthur T. Hatto has amply documented the genre in *Eos: An Enquiry into the Theme of Lovers' Meetings and Partings at Dawn* (London: Mouton, 1965). See also Peter Dronke, "The Alba," in *The Medieval Lyric* (London: Hutchinson, 1968), pp. 167–185; Elizabeth Wilson Poe, "New Light on the Alba: A Genre Redefined," *Viator* 15 (1984): 139–150; Ezra Pound, *The Spirit of Romance* (New York: New Directions, 1968), p. 11.
31. Jacopo writes: "Incontrò al detto Titone di quello che spesso incontra alli uomini del mondo, ch' elli non si contentano delle moglieri; invaghiò della figliuola della Luna, la quale similemente avea nome Aurora, e seppe sì fare, ch' elli ebbe suo intendimento di quella, e teneala per concubina overa bagascia, e spesse fiate similemente andava con la luna da oriente a mezzo díe, e poi in ponente con la sua concubina fornicando, poi sotto terra ritornava in oriente." Benvenuto da Imola had already recognized that if Dante meant to indicate any such "lunar aurora" it was purely of his own invention. For both, see G. A. Scartazzini's digression on "Titone" in his *Enciclopedia dantesca,* vol. 2 (Milan: Hoepli, 1899), pp. 1952–1974.
32. Scartazzini, "Titone," p. 1959: "Ma una bella e giovine dea, come dovremmo immaginarci questa nuova divinità mitologica, che si innamora di un vecchio decrepito, rimbambito ed impotente, che esce fuori dalle braccia illanguidite di quel povero vecchio—ma quel vecchio stesso che si tiene una concubina nella sua culla da bimbo—oibò, che sozza im-

magine! Immagine nauseante questa, indegna del più mediocre Poeta nonche di un Dante!. . . noi dal canto nostro svolgiamo con nausea e con ribrezzo gli occhi da cotal sozza pittura e proseguiamo alla seconda interpretazione."

33. "Omnes interpretes a veritate aberraverunt, quia et Aurora et Noctem in uno hemisphoerio Purgatorii quoerentes, ne leviter quidem suspicati sunt, duo diversa loca a Poeta designari, in quorum uno nox esset, in altero aurora." Bartolommeo Perazzini, *In Dantis Comoediam correctiones et adnotationes* (Verona, 1775; reprint, Venice, 1844), trans. G. G. Dionisi, "Sopra Dante Cap. IX," *Serie di Aneddoti,* vol. 4 (Verona, 1788), pp. 47–62. For two graphic versions of this interpretation that predate Perazzini's, see Alison Cornish, "Interpretazioni fiorentine della 'concubina di Titone antico,'" in *Studi danteschi* 62 (1991): 85–95.

34. Alessandro Vellutello was perhaps the first to make this point; *Dante con l'espositioni di Christoforo Landino, et d'Alessandro Vellutello, ecc.* (Venice: Sessa, 1564), fol. 194v: "L'aurora veniva ad occupare col resto di lei, cioè, da la fronte in giù, tutti quei segni, che seguono dietro ad esso Scorpion, e che precedono al detto Ariete, e che saliti erano fuori." See also Manfredi Porena's comment to the passage in Dante Alighieri, *La Divina Commedia,* ed. M. Porena (Bologna: Zanichelli, 1955); and Franca Brambilla Ageno, "Alcuni passi danteschi d'interpretazione controversa," *Studi danteschi* 53 (1981): 85–95.

35. *Paradiso* 31.118–128: "Io levai li occhi; e come da mattina / la parte orïental de l'orizzonte / soverchia quella dove 'l sol declina, / così, quasi di valle andando a monte / con li occhi, vidi parte ne lo stremo / vincer di lume tutta l'altra fronte." Cf. Bonaventure's comparison of the beauty of the rising sun to the Virgin in *Sermones de B. V. M.* 2.9, *Opera omnia,* vol. 9 (Quaracchi, 1882–1902), pp. 708–709.

36. *Purgatorio* 2.7–9: "Sì che le bianche e le vermiglie guance, / là dov'i' era, de la bella Aurora / per troppa etate divenivan rance." *Paradiso* 30.7–8: "E come vien la chiarissima ancella / del sol più oltre, così 'l ciel si chiude."

37. *Convivio* 2.14.20. Canticum Canticorum 6.7–8: "Sexaginta sunt reginae et octoginta concubinae et adulescentularum non est numerus. Una est columba mea perfecta mea." Virgil used the same line about Aurora no less than three times: *Aeneid* 4.584–5 and 9.460 and *Georgics* 1.446–447.

For the rich catalogue of allusion contained in Dante's verses, see Ezio Raimondi, "Analisi strutturale e semantica del canto IX del 'Purgatorio,'" *Studi danteschi* 45 (1968): 121–146.

38. Gino Casagrande, "Il 'freddo animale' e la 'concubina'; (*Purgatorio* IX, 1–6)," in *Filologia e critica dantesca: Studi offerti a Aldo Vallone* (Florence: Olschki, 1989), pp. 141–159.

39. Warren Ginsberg, "Dante's Dream of the Eagle and Jacob's Ladder," *Dante Studies* 100 (1982): 41–69. For Dido's similarity to Aurora, see Raimondi, "Analisi strutturale," p. 122.

40. See Ptolemy, *Tetrabiblos* 1.11–12; Macrobius, *Saturnalia* 1.21–25; Hipparchus, *Treatise on the Twelve Signs;* and others exhaustively discussed by Luigi Aurigemma, *Le signe zodiacale du Scorpion dans les traditions occidentales de l'Antiquité greco-latine à la Renaissance* (Paris, 1976). See also Casagrande, "Il 'freddo animale,'" 147f. Alain de Lille in his *Distinctiones* equates *scorpio* with *desperatio:* "Quae retro pungit sicut scorpio . . . cum enim spes in anteriora se extendit, desperatio retro afficit" (*PL* 210.714 and 937). See Raimondi, "Analisi strutturale," p. 125. The front-and-back distinction of hope and despair is suggestive for the opposition of Aurora's *fronte* to the scorpion that attacks from behind.

41. In Cesare Ripa's *Iconologia* (Rome, 1603), pp. 150–151, *libidine* is represented as a woman holding a scorpion. The scorpion itself was often depicted with the face of a girl. Casagrande, "Il 'freddo animale,'" amply demonstrates the negative feminine associations of Scorpio, even to its etymology based on *scortum,* "harlot" or "prostitute."

42. Baldassare Castiglione, *Il cortegiano* 1.9, ed. Ettore Bonora (Milan: Mursia, 1972), p. 41. For a reproduction of the late fifteenth-century portrait, variously attributed to Mantegna, Gianfrancesco Caroto, or Raphael, and an English translation of *Il cortegiano,* see Baldassare Castiglione, *The Book of the Courtier,* ed. and trans. Charles S. Singleton (New York: Anchor, 1959). The *S* on her forehead, talked of there, is often thought to stand for the scorpion represented in the portrait. See Cordié's note to the passage in *Il cortegiano* (Milan: Mondadori, 1991), p. 26; and John Robert Woodhouse, *Baldesar Castiglione: A Reassessment of the Courtier* (Edinburgh: Edinburgh University Press, 1978).

43. A. Pease and J. Coon, "Eos," in *Paulys Real-Encyclopädie der Classischen Altertumswissenschaft,* ed. Georg Wissowa, vol. 5 (Stuttgart: Metzler,

1905), pp. 2658–2670. See also Froma Zeitlin, "Configurations of Rape in Greek Myth," in *Rape,* ed. Sylvana Tomaselli and Roy Porter (Oxford: Basil Blackwell, 1986), p. 144.

44. Carina Weiss, "Eos," in *Lexicon iconographicum mythologiae classicae* (Zurich: Artemis, 1986), pp. 747–789.

45. J. Fontenrose, *Orion: The Myth of the Hunter and the Huntress* (Berkeley: University of California Press, 1981).

46. *Purgatorio* 9.13–15, 22–24, and 34–39. The theme of sexual violence in these passages, as well as that of the eagle burning together with Dante in his dream, has been noted by Francis Fergusson, *Dante's Drama of the Mind* (Princeton: Princeton University Press, 1953), p. 35; and Mark Musa, *Dante's Purgatory* (Bloomington: University of Indiana Press, 1981), p. 103.

47. Giorgio Stabile, "Cosmologia e teologia nella 'Commedia,'" *Letture classensi,* vol. 12 (Ravenna: Longo, 1983), pp. 139–173.

48. *Convivio* 3.5.8–22. See Patrick Boyde, *Dante: Philomythes and Philosopher* (Cambridge: Cambridge University Press, 1981), pp. 151–152.

49. André Pézard, *"La Rotta Gonna": Gloses et corrections aux textes mineurs de Dante,* vol. 1 (Paris: Didier, 1979), pp. 177f. Rachel Jacoff and William A. Stephany, *Inferno II,* Lectura Dantis Americana (Philadelphia: University of Pennsylvania Press, 1989), pp. 29–38.

50. John Donne, "A Nocturnall upon S. Lucies Day, Being the Shortest Day," in *The Complete Poetry and Selected Prose of John Donne,* ed. Robert Sillman Hillyer (New York: Modern Library, 1946), pp. 29–30.

51. *Convivio* 3.5.17.

52. *Convivio* 3.5.21: "Per che vedere omai si puote che per lo divino provedimento lo mondo è sì ordinato che, volta la spera del sole e tornata ad uno punto, questa palla dove noi siamo in ciascuna parte di sé riceve tanto tempo di luce quanto di tenebre. O ineffabile sapienza che così ordinasti, quanto è povera la nostra mente a te comprendere! E voi a cui utilitade e diletto io scrivo, in quanta cechitade vivete, non levando li occhi suso a queste cose, tenendoli fissi nel fango de la vostra stoltezza!"

53. On this passage Natalino Sapegno comments: "Questo esordio astronomico . . . è nel gusto prezioso ed ermetico delle rime pietrose." Dante Alighieri, *La Divina Commedia,* ed. N. Sapegno (Milan: Ricciardi, 1957), p. 489.

54. "Io son venuto," pp. 63–64: "Non son però tornato un passo a retro, /

né vo' tornar." On this poem I am indebted to the cosmic associations pointed out by Robert Durling and Robert Martinez, *Time and the Crystal: Studies in Dante's "Rime Petrose"* (Berkeley: University of California Press, 1990), pp. 71–108, and also by Durling in "'Io son venuto': Seneca. Plato, and the Microcosm," *Dante Studies* 93 (1975): 95–129. Although Durling and Martinez find the message of the petrose ultimately to be an optimistic one, they too see this "first astronomical description in Dante's poetry" as representing "the first half of a pattern of descent followed by ascent" (*Time and the Crystal,* pp. 79 and 76).

55. *Bedae venerabilis De temporum ratione* 7, ed. W. Jones, *Corpus Christianorum Series Latina,* vol. 123B (Turnhout, Belgium: Brepols, 1977), pp. 296–297: "Eo quod circa fines telluris solis splendor undique diffusus, ea libere quae telluri procul absunt aspiciat; ideoque aetheris quae ultra lunam sunt spatia diurnae lucis plena semper efficiat, vel suo videlicet vel siderum radiata fulgore. Et quomodo nocte caeca procul accensas faces intuens circumposita quaeque loca eodem lumine perfundi non dubitas, tametsi tenebris noctis obstantibus non amplius quam solas facium flammas cernere praevaleas."

56. *Bedae venerabilis De temporum ratione* 5, p. 289: "Ipsa mutatio temporis nos quoque a paradisi quondam lumine translatos in conuallem lacrymarum, iam modo a peccatorum tenebris ad caeleste gaudium transferendos esse designat."

57. *Paradiso* 3.14.

58. *Purgatorio* 2.75.

59. Bernard of Clairvaux, *Sermones de tempore, PL* 183.711–712: "Aurora quippe finis est noctis et initium lucis. Nox autem vitam peccatoris, lux significat vitam justi. Aurora ergo quae fugat tenebras, lucem nuntiat, merito humilitatem designat, quia sicut illa diem et noctem, ita ista dividit iustum et peccatorem." Cited by Raimondi, "Analisi strutturale," p. 125.

60. *Epistola* 13.17: "Istius operis non est simplex sensus, ymo dici potest polisemos, hoc est plurium sensuum."

CHAPTER FIVE: LOSING THE MERIDIAN

1. Ilvano Caliaro ("Per una poetica dell'astronomia dantesca," *Atti dell'Istituto Veneto di Scienze, Lettere ed Arti* 137 [1978–79]: 186) notes that the as-

tronomical passages move from concrete to metaphysical, astrological, and poetic in a process of disintegration and abstraction. James T. Chiampi has also noted the progressive abstraction of astronomical references in "Dante's *Paradiso* from Number to *Mysterium*" (*Dante Studies* 110 [1992]: 225−278). Robert Durling and Ronald Martinez (*Time and the Crystal* [Berkeley: University of California Press, 1990], p. 209) note the prominence of the horizon in the *Purgatorio*. In *Monarchia* 3.16, Dante refers to the notion that man can be compared to a horizon because he links two hemispheres. In her chapter "Problems in Paradise," Teodolinda Barolini emphasizes that the alleged absence of temporality in the *Paradiso* is what puts its poet in difficulty (*The Undivine Comedy* [Princeton: Princeton University Press, 1992], pp. 166−193). Rachel Jacoff remarks in her "Introduction to the *Paradiso*" (in *The Cambridge Companion to Dante,* ed. R. Jacoff [Cambridge: Cambridge University Press, 1993], p. 223) that the last canticle "oscillates between statements of its daring originality and confessions of its impossibility."

2. Francis X. Newman, "St. Augustine's Three Visions and the Structure of the Comedy," in *Modern Language Notes* 82 (1967): 56−78. Marguerite Mills Chiarenza, "The Imageless Vision and Dante's *Paradiso*," *Dante Studies* 90 (1972): 77−91. John Freccero, "Introduction to the *Paradiso*," in *Dante: The Poetics of Conversion* (Cambridge: Harvard University Press, 1986); and "Introduction to *Inferno*," in *The Cambridge Companion.*

3. On different modes of perception in general in the *Commedia,* see Patrick Boyde, *Perception and Passion in Dante's "Comedy"* (Cambridge: Cambridge University Press, 1993).

4. Statius, *Thebaid* 1.692−693, in *Statius* (Cambridge: Harvard University Press, 1955): "Et iam temone supino / languet Hyperboreae glacialis portitor Ursae"; and 3.414: "Et erecto currum temone supinant."

5. *Purgatorio* 29.16−21: "Ed ecco un lustro sùbito trascorse / da tutte parti per la gran foresta, / tal che di balenar mi mise in forse. / Ma perché balenar, come vien, resta, / e quel, durando, più e più splendeva, / nel mio pensier dicea: 'Che cosa è questa?'"

6. *Purgatorio* 29.53−54: "Più chiaro assai che luna per sereno / di mezza notte nel suo mezzo mese"; *Purgatorio* 29.77−78: "Tutte in quei colori / onde fa l'arco il Sole e Delia il cinto"; *Purgatorio* 29.82: "così bel ciel."

7. *Purgatorio* 29.91: "sì come luce luce in ciel seconda." Benvenuto da Imola (*Comentum super Dantis Aldigherij Comoediam,* ed. G. Barbera, vol. 4 [Florence: G. Barbera, 1887], p. 194) affirms the appropriateness of comparing the ancient books to stars that illuminate the world at night: "Et est propria comparatio, quia sicut in coelo una stella oritur post aliam ad illuminandum mundum tempore noctis, ita primo libri antiqui luxerunt in mundo in tempore tenebrarum; postea venerunt maiores luces in tempore gratiae, scilicet libri evangelistarum."

8. *Purgatorio* 29.117–120: "Ma quel del Sol saria pover con ello; / quel del Sol che, svïando, fu combusto / per l'orazion de la Terra devota, / quando fu Giove arcanamente giusto."

9. *Purgatorio* 31.106: "Noi siam qui ninfe e nel ciel siamo stelle." The two constellations are described in cantos 1.23–24 and 8.85–93.

10. On Dante's use of historical personages as types or figures, see Erich Auerbach's influential essay "Figura," in *Scenes from the Drama of European Literature* (Minneapolis: University of Minnesota Press, 1984).

11. Classic studies aimed at decoding the allegories of these cantos are Robert E. Kaske, "Dante's *DXV,*" in *Dante: A Collection of Critical Essays,* ed. J. Freccero (Englewood Cliffs, N.J.: Prentice-Hall, 1965); and Kaske, "The Seven Status Ecclesiae in *Purgatorio* XXXII and XXXIII," in *Dante, Petrarch, Boccaccio: Studies in the Italian Trecento in Honor of Charles S. Singleton,* ed. Aldo S. Bernardo (Binghamton, N.Y.: Center for Medieval and Early Renaissance Studies, 1983). See, more recently, Richard Lansing, "Narrative Design in Dante's Earthly Paradise," in *Dante: Contemporary Perspectives,* ed. Amilcare Iannucci (Toronto: University of Toronto Press, 1997).

12. Zygmunt G. Barański, "Dante's Signs: An Introduction to Medieval Semiotics and Dante," in *Dante and the Middle Ages: Literary and Historical Essays,* ed. John C. Barnes and Cormac ó Cuilleanáin (Dublin: Irish Academic Press, 1995), pp. 139–180.

13. John 16:25: "Haec in proverbiis locutus sum vobis. Venit hora cum iam non in proverbiis loquar vobis sed palam de Patrem adnuntiabo vobis."

14. *Purgatorio* 33.82–83: "Tanto sovra mia veduta / vostra parola disïata vola."

15. *Purgatorio* 33.88–90: "E veggi vostra via da la divina / distar cotanto, quanto si discorda / a terra il ciel che più alto festina."

16. *Macrobius,* ed. F. Eyssenhardt (Leipzig, Germany: Teubner, 1893), p. 547: "Duo qui ad numerum praedictum supersunt, meridianus et horizon, non scribuntur in sphaera, quia certum locum habere non possunt, sed pro diversitate circumspicientis habitantisve variantur. Meridianus est enim quem sol, cum super hominum verticem venerit, ipsum diem medium efficiendo designat: et quia globositas terrae habitationes omnium aequales sibi esse non patitur, non eadem pars caeli omnium verticem despicit: et ideo unus omnibus meridianus esse non poterit, sed singulis gentibus super verticem suum proprius meridianus efficitur. Similiter sibi horizontem facit circumspectio singulorum." Translation modified from Macrobius, *Commentary on the Dream of Scipio,* trans. W. H. Stahl (New York: Columbia University Press, 1952), p. 151. Cf. *Remigii Autissiodorensis Commentum in Martianum Capellam* 8.434.22, ed. Cora E. Lutz, vol. 2 (Leiden: Brill, 1965), p. 258: "ORIZON est quicquid subiacet nostro aspectui, ergo ratio orizontis terra est ORIENS quia ibi videtur oriri sol."

17. For a fanciful meditation on the implications of meridians in what became known as the problem of longitude, see Umberto Eco, *L'isola del giorno prima* (Milan: Bompiani, 1994).

18. It is true that between Dante's two looks back at the earth from the height of the fixed stars, he can tell that six hours have passed (*Paradiso* 21.133–154 and 27.79–87), but this is not the same as knowing what time it is now for him, as was possible in the highly localized time-references of the *Purgatorio.*

19. Peter Dronke, *Dante and Medieval Latin Traditions* (Cambridge: Cambridge University Press, 1986), p. 81: "Applying Geoffrey of Vinsauf's conception, we see the fluctuations of inner and outer meaning. . . . [The enigmas might be] nodal points of concentration where inner and outer significance are tied together. Tree and chariot and eagle, dragon and giant and prostitute, not only gather up inherited meanings: they generate a fuller meaning that embraces 'within and without, here and there'—the subjective and the universal."

20. Geoffrey of Vinsauf, *Poetria Nova* 245–255, trans. Margaret F. Nims (Toronto: Pontifical Institute, 1967), p. 25. Latin text in *Les arts poétiques du XIIe et du XIIIe siècle,* ed. E. Faral (Paris: E. Champion, 1924), pp. 204–205, lines 247–255: "Quae fit in occulto, nullo venit indice signo; / Non

venit in vultu proprio, sed dissimulato, / Et quasi non sit ibi collatio, sed nova quaedam / Insita mirifice transsumptio, res ubi caute / Sic sedet in serie quasi sit de themate nata: / Sumpta tamen res est aliunde, sed esse videtur / Inde; foris res est, nec ibi comparet; et intus / Apparet, sed ibi non est; sic fluctuat intus / Et foris, hic et ibi, procul et prope; distat et astat."

21. See Marsh H. McCall, Jr., *Ancient Rhetorical Theories of Simile and Comparison* (Cambridge: Harvard University Press, 1969).

22. Chiarenza, "Imageless Vision."

23. Martianus Capella, *De Nuptiis,* 8.816, ed. A. Dick (Leipzig, Germany: Teubner, 1925), pp. 431–432: "Nos igitur circulos non ita dicemus, ut linquentis naturae discrimina corpulenta fingamus, sed ut ascensus descensusque ad nos errantium demonstremus. Neque enim vel axem polosque, quos in sphaera aenea, quae cricote dicitur, ad intellegentiae compendia adfinxere mortales, ego robori mundanae rationis apponam, cum nihil solidius terra sit, quod eam valeat sustinere; deinde cum poli velut perforatae exterioris sphaerae cavernis emineant, et hiatus quidam cardinesque fingantur, quod utique subtilibus aethereisque accidere non potuisse compertum. Sicubi igitur intelligentiae edissertandique proposito vel axem vel polos vel circulos perhibebo, ideali quadam prudentia, non diversitate caeli discreta, sed spatiorum rationibus dispensetur. Sicque habeatur cum evexem devexumque mundum dixero, cum similis cunctis suis partibus sit sublimeturque vel lateat pro condicione horizontis positioneque terrarum." English translation from *Martianus Capella and the Seven Liberal Arts,* trans. W. H. Stahl, vol. 2 (New York: Columbia University Press, 1971), p. 319.

24. *Theorica Planetarum* 6.96, in Edward Grant, *A Source Book in Medieval Science* (Cambridge: Harvard University Press, 1974), p. 462.

25. Lynn Thorndike, *The "Sphere" of Sacrobosco and Its Commentators* (Chicago: University of Chicago Press, 1949), p. 90: "Dicitur autem colurus a colon, quod est membrum, et uros, quod est bos silvester, quoniam quemadmodum cauda bovis silvestris erecta, que est eius membrum, facit semicirculum et non perfectum, ita colurus semper apparet nobis imperfectus, quoniam tantum una est eius medietas apparens."

26. Macrobius, trans. Stahl, p. 151.

27. Pietro Caligaris ("L'ora della salita di Dante al Paradiso," *Studi danteschi*

e altre noterelle [Brescia, Italy: Paideia, 1973], pp. 13–21, p. 17), using a diagram supplied him by G. Maccone and M. Baratella, counts the fourth intersection with the other (equinoctial) colure, rather than with the horizon. For other interpretations, see Pietro Cuscani Politi, "I quattro cerchi che formano le tre croci: Interpretazione di un verso dantesco," *Studi danteschi* 32, no. 1 (1954): 65–70; and André Pézard, "Appendices," in Dante Alighieri, *Oeuvres complètes* (Paris: Gallimard, 1965), pp. 1699–1701.

28. Hermes Trismegistus, *Corpus Hermeticum . . . Ascleplius* 317.18, ed. A. D. Nock and A. J. Festugière (Paris: Belles Lettres, 1945).

CHAPTER SIX: THE SHADOWS OF IDEAS

1. Michel Serres, "Mathematics and Philosophy: What Thales Saw," in *Hermes: Literature, Science, Philosophy,* ed. Josué V. Harari and David F. Bell (Baltimore: Johns Hopkins University Press, 1982), p. 91.

2. Plato, *Republic* 7.516a, in *The Portable Plato* (New York: Viking, 1948), p. 548.

3. Michel Serres, "Gnomon: Les débuts de la géométrie en Grèce," in *Eléments d'histoire des sciences,* ed. M. Serres (Paris: Bordas, 1989), p. 69.

4. *Paradiso* 10.76–78 and 10.42.

5. The theory of sunlight being recycled in starlight is perhaps also behind these lines of John Donne's "Nocturnall on Saint Lucy's Day": "The Sunne is spent, and now his flasks / Send forth light squibs, no constant rayes" (*The Complete Poetry and Selected Prose of John Donne* [New York: Modern Library, 1946], p. 29).

6. *Paradiso* 10.53–54.

7. *Paradiso* 10.46–48: "E se le fantasie nostre son basse / a tanta altezza, non è maraviglia; / ché sopra 'l sol non fu occhio ch'andasse."

8. *Paradiso* 10.121.

9. Alfragano, *Il "Libro dell'aggregazione delle stelle,"* ed. Romeo Campani (Florence, 1910), pp. 142–143.

10. Aristotle, *De mundo* 6.399a–400b, trans. D. J. Furley (Cambridge: Harvard University Press, 1955), pp. 393–395. God is the "chorus-leader" of this dance: "The single harmony that is produced by all these as they sing and dance in concert round the heavens has one and the same beginning and one and the same end, in a true sense giving to the whole the name

of order (*kosmos*) and not disorder (*akosmica*). Just as in a chorus at the direction of the leader all the chorus of men, sometimes of women too, join in singing together, creating a single pleasing harmony with their varied mixture of high and low notes, so also in the case of the god who controls the universe."

11. *Convivio* 4.2.6: "Lo tempo, secondo che dice Aristotile nel quarto della Fisica, è 'numero di movimento secondo prima e poi,' e 'numero di movimento celestiale,' lo quale dispone le cose di qua giù diversamente a ricevere alcuna informazione." Some have thought that Dante's expression meant moving in harmony, in the same direction, one following the example of the first. See, e.g., *Commento di Francesco da Buti sopra la Divina comedia di Dante Alighieri* (Pisa: Nistri, 1858). Grandgent makes the curious comment, "That one should start at the word 'First!' and the other at the word 'Next!'" Dante Alighieri, *La Divina Commedia,* ed. C. H. Grandgent (Cambridge: Harvard University Press, 1972), p. 741.

12. See Albertus Magnus' discussion and refutation of Alpetragius' theory of retardation in his commentary on Aristotle's *Metaphysics* 12, Albertus Magnus, *Metaphysica* 11, tract. 2, cap. 10, *Opera Omnia,* vol. 16, ed. Bernhard Geyer (Münster, Germany: Aschendorff, 1964), pt. 2; and Pierre Duhem, *Le système du monde* (Paris: Hermann, 1913–1959), vol. 3, pp. 328–330.

13. Ronald Martinez has described this passage as an enactment of "the education of the mind to an imitation of the cosmic motions." "Ovid's Crown of Stars (Paradiso 13.1–27)," in *Dante and Ovid: Essays in Intertextuality,* ed. Sowell Madison (Binghamton: Medieval & Renaissance Texts & Studies, 1991), p. 127. Teodolinda Barolini says that the opening of canto 13 is part of a lyrical "antinarrative" (*The Undivine Comedy* [Princeton: Princeton University Press, 1992], p. 211).

14. Plato, *Timaeus* 36b–c. Francis MacDonald Cornford, *Plato's Cosmology: The "Timaeus" of Plato Translated with a Running Commentary* (London: Routledge and K. Paul, 1952), p. 73. John Freccero has made much of this Platonic topos in Dante's *Paradiso.* See, especially, his "Dance of the Stars" in *Dante: The Poetics of Conversion* (Cambridge: Harvard University Press, 1986).

15. Guillaume de Conches, *Glosae super Platonem,* ed. Edouard Jeauneau (Paris: J. Vrin, 1965), p. 167. Etienne Gilson ("La cosmogonie de Bernard

Silvestre," *Archives d'histoire doctrinale et littéraire du moyen âge* 3 [1928]: 7) writes: "The *Timaeus* and also therefore Bernard Sylvester's *Cosmographia* are concerned with creation not from the point of view of existence—from non-being to being—but from the point of view of disposition, ornamentation" (translation mine). See also J. Festugière, *La révélation d'Hermes Trimégiste* (Paris: Lecoffre, 1954), vol. 4, pp. 275–292; and Tullio Gregory, *Anima mundi* (Florence: Sansoni, 1955), p. 47.

16. Thomas Aquinas, *ST* 1.45.6 ad 2: "Filio autem appropriatur sapientia, per quam agens per intellectum operatur, ed ideo dicitur de Filio, *per quem omnia facta sunt.*"

17. *ST* 1.44.3, resp.: "Haec autem formarum determinatio oportet quod reducatur, sicut in primum principium, in divinam sapientiam, quae ordinem universi excogitavit, qui in rerum distinctiones consistit. Et ideo oportet dicere quod in divina sapientia sunt rationes omnium rerum, quas supra diximus ideas, idest formas exemplares in mente divina existentes."

18. Wisdom 7:17–21.

19. See Henri Corbin, *Creative Imagination in the Sufism of Ibn Arabi* (Princeton: Princeton University Press, 1981), p. 179; and Alexandre Koyré, *Mystiques, spirituels, alchimistes* (Paris: A. Colin, 1955), p. 59: "L'imagination . . . est la production magique d'une image. Plus exactement elle est l'expression par une image d'une tendance de la volonté, et, si l'on y fait attention, on verra bien que l'imagination est la force magique par excellence. . . . L'image est un corps dans lequel s'incarnent la pensée et la volonté de l'âme. . . . C'est exactement de la même manière, en l' 'imaginant' que Dieu a créé l'univers."

20. Richard of St. Victor, *Benjamin Major* 4.20, *PL* 196.162: "Si miraris quomodo ille omnium opifex Deus tot et tam varias rerum species, prout voluit, in ipso mundi exordio ex nihilo in actum produxit, cogita quam sit humanae animae facile omni hora quaslibet rerum figuras per imaginationem fingere, et quasdam quasi sui generis creaturas quoties volverit sine praejacenti materia, et velut ex nihilo formare, et incipiet minus esse mirabile, quod prius forte videbatur incredibile. In quo et illud invenies valde notabile, quod rerum veritatem, quae summa veritatis est, reservavit sibi, rerum vero imagines qualibet hora formandas suae concessit imagini." English translation from *Richard of St. Victor,* trans. Grover A. Zinn (New York: Paulist, 1979), p. 298.

21. Richard Kearney, *The Wake of the Imagination: Ideas of Creativity in Western Culture* (London: Hutchinson, 1988), p. 73.

22. For a discussion of this aspect of the imagination in Coleridge, see M. H. Abrams, *The Mirror and the Lamp: Romantic Theory and the Critical Tradition* (New York: Oxford University Press, 1953), p. 272f.

23. Benedetto Croce (*La poesia di Dante* [Bari, Italy: Laterza, 1956], p. 56) used the language of demiurgic creation when he remarked: "Qui invece l'immaginazione interviene come demiurgo e compie un'opera affatto pratica, qual'è quella di foggiare un oggetto che adombri a uso dell'immaginazione l'idea dell'altro mondo, dell'eterno" (But here the imagination intervenes as demiurge and achieves a wholly practical task: to forge an object that with the use of the imagination adumbrates the idea of the other world and of eternity).

24. *Paradiso* 30.130–132: "Vedi oltre fiammeggiar l'ardente spiro / d'Isidoro, di Beda e di Riccardo, / che a considerar fu più che viro."

25. Romans 1:20. Richard of St. Victor, *Benjamin Major* 1.3 and 1.12; Zinn, *Richard,* pp. 156, 190.

26. *Les douze patriarches ou Beniamin Minor,* ed. and trans. J. Châtillon and M. Duchet-Suchaux (Paris: Editions du Cerf, 1997), p. 132: "Rationalis autem est illa, quando ex his quae per sensum corporeum nouimus, aliquid imaginabiliter fingimus. Uerbi gratie: aurum uidimus, domum uidimus, auream autem domum nunquam uidimus; auream tamen domum imaginari possumus, si uolumus."

27. *Beniamin Minor,* pp. 136–138: "Nemo fidelium, cum infernum, flammam gehennae, tenebras exteriores in Scripturis sanctis legit, haec figuraliter dicta credit, sed ista ueraciter et corporaliter alicubi esse non diffidit. . . . Sed cum terram lacte et melle manatem, coelestis Ierusalem muros ex lapidibus pretiosis, portas ex margaritis, plateas ex auro legerit, quis sani sensus homo haec iuxta litteram accipere uelit? Vnde statim ad spiritualem intelligentiam recurrit, et quid ibi misticum contineatur exquirit." English translation in Zinn, *Richard,* p. 70. See Giuseppe Mazzotta's discussion of Dan and Naphtali in *Dante's Vision and the Circle of Knowledge* (Princeton: Princeton University Press, 1992), p. 129.

28. John Freccero ("Introduction to the Paradiso," in *Dante: The Poetics of Conversion* [Cambridge: Harvard University Press, 1986], p. 210) summarizes the shift in poetic mode among the three canticles of the *Com-*

media as "the gradual attenuation of the bond between poetry and representation, from the immediacy of the *Inferno* to the dreamlike meditation of the *Purgatorio* to the attempt to create a non-representational poetic world in the last *cantica*."

29. *Beniamin Minor*, p. 148: "Quanta namque, putas, erit lux illa quae erit nobis communis cum angelis, si tanta est ista quam habemus communem cum bestiis. . . . Quaerit ergo quae lux ista sit incorporea quam inhabitat inuisibilis et incorporea Dei natura, et inuenit quia lux ista est ipsa Dei sapientia, quia ipsa est lux uera"; Zinn, *Richard*, p. 74. Because the Victorines thought of the created universe as God's "other book," as would Bonaventure after them, we see that examples taken from natural objects are equivalent to figurative statements in the Bible. Biblical exegesis and the study of nature in fact make use of similar methods. Tullio Gregory ("L'idea di natura nella filosofia medievale prima dell'ingresso della fisica di Aristotele: Il secolo XII," in *Filosofia della natura nel medioevo* [Milan: Società Editrice Vita e Pensiero, 1966], p. 27) wrote about the interpretation of nature: "Tale lettura utilizzerà quindi le stesse tecniche ermeneutiche applicate a testi letterari e soprattutto all'esegesi del testo sacro." See also E. R. Curtius, "The Book as Symbol," in *European Literature and the Latin Middle Ages* (Princeton: Princeton University Press, 1943); Eugenio Garin, "La nuova scienza e il simbolo del libro," in *La cultura filosofica del Rinascimento italiano* (Florence: Sansoni, 1961), pp. 451f.

30. *Beniamin Minor*, chap. 23; Zinn, *Richard*, pp. 75–76. This is how Richard interprets Jacob's description of Naphtali as "ceruus emissus et dans eloqui pulchritudo" in Genesis 49:21.

31. Hugh of St. Victor, *Didascalicon* 7.25; *PL* 176.835: "In sapientia Dei est veritas, in rationali creatura imago veritatis, in corporea creatura umbra imaginis." *Umbra, imago,* and *veritas* also make up an exegetical trio in biblical allegory; Henri de Lubac, *Exégèse médiévale: Les quatre sens de l'e-criture* (Paris: Aubier, 1964), pt. 2, vol. 2, p. 286.

32. Mary Carruthers, *The Book of Memory: A Study of Memory in Medieval Culture* (Cambridge: Cambridge University Press, 1990), pp. 197 and 59, respectively. Carruthers argues persuasively that reading, meditation, and wisdom itself were thought of as coextensive with memory. The fundamental works on the history of trained recollection are Frances Yates, *The Art of Memory* (Chicago: University of Chicago Press, 1966); and Paolo

Rossi, *Clavis Universalis: Arti mnemoniche e logica combinatoria da Lullo a Leibniz* (Milan: Ricciardi, 1960). On the history of the imagination, see Murray Wright Bundy, *The Theory of the Imagination in Classical and Medieval Thought,* University of Illinois Studies in Language and Literature, vol. 12 (Urbana: University of Illinois Press, 1927); and David Novitz, *Knowledge, Fiction, and Imagination* (Philadelphia: Temple University Press, 1987).

33. Augustine, *De Trinitate* 11.8.13. English translation in *A Select Library of the Nicene and Post-Nicene Fathers of the Church,* ed. Philip Schaff (W. B. Eerdmans, 1956), vol. 3, p. 152.

34. Augustine, *Confessions* 10.11, trans. R. S. Pine-Coffin (New York: Penguin, 1964), pp. 218–219; and 10.24 for God's presence in the memory.

35. Augustine, Epistle 7, to Nebridius; *PL* 33.68. English translation from *A Select Library,* vol. 1, p. 224.

36. Marguerite Mills Chiarenza, "The Imageless Vision and Dante's *Paradiso,*" *Dante Studies* 90 (1972): 77–91.

37. Yates, *Art,* p. 43. For a discussion of the possible allusion to Solomonic magical treatises, see Alison Cornish, "La sapienza di Salomone e le arti magiche," in *Dante: Mito e poesia,* ed. M. Picone and T. Crivelli (Florence: Franco Cesati Editore, 1998), pp. 391–403.

38. Yates, *Art,* pp. 200–216. See also Lynn Thorndike, "Cecco d'Ascoli," in *A History of Magic and Experimental Science* (New York: Macmillan, 1923–41), vol. 2, chap. 71.

39. Plato, *Timaeus, a Calcidio translatus,* ed. J. Waszink (Leiden: Brill, 1962), p. 270: "Ut mentis providentiaeque circuitus, qui fiunt in caelo, notantes eorum similes constituerent in suis mentibus, hoc est, motus animi, qui deliberationes vocantur, quam simillimos instituerent divinae mentis providis motibus placidis tranquillisque perturbatos licet." Calcidius adds that what is meant by this imitation is moral reform: "Quod est morum vitaeque correctio." See Martinez, "Ovid's Crown."

40. Aristotle, *Metaphysics* 980a22; Dante, *Convivio* 1.1.1. *Intelligere cupio* is the repeated remark of interlocutors in scholastic dialogues. See, e.g., Albertus Magnus, *De Apprehensione* 4, *Opera Omnia,* vol. 5, ed. A. Borgnet (Paris: Vives, 1890), p. 583.

41. Augustine, *De Trinitate* 10.11.18, ed. W. J. Mountain (Turnhout, Belgium: Brepols, 1968), p. 330: "Haec igitur tria, memoria, intelligentia, voluntas,

quoniam non sunt tres vitae sed una vita, nec tres mentes sed una mens." It was Bonaventure's incorporation of this image into his hierarchy of contemplation that would make memory, understanding, and will the focus and the starting point of devotional exercises and metaphysical poetry for centuries to come. See Louis L. Martz, *The Poetry of Meditation: A Study in English Religious Literature of the Seventeenth Century* (New Haven: Yale University Press, 1962).

42. Augustine, *De Trinitate* 11.3.6, p. 340: "Atque ita fit illa trinitas ex memoria et interna visione et quae utrumque copulat voluntate, quae tria eum in unum coguntur ab ipso coactu cogitatio dicitur"; 12.7.10, pp. 364–365: "Sicut de natura hominae mentis diximus quia et si tota contempletur veritatem, imago dei est."

43. *The Garden of Eloquence* (1593; facsimile ed. by W. G. Crane [Gainesville, Fla., 1954], pp. 25–26), quoted in Angus Fletcher, *Allegory: The Theory of a Symbolic Mode* (Ithaca: Cornell University Press, 1964), pp. 96–97.

44. Jacques Derrida, "White Mythology: Metaphor in the Text of Philosophy," in *Margins of Philosophy,* trans. Alan Bass (Chicago: University of Chicago Press, 1982), p. 268.

45. Johannes Scotus Eriugena, *De divisione naturae* 3.2; *PL* 122.689: "Deus enim omnia in omnibus erit, et omnis creatura obumbrabitur, in Deum videlicet conversa, sicut astra sole oriente."

CHAPTER SEVEN: THE SUFFICIENT EXAMPLE

1. Plato, *The Republic* 529b–c, trans. Desmond Lee (Harmondsworth, England: Penguin, 1955), pp. 337–338.

2. Calcidius, *Timaeus a Calcidio translatus commentarioque instructus* 105, ed. J. H. Waszink (London: Warburg Institute, 1962), p. 154.

3. Lynn Thorndike, *The "Sphere" of Sacrobosco and Its Commentators* (Chicago: University of Chicago Press, 1949), p. 80: "Mundus sensibilis factus est ad similitudinem mundi architipi, in quo non est finis neque principium." English translation in ibid., p. 120.

4. Marie-Dominique Chenu, "The Symbolist Mentality," in *Nature, Man, and Society in the Twelfth Century* (Chicago: Chicago University Press, 1968), p. 113; Robert Anglicus' paraphrase of Ptolemy, *quasi semita ducens ad deum,* in Thorndike, *The "Sphere,"* p. 143.

5. *Timaeus* 29C; Francis M. Cornford, *Plato's Cosmology: The "Timaeus" of*

Plato (London: Routledge and K. Paul, 1952), pp. 23, 30. Calcidius, *Timaeus,* p. 22: "At vero eius quae ad similitudinem constantis perpetuaeque rei facta est ratio, utpote imaginis imaginaria simulacrumque rationis, perfunctoriam similitudinem mutuatur."

6. Aristotle, *De caelo* 288a13−b7. Latin text in Thomas Aquinas, *In Aristotelis libros De caelo et mundo* 2.8, ed. R. Spiazzi (Turin: Marietti, 1952), p. 181.

7. *Paradiso* 28.13−15: "E com'io mi rivolsi e furon tocchi / li miei da ciò che pare in quel volume, / quandunque nel suo giro ben s'adocchi."

8. *Paradiso* 28.16−21, 22−27.

9. *Paradiso* 28.41−42. Aristotle, *Metaphysica* 12.7. On the modern implications of Dante's use of this Aristotelian principle, see Mark Peterson, "Dante and the 3-Sphere," *American Journal of Physics* 47, no. 12 (1979): 1031−1035.

10. Titus Burckhardt, in his essay "Because Dante is Right" (in *Mirror of the Intellect: Essays on Science and Sacred Art,* trans. William Stoddart [Cambridge, England: Quinta Essentia, 1987], pp. 82−97), remarks that "every picture of the universe that man makes for himself can only possess a conditional and provisional accuracy."

11. Benvenuto da Imola (*Comentum super Dantis Aldigherij Comoediam,* vol. 5 [Florence: G. Barbera, 1887], p. 413) glosses the "angelic temple" as the primum mobile in which the angelic orders appear, and defines exemplum as that which is drawn from the exemplar. For the range of opinions, see Enrico Malato, "Essemplare," in *ED,* vol. 2, p. 733.

12. *Macrobius,* ed. F. Eyssenhardt (Leipzig, Germany: Teubner, 1893), p. 539: "Bene autem uniuersus mundus dei templum uocatur propter illos, qui aestimant, nihil esse aliud deum nisi caelum ipsum et caelestia ista, quae cernimus. Ideo ut summi omnipotentiam dei ostenderet posse uix intellegi, numquam uideri, quicquid humano subicitur aspectui, templum eius uocauit, qui sola mente concipitur, ut qui haec ueneratur ut templa, cultum tamen maximum debeat conditori, sciatque quisquis in usum templi huius inducitur, ritu sibi uiuendum sacerdotis." English translation from Macrobius, *Commentary on the Dream of Scipio* 1.14.2, trans. W. H. Stahl (New York: Columbia University Press), p. 142.

13. Albertus Magnus, *Metaphysica* 11.2.24, in *Opera omnia,* vol. 16, pt. 2, ed. Bernhard Geyer (Münster, Germany: Aschendorff, 1964), p. 514: "Tertia autem opinio est ab antiquis derivata, sed nuper per ALPETRAGIUM quen-

dam Arabem Hispanum renovata. Hic enim omnes sphaeras dicit moveri ab oriente in occidentem et quod omnes moventur motore uno, sicut habent motum unum; sed quia virtus illius motoris fortior est in caelo immediato sibi quam in eo quod iungitur ei per medium, ideo motum circuli perficit in primo caelo in spatio viginti quattuor horarum. In caelo autem secundo, quod est Saturni, non perficit totam circulationem, sed remanet aliquantulum, et illae remanentiae quotidianai simul collectae diminuunt unam circulationem in spatio triginta annorum. Et ideo videtur Saturnus moveri contra firmamentum secundum ordinem signorum et in triginta annis complere circulum. In caelo autem Iovis iterum plus diminuitur virtus motoris, et ideo excrescunt morae eius ad circulationem in duodecim annis." See also Albert's commentary on *De caelo* 1.3.6, in *Opera omnia,* vol. 5, pt. 1, p. 66. Attilio Mellone ("Il canto XXVIII del 'Paradiso,'" *Paradiso: Letture degli anni 1979–'81,* ed. Silvio Zennaro [Rome: Bonacci, 1989], pp. 731–754) pointed out the relevance of the Alpetragian theory to Dante's image.

14. *Paradiso* 28.64–65.

15. *De motibus celorum: Critical Edition of the Latin Translation of Michael Scot,* ed. Francis J. Carmody (Berkeley: University of California Press, 1952). English translation of Alpetragius from Bitruji, *On the Principles of Astronomy,* trans. B. Goldstein (New Haven: Yale University Press, 1991), p. 66. See Bruno Nardi, "Dante e Alpetragio," *Saggi di filosofia dantesca* (Florence: La Nuova Italia, 1967), pp. 139–166.

16. Aristotle, *De caelo* 2.10 (291b.11); Aquinas, *In Aristotelis libris De caelo,* p. 215: "Accidit autem secundum rationem fieri uniuscuiusque motus elongationibus, propter hos quidem esse velociores, hoc autem tardiores. Quoniam enim supponitur extremam caeli circulationem simplicem esse et velocissimam, aliorum autem tardiores et plures (unumquodque enim contra fertur caelo secundum sui ipsius circulum) rationabile iam propinquissimo quidam simplici et primae circulationi in plurimo tempore pertransire sui ipsius circulum, maxime autem distanti in minimo, aliorum autem propinquius semper in pluri, distantius autem in minori; propinquissimo enim maxime praevalet, distanti autem maxime omnium minime propter distantiam."

17. Gianfranco Contini, in "Un esempio di poesia dantesca: Il canto XXVIII" (in his *Un'idea di Dante* [Turin: Einaudi, 1970], p. 193), suggests

that the repetition of the word *truth* in this canto suggests a notion of truth that is no longer simply the opposite of falsehood, as it may have been in the *Inferno*, but rather an approximation (*adaequatio*) of reality.

18. *Paradiso* 3.16–18: "Tali vid'io più facce a parlar pronte; / per ch'io dentro a l'error contrario corsi / a quel ch'accese amor tra l'omo e 'l fonte."

19. *Vita nuova* 1.1.

CHAPTER EIGHT: PLANETS AND ANGELS

A version of this chapter appeared as "Planets and Angels in *Paradiso* XXIX: The First Moment," in *Dante Studies* 108 (1990): 1–28.

1. Genesis 1:16: "Fiant luminaria in firmamento caeli ut dividant diem ac noctem et sint in signa et tempora et dies et annos."

2. Claude Lévi-Strauss, *Tristes tropiques* (Paris: PLON, 1955), pp. 48–49: "Pour les savants, l'aube et le crépuscule sont un seul phénomène et les Grecs pensaient de même puisqu'ils les désignaient d'un mot que l'on qualifiait autrement selon qu'il s'agissait du soir ou du matin. Cette confusion exprime bien le prédominant souci des spéculations théoriques et une singulière négligence de l'aspect concret des choses. Qu'un point quelconque de la terre se déplace par un mouvement indivisible entre la zone d'incidence des rayons solaires et celle où la lumière lui échappe ou lui revient, cela se peut. Mais en réalité, rien n'est plus différent que le soir et le matin."

3. Bede, following Isidore, defines twilight as follows: "Crepusculum est dubia lux, nam creperum dubium dicimus, hoc est inter lucem et tenebras." *Bedae venerabilis De temporum ratione,* ed. W. Jones, *Corpus Christianorum Series Latina,* vol. 123B (Turnhout, Belgium: Brepols, 1977), p. 299.

4. Augustine, *De civitate Dei,* book 11, chaps. 19–21, ed. B. Dombart and A. Kalb, *Opera, Corpus Christianorum Series Latina,* vol. 48, pt. 14.2 (Turnhout, Belgium: Brepols, 1955), p. 338: "Si, cum lux prima illa facta est, angeli creati intelleguntur, inter sanctos angelos et inmundos fuisse discretum, ubi dictum est 'et divisit Deus inter lucem et tenebras et vocavit Deus lucem diem et tenebras vocavit noctem.'"

5. Robert Durling and Ronald Martinez (*Time and the Crystal* [Berkeley: University of California Press, 1990], p. 208) have also observed that the whole passage is related to the question raised later in the canto of the interval between creation and the angels' fall. Erich von Richthofen saw the

image as one of justice related to others in Dante's works; "The twins of Latona and other symmetrical symbols for justice in Dante," in *The Worlds of Dante*, ed. B. Chandler and J. A. Molinaro (Toronto: University of Toronto Press, 1966).

6. Ptolemy, *Almagestum* (Venice: 1515), p. 71v: "Sectiones autem orientales et occidentales quae fuerint ex sectione orbis horizontis et capite arietis et capite libre (quorum longitudines ab orbe meridiei sunt semper quarte equales) vocabimus orientale equalitatem et occidentale equalitatem."

7. Ibid., p. 71r: "Et videtur similiter declinatio inclinationum tenebrarum apud orbem medij signorum in orbe magno descripto super duo centra lune et umbre et super duo centra lune et solis. Igitur necessarium est etiam propter transitum centri lune in tempore eclypsis: ut alteretur locus orbis magni descripti super duo centra: et fiat locus eius alteratus semper in orbe signorum: et ut sint anguli quos continent sectiones eorum in omne hora non equales."

8. Manfredi Porena, "Noterelle dantesche," in *Studj romanzi,* ed. V. Rossi (Rome: Società Filologica Romana, 1930), pp. 201–206. Although it is true that a large majority of the commentators have thought that the simile describes a mathematical instant, it is not the case that Porena contradicts "tutti i commentatori." Early on, Alessandro Vellutello had already proposed that perhaps a total rising or setting was intended, yielding an interval of a certain length. For a concise rendering of his and other commentators' opinions, see *La "Divina Commedia" nella figurazione artistica e nel secolare commento,* vol. 3, ed. G. Biagi et al. (Turin, Italy: UTET, 1924–1927), p. 639. The notion of both planets fully setting or rising was suggested by Poggiali in *La Divina Commedia di Dante Alighieri già ridotta a miglior lezione dagli accademici della Crusca,* vol. 4, ed. G. Poggiali (Livorno, Italy: T. Masi, 1813), p. 441: "Che ambedue quegli Astri si disimpegnano dalla detta fascia cambiando emisferio, cioè uno dall' orizzonte totalmente emergendo, l'altro sotto l'orizzonte totalmente immergendosi, per tanto tempo, e non più, Beatrice si tacque."

9. These expressions are taken, in order, from the commentaries of Venturi; from those of Lombardi; from Giorgio Petrocchi, *La lezione sugli angeli,* Lectura Dantis Romana (Rome: Società Editrice Internazionale, 1965), p. 22; and from C. H. Grandgent's notes on *La Divina Commedia* (Cambridge: Harvard University Press, 1972). Not one of them seems to ap-

preciate the contradiction entailed in describing a single mathematical instant with adjectives like "very short," "infinitesmally small," "intermediate," and so on: an instant has no extension whatever, however brief.

10. Aristotle's discussion of time is in *Physics* 4.10–14, 218a–224a. See Sarah Waterlow, *Nature, Change, and Agency in Aristotle's "Physics"* (Oxford: Clarendon Press, 1982), pp. 132f: "[In instantaneous transition] the object must not be described as in process of changing *at* the instant in question. It is changing *as from* this instant, and at every subsequent instant (up to the latter end of the change) it is true of it that it has already been changing. There is no moment which is the first at which the thing has changed."

11. I have taken the liberty of rephrasing Richard Sorabji's example of the "instant after two o'clock" in terms of Dante's simile. Richard Sorabji, *Time, Creation and the Continuum: Theories in Antiquity and the Early Middle Ages* (Ithaca: Cornell University Press, 1983), p. 412. See also G. E. L. Owen, "Aristotle on Time," in *Motion and Time, Space and Matter*, ed. P. K. Machamer and R. G. Turnbull (Columbus: Ohio State University Press, 1976), pp. 3–27.

12. *La Divina Commedia di Dante Alighieri*, comm. M. Porena, vol. 3 (Bologna, Italy: Zanichelli, 1955), p. 283. For a reading of this eclipse in the context of others in the *Paradiso*, see John Kleiner, "The Eclipses in the *Paradiso*," *Stanford Italian Review* 9, nos. 1–2 (1990): 5–32; and Kleiner, *Mismapping the Underworld* (Stanford: Stanford University Press, 1994).

13. Because the sun is much larger than the earth, the terrestrial shadow extends into space away from the sun in the shape of a cone. If the two globes were of the same size, the shadow would be cylindrical; if the earth were larger than the sun, the shadow would extend outward like a funnel and engulf all the stars in the night sky, as Calcidius explains (*Timaeus a Calcidio translatus commentarioque instructus*, ed. J. H. Waszink [London: Warburg Institute; Leiden: Brill, 1962], p. 141). A lunar eclipse does not occur every month with the full moon because it is usually either to the north or south of the sun's path (the ecliptic) and avoids the conical umbra of the earth.

14. Ibid., p. 139: "Igitur si utrosque orbes epipedos, id est planos et sine ulla soliditate, tam solis quam lunae consideremus animo positos adversum

se ita directa positione, ut una per medios orbes ducta linea spinam duobus planis orbibus insigniat, erit diametrus amborum eadem linea et eius summa pars scindens proximum circulum catabibazon appellatur, ima vero secans aeque sursum versum maiorem orbem anabibazon." It should be said that here Calcidius is describing the solar eclipse, but as regards alignment it is equally applicable to the discussion of the lunar eclipse that follows. Cf. the discussion of eclipses in Alfragano, *Il "libro dell'aggregazione delle stelle,"* chaps. 28–29, ed. Romeo Campani (Florence, 1910), pp. 165–170; and in Bede, *De temporum ratione,* p. 297.

15. *Paradiso* 29.97–102: "Un dice che la luna si ritorse / ne la passion di Cristo e s'interpuose, / per che 'l lume del sol giù non si porse; / e mente, ché la luce si nascose / da sé: però a li Spani e a l'Indi / come a' Giudei tale eclissi rispuose." *Paradiso* 29.79–80: "Non hanno vedere interciso / da novo obietto."

16. *Paradiso* 29.16–30: "In sua etternità di tempo fore, / fuor d'ogne altro comprender, come i piacque, / s'aperse in nuovi amor l'etterno amore. / Né prima quasi torpente si giacque; / ché né prima né poscia procedette / lo discorrer di Dio sovra quest'acque. / Forma e materia, congiunte e purette, / usciro ad esser che non avia fallo, / come d'arco tricordo tre saette. / E come in vetro, in ambra o in cristallo / raggio resplende sì, che dal venire / a l'esser tutto non è intervallo, / così 'l triforme effetto del suo sire / ne l'esser suo raggiò insieme tutto / sanza distinzione in essordire."

17. Thomas Aquinas, *ST* 1.45.2 ad 3: "In his quae fiunt sine motu, simul est fieri et factum."

18. *Paradiso* 29.31–33: "Concreato fu ordine e costrutto / a le sustanze; e quelle furon cima / nel mondo in che puro atto fu produtto." Dante's description of angels as pure act exceeds the limits set forth for them by scholastic metaphysics, in which God alone is defined as *actus purus.* It is equally foreign to Thomism to conceive of prime matter coming into existence as pure potency, as Dante asserts. *Paradiso* 29.34: "Pura potenza tenne la parte ima."

19. Attilio Mellone disagrees with most commentators on this point. He believes that *quest'arte* which the good angels began after the bad ones fell is not the moving of the spheres but the contemplative orbits around God:

"Il giro dei nove cori angelici intorno a Dio, giro simboleggiante la visione beatifica." It is hard to distinguish these two activities so sharply, however, as in the previous canto it was explained that the spiritual revolutions of the angels around God in some fashion cause the movements of the celestial spheres. Attilio Mellone, "Il canto XXIX del 'Paradiso' (una lezione di angelologia)," *Nuove letture dantesche* 7 (1974): 194–213, 202.

20. *Paradiso* 29.44–45: "Che non concederebbe che 'motori / sanza sua perfezion fosser cotanto." Ecclesiasticus 18:1: "Qui vivit in aeternum creavit omnia simul." Aquinas himself (*ST* 1.61.3 ad 3, vol. 9, p. 212) says that the opening words of Genesis must be reinterpreted if the view of simultaneous creation is to be abandoned.

21. I Ezekiel 28:13,14: "In deliciis paradisi Dei fuisti, omni labide pretioso ornatus es. Ambulasti in diebus tuis sine vitio." Isaiah 14:12: "Quomodo cecidit Lucifer, qui mane oriebatur." This line, explicitly indicating the Prince of Tyre, is traditionally interpreted as a reference to Satan.

22. Peter Lombard, *Sententiarum libri quatuor* 2.2; *PL* 192.637–660: "Quales facti fuerint angeli, et quod quatuor eis attribuita sunt in ipso initio suae conditionis"; Albertus Magnus, *In II sententiarum* 3.14, *Opera omnia,* vol. 2, p. 116; Bonaventure, *In II sententiarum* 3.2, a. 1, q. 2, concl., *Opera Omnia,* vol. 2 (Quaracchi, 1882–1902), p. 117: "Ideo tamquam magis veram et catholicam, et magis probabilem et communem opinionem . . . quod morulam fuit inter creationem et lapsum." For a summary of the major arguments, see Edward J. Montano, *The Sin of the Angels* (Washington, D.C.: Catholic University of America Press, 1955), pp. 232–281.

23. *Paradiso* 29.49–50. See discussion below.

24. John 8:44. Augustine, *De Genesi* 11.16.21, *PL* 34.437.

25. Augustine, *De Genesi* 11.17.22, *PL* 34.438.

26. Augustine, *De Genesi* 11.23.30, *PL* 34.441: "Neque enim cecidit, si talis est factus. Sed factus continuo se a luce veritatis avertit, superbia tumidus, et propriae potestatis delectatione corruptus: unde beatae atque angelicae vitae dulcedinem non gustavit." Translations of the *De Genesi* are from Augustine, *The Literal Meaning of Genesis,* trans. John H. Taylor (New York: Newman, 1982).

27. Augustine, *De civitate Dei* 11.15, p. 335.

28. Augustine, *De civitate* 11.17, p. 337: "Diabolus institutione illius bonus, voluntate sua malus."

29. Augustine, *De Genesi* 4.30.47, *PL* 34.316: "Quis non videat, si attendere velit, et diem ubi sol est, et noctem ubi non est, et vesperam unde discedit, et mane quo accedit, simul habere? Sed nos plane in terris haec omnia simul habere non possumus: nec ideo tamen istam terrenam conditionem lucisque corporae temporalem localemque circuitum illi patriae spirituali coaequare debemus, uti semper est dies in contemplatione incommutabilis veritatis, semper vespera in cognitione in seipsa creaturae, semper mane etiam ex hac cognitione in laude Creatoris." *Literal Meaning,* vol. 1, p. 137.

30. Augustine, *De Genesi* 4.32.49, *PL* 34.317: "Post hoc si eo modo sibi placeret, ut amplius seipsa quam Creatore suo delectaretur, non fieret mane, id est non de sua cognitione in laudem Creatoris assurgeret." *Literal Meaning,* vol. 1, p. 139.

31. 1 Corinthians 15:52: *in ictu oculi. De Genesi* 4.34.54–55; *PL* 34.319–320.

32. See Sorabji, *Time,* pp. 31–32: "*City* XII.16 contains a further and very unexpected idea, namely the theory of angelic time. Hours, days, months and years, which are ordinarily called time, began with celestial motion. But we can also distinguish a kind of time which depends on the *mental* movements of the angels. . . . Besides the times which began with celestial motion, there is also a quasi-time which depends on quasi-change in angelic minds. But since this change is only a quasi-change, the angels can also be viewed as poised between time and eternity."

33. *ST* 1.63.5 resp., vol. 9, p. 264: "Sed si sunt mutationes instantaneae, simul et in eodem instanti potest esse terminus primae et secundae mutationis; sicut in eodem instanti in quo illuminatur luna a sole, illuminatur aër a luna."

34. *ST* 1.63.6 resp., vol. 9, p. 266: "Diabolus in primo instanti, in gratia creatus, meruit, statim post primum instans beatitudinem accepisset, nisi statim impedimentum praestitisset peccando." Ibid., ad 3, p. 268: "Et ideo nisi statim post primum instans, in quo naturalem motum habuit ad bonum, impedimentum beatitudini praestitisset, fuisset firmatus in bono."

35. Thomas Aquinas, *De malo* 16.4, *Quaestiones disputatae, Opera omnia,* vol. 8 (New York: Misurgia, 1949), p. 401: "Quantum est ex creatione Dei, Angelus in primo instanti habuit naturam omnino integram, ita tamen quod haec integritas fuerit mox impedita per resistentiam angelicae vol-

untatis; sicut radius solis impediatur ne illuminet aerem in ipso solis exortu."

36. The proposition condemned in Paris in 1240 reads as follows: "Quod malus angelus in primo instanti suae creationis fuit malus et nunquam nisi malus." *Collect. iudicior.*, d. 23 *in fine,* vol. 1., p. 186 et infra, quoted in Bonaventure, *II sententiarum,* p. 117.

37. Peter Lombard 2.3, a. 5, *PL* 192.658: "Putaverunt enim quidam angelos qui ceciderunt creatos esse malos, et non libero arbitrio in malitiam declinasse, sed etiam in malitia a Deo factos esse; nec aliquam fuisse moram inter creationem et lapsum, sed ab initio apostatasse; alios vero creatos fuisse plene beatos."

38. Peter Lombard, ibid., a. 6: "Aliquam etiam fuisse morulam aiunt inter creationem et lapsum ac confirmationem, et in illa brevitate temporis omnes boni erant, non quidem per usum liberi arbitrii, sed per creationis beneficium." Cf. Bonaventure, *II sententiarum* 3.2, a. 1, q. 2, p. 116: "Ideo tanquam magis veram et catholicam, et magis probabilem et communem opinionem dico illam esse tenendam, quod morula fuit inter creationem et lapsum, licet parvula." Because this delay was so brief, however, saints, exegetes, and the Scriptures themselves sometimes refer to it as if it were no space of time whatever: "Propter quam Sancti et expositores et ipsa Scriptura loquitur de malitia diaboli, quasi semper fuisset in ea, quia illud modicum quasi pro nihilo reputatur."

39. Peter Lombard 2.3, a. 8; *PL* 192.658.

40. Bonaventure (*II sententiarum,* p. 116) had argued that every sin is preceded by deliberation, and therefore succession of time: "Omne peccatum actuale exit in esse per actum deliberationis; sed ubi deliberatio, ibi collatio et successio de necessitate: ergo si peccatum sequitur deliberationem Angeli, peccatum sequitur Angelum non tantum *natura,* verum etiam *duratione. Si tu dicas,* quod Angelus propter intellectum deiformem deliberat in instanti, et simul videt et deliberat, *ostendo,* quod non potest esse." Bonaventure also differs from Aquinas in that he believed that the angels consisted in a certain composition of form and matter. See Etienne Gilson, "The Angels," in *The Philosophy of Saint Bonaventure* (London: Sheed and Ward, 1938), pp. 238–270.

41. Aquinas, *De malo* 16.4, p. 401.

42. See Montano, p. 234.

43. Aquinas, *De malo* 16.4, p. 401. Aristotle, *Physics* 4.14.223b: "Uniform circular motion is the best measure because the 'number' belonging to it is best known. . . . This is also the reason why time has been identified by some with the motion of the celestial sphere: other movements are measured by means of it; and time, by means of this motion" *(Aristotle's Physics,* trans. Richard Hope [Lincoln: University of Nebraska Press, 1961], p. 88).

44. Augustine had said that "God moves his spiritual creature through time." *De Genesi,* book 8, chaps. 20 and 39, *PL* 34.388: "Ita per tempus movet conditum spiritum." On the question of the angels' duration, see James Collins, "Angelic Duration," in *The Thomistic Philosophy of the Angels,* (Washington, D.C.: Catholic University of America Press, 1947), pp. 329–367; and Frank Herbert Brabant, "The Perpetuity of the Angels," in *Time and Eternity in Christian Thought* (London: Longmans, Green, 1937), pp. 74–84.

45. Aquinas, *De malo* 16.4, p. 401b: "In ea igitur quae secundum unam speciem Angelus apprehendere non potest, necesse est quod moveatur in diversis instantibus sui temporis."

46. *De malo* 16.4, p. 401b: "Angelus in primo instanti suae creationis non fuit neque beatus per conversionem perfectam in Deum, neque peccator per aversionem ab ipso."

47. *ST* 1.63.6 ad 4, vol. 9, p. 268: "Sic igitur instans primum in angelis intelligitur respondere operationi mentis angelicae, qua se in seipsam convertit per vespertinam cognitionem, quia in primo die commemoratur vespere, sed non mane. Et haec quidem operatio in omnibus bona fuit. Sed ab hac operatione quidam per matutinam cognitionem ad laudem Verbi sunt conversi, quidam vero, in se ipsis remanentes, facti sunt nox, per superbiam intumescentes, ut Augustinus dicit 4 Super Gen. ad litt. Et sic prima operatio fuit omnibus communis; sed in secunda sunt distincti. Et ideo in primo instanti omnes fuerunt boni, sed in secundo fuerunt boni a malis distincti."

48. *ST* 1.63.6 obj. 4, vol. 9, p. 266: "Aliud instans fuit in quo diabolus peccavit, ab instanti in quo creatus fuit. Sed inter quaelibet duo instantia cadit tempus medium. Ergo aliqua mora fuit inter creationem ejus et lapsum."

49. If "a philosophical position is definitely characterized by its attitude towards Time," the question of the angels' deferral of sin is a defining point

in Thomistic philosophy. See William Ralph Inge, *God and the Astronomers* (London: Longmans, Green, 1933), p. 71. Concerning angelic time Aquinas writes: "Tempus autem quod mensurat eorum actiones non est continuum." "De instantibus," *Opera omnia,* vol. 6, ed. Roberto Busa (Stuttgart: Frommann-Holzboog, 1980), p. 558. Even as early as the commentary on the *Sentences,* Aquinas was already formulating an original idea of angelic time in response to various speculations about the nature of the first instant of creation. It had been argued that because any *nunc* on the continuum of time can logically be conceived of as both the end of the past and the beginning of the future (while really one and the same), it might therefore be possible for the angels to have been first good and then evil within the same instant: "In eodem instanti angelus fuit primo bonus, et post malus, et illud instans quamvis sit unum re, tamen differt ratione, secundum quod est finis praeteriti et principium futuri," *Commentum in quatuor libros sententiarum* I.3, q. 2, a. 1 in *Opera omnia,* vol. 6, p. 135. This notion, apparently derived from *Physics* 8.8, is perhaps related to a fourteenth-century school of thought that Norman Kretzmann has called Quasi-Aristotelianism, which posited various "instants of nature" existing in a given order within single instants of time. See Kretzmann, "Continuity, Contrariety, Contradiction, and Change," in *Infinity and Continuity in Ancient and Medieval Thought,* ed. N. Kretzmann (Ithaca: Cornell University Press, 1982), pp. 270–274. Paul Vincent Spade, in his response to Kretzmann in the same volume (pp. 297–307) entitled "Quasi-Aristotelianism," proposes that the special circumstances surrounding the doctrine of creation may have motivated the theory of instants of nature. See also Richard Sorabji, "Atoms and Time Atoms," in *Infinity and Continuity,* pp. 37–86.

50. *ST* 1.63.6 ad 4, vol. 9, p. 268: "Ad quartum dicendum quod inter quaelibet duo instantia esse tempus medium, habens veritatem, inquantum tempus est continuum, ut probatur in 6 Physic. Sed tamen in angelis, qui non sunt subjecti coelesti motui, qui primo per tempus continuum mensuratur, tempus accipitur pro ipsa successione operationum intellectus, vel etiam affectus."

51. For modern discussions of the aevum and its possible relation to the Bergsonian *durée,* see Frank Kermode, *The Sense of an Ending: Studies in the Theory of Fiction* (New York: Oxford University Press, 1967), pp. 67–89; and Inge, *God and the Astronomers,* p. 279.

52. *ST* 1.10.5 resp., vol. 2, p. 148: "Sic ergo tempus habet prius et posterius: aevum autem non habet in se prius et posterius, sed ei coniungi possunt: aeternitas autem non habet prius neque posterius, neque ea compatitur. . . . Creaturae spirituales, quantum ad affectiones et intelligentias, in quibus est successio, mensurantur tempore. . . . Quantum vero ad eorum esse naturale, mensurantur aevo. Sed quantum ad visionem gloriae, participant aeternitatem." "De instantibus," p. 558: "Ideo tempus quo mensuratur successio in actionibus Angelorum est ex indivisibilibus." *ST* 1.10.2 obj. 1: "dicit enim Boetius (*De. Trin.* 4) quod 'nunc fluens facit tempus, nunc stans facit aeternitatem.'" Cf. Boethius, *De Sancta Trinitate,* ch. 4, *Philosophiae consolationis libri 5,* ed. R. Peiper (Leipzig, Germany: Teubner, 1871), p. 158: "Nostrum nunc quasi currens tempus facit et sempiternitatem, divinum vero nunc permanens neque movens sese atque consistens aeternitatem facit."

53. Later Duns Scotus would deny that the angels acted in time. The succession was to be attributed to the aevum itself. In his *Lectura in librum secundum sententiarum,* distinctiones 4 and 5 (*Opera omnia,* vol. 18, ed. P. J. Vaughn [Vatican City: Typis Polyglottis Vaticanis, 1982], pp. 361–370), Scotus argues against Aquinas that there was a *mora,* but refers to the Thomistic opinion itself in terms of two consecutive morae, not instants. His own opinion involves three or more such morae. See Etienne Gilson, *Jean Duns Scot: Introduction à ses positions fondamentales* (Paris: J. Vrin, 1952), p. 404f.

54. For example, Albert asserts that *mox ut* means *postquam; post* implies some time between creation and sin; and *ab initio* for him means *cito post initium.* Therefore *statim post* implies that there was a *morula* or *mora* between the instant of creation and the instant of aversion from the highest good: "*Statim ab initio,* hoc est, *statim post initium:* ut per adverbium *statim,* et praepositionem *post,* notetur mora temporis quod fuit inter instans creationis et instans apostatsiae." Albert did not believe that an angel could move in any indivisible *nunc,* let alone the very first moment of creation, because decision-making takes time, and therefore delay. *Summa Theologica* 2, tract. 4, q. 18, art. 1, *Opera omnia,* vol. 32, ed. A. Borgnet (Paris: Vives, 1895), p. 232.

55. *ST* 1.63.6 ad 3, vol. 9, p. 268: "Angelus habet liberum arbitrium inflexibile post electionem. Et ideo nisi statim post primum instans, in quo nat-

uralem motum habuit ad bonum, impedimentum beatitudini praestitisset, fuisset firmatus in bono."

56. *ST* 1.63.6 ad 4, vol. 9, p. 232: "Et ideo in primo instanti omnes fuerunt
boni; sed in secundo fuerunt boni a malis distincti." See also *ST* 1.62.5 ad
2, vol. 9, p. 232: "Angelus est supra tempus rerum corporalium. Unde instantia diversa in his quae ad angelos pertinent, non accipiuntur nisi secundum successionem in ipsorum actibus. Non autem potuit simul in eis
esse actus meritorius beatitudinis, et actus beatudinis, qui est in fruitione,
cum unus sit gratiae imperfectae, et alius gratiae consummatae. Unde re-
linquitur quod oportet diversa instantia accipi, in quorum uno meruerit
beatitudinem, et in alio fuerit beatus." Cf. Etienne Gilson, *The Christian
Philosophy of St. Thomas Aquinas* (London: Victor Gollancz, 1957), p. 251;
and Jacques Maritain, "Les deux instants de l'ange," in *Le péché des anges:
Oeuvres complètes* (Paris: Editions Saint-Paul, 1982), p. 1017f.

57. *Convivio* 2.5.12: "Dico che di tutti questi ordini si perderono alquanti
tosto che furono creati, forse in numero della decima parte: alla quale
restaurare fu l'umana natura poi creata."

58. Bruno Nardi, *La caduta di Lucifero e l'autenticità della Quaestio de aqua
et terra* (Turin: Società editrice internazionale, 1959), p. 20: "gli angeli ri-
belli invece non furono così rapidi."

59. Attilio Mellone criticized Nardi for this concept of two different lengths
of time for the same angelic decision, depending on whether they were
to become angels or demons. Mellone also rightly points out that the
verse *Né giugneriesi, numerando, al venti* refers to the actual fall, not the
first moment of sin, although he believes that there was a *morula* for both:
"Si tratta del tempo intercorso non tra la creazione e il peccato, ma tra la
creazione e l'espulsione dal cielo. "Il canto XXIX,'" pp. 202–203.

60. Whether the *suggetto* of the elements is prime matter or the lowest-lying
element, earth, has been hotly debated, chiefly between Bruno Nardi and
Giovanni Busnelli. See the summary in the appendix "Angels and Prime
Matter" in Stephen Bemrose, *Dante's Angelic Intelligences: Their Importance in the Cosmos and in Pre-Christian Religion* (Rome: Edizioni di Storia e Letteratura, 1983), pp. 185–201. Whatever the case may be, the *suggetto* certainly describes a *terminus ad quem* not as regards Satan's choice
for evil, but for his spatial displacement from heaven to hell. See John
Freccero, "Satan's Fall and the 'Quaestio de aqua et terra'" (*Italica* 38

[1961]: 109), where he notes the Christian adaptation of the giants' mythological ten-day fall to earth to the angels and a nine-sphere cosmology. See also Freccero, "The Neutral Angels," in *Dante: The Poetics of Conversion*, ed. Rachel Jacoff (Cambridge: Harvard University Press, 1986), pp. 110–118.

61. Benvenutus de Rambaldis de Imola, *Comentum super Dantis Aldigherij Comediam*, vol. 5 (Florence: G. Barbera, 1887), p. 431: "Idest, non posses numerare usque ad viginti, immo non ad duo, quia peccaverunt in instanti suae creationis." The notion that the devil could have sinned either naturally or spontaneously in the first instant of creation was condemned doctrine—which suggests its prevalence. This may be why the Italian translation of this commentary reduces this entire statement, involving the controversial opinion of sin in the first moment, to simply "non potresti contare fino al numero venti tanto presto." Benvenuto Rambaldi da Imola, *Commento latino sulla Divina Commedia di Dante Alighieri* (Imola: Galeati, 1856), p. 501. Brabant (*Time and Eternity*, p. 71) also evidently sees Dante's account as compatible with Aquinas' notion of discontinuous angelic time.

62. Albertus Magnus, "Quando ceciderit malus Angelus?" *Summa Theologica* 2, tract. 5, q. 24, pp. 267–268: "Quod secundo die ceciderunt Angeli: et de hoc assignaverunt tres rationes: quarum prima accipitur ex ipso numero: binarius enim prius recedit ab unitate: et hoc competenter significabat recessum Angeli a monade Deo, Deus enim monas est propter individuitatem et simplicitatem."

63. *Convivio* 2.14.3, p. 132: "Ché per lo due s'intende lo movimento locale, lo quale è da uno punto ad un altro di necessitade. E per lo venti [si] significa lo movimento dell'alterazione: ché, con ciò sia cosa che dal diece in sù non si vada se non esso diece alterando colli altri nove e con se stesso, e la più bella alterazione che esso riceva sia la sua di se medesimo, e la prima che riceve sia venti, ragionevolemente per questo numero lo detto movimento [si] significa." These numerological expositions are meant to explain why the *stellatum* heaven, with its 1,022 fixed stars, should represent the science of physics, which studies movement (2), change (20), and growth (1,000). Etienne Gilson discusses this passage in *Dante and Philosophy*, trans. David Moore (London: Harper Torch Books, 1963), p. 103.

64. Creation itself, it should be recalled, is not a change, but the fall of the

angels is perhaps the most important change the world had to undergo. It is therefore more suitable that Dante's simile, describing the planets as they *change* hemispheres (*cambiando emisperio*) should refer to the first choice of the angels rather than to the fact of creation itself.

65. Bruno Nardi, "Il Canto XXIX del *Paradiso*," *Convivium* 24 (1956): 294–302.

66. Nardi, *La caduta,* p. 21.

67. Petrocchi, *La lezione,* p. 16: "Il Poeta dovrà ricorrere ad una misurazione del tempo svolta in guisa non molto differente da quella adoperata per cronometrare il silenzio di Beatrice." Apropos of the opening simile, Petrocchi is content to use such imprecise expressions as *baleno di tempo* and *un istante infinitesimalmente piccolo.* He calls Beatrice's silence both absolute and extremely brief. As for the question of Lucifer's fall, he assumes that Dante was as little interested in it as he: "È indubbio che, di tutta la lezione di Beatrice, questa è la meno interessante per Dante, e peraltro la meno necessaria."

68. See Sorabji, *Time,* p. 413: "Thus although [Aristotle] denies that things can *change* or *remain* in the same state at an instant, he concedes that there are many other things that can be true of them at an instant. He is quite prepared to allow that what is moving can be at a point, or level with something at an instant." Cf. Aristotle, *Physics* 8.8, 262a30, b20 and 6.8, 239a35–b3.

69. *ST* 1.46.3 ad 3, p. 88: "Non quia in ipso primo *nunc* sit tempus, sed quia ab eo incipit tempus."

70. *ST* 1.10.5 resp., vol. 2, p. 148: "Sicut patet in corporibus caelestibus quorum esse substantiale est intransmutabile, tamen esse intransmutabile habent cum transmutabilitate secundum locum. Et similiter patet de angelis quod habent esse intransmutabile cum transmutabilitate secundum electionem." Brabant (*Time and Eternity,* p. 79) assumes that "election" refers precisely to the primordial conversion or aversion of the angels. Cf. also Aquinas, "De instantibus," p. 558: "Sicut patet de corpore caelesti, quod secundum suum esse quod est intransmutabile, mensuratur aevo quod est instans permanens. Sed quia idem corpus habet transmutationem adjunctam motui, movetur enim secundum locum; tempus autem est mensura motus, ut dictum est; ideo hoc instans, licet sit intransmutabile, est tamen mutationi adjunctum ratione sui subjecti, quod

movetur secundum locum, ut dictum est: et sic accidentaliter habet mutationem adjunctam, sive alterationem. Similiter in substantiis separatis reperitur quidam motus affectionum et intellectionum, non autem secundum suum esse; unde ubicumque reperitur natura istius nunc, semper est reperire motum aliquem adjunctum."

71. *Paradiso* 28.116–117.

72. Patrick Boyde (*Dante Philomythes and Philosopher* [Cambridge: Cambridge University Press, 1981], p. 240) pointed out that the planets were in the positions in which they were created.

73. *Paradiso* 29.12.

CONCLUSION

1. *Paradiso* 25.70.
2. *Paradiso* 26.7–8.
3. *Paradiso* 26.38.
4. *Paradiso* 24.130–132.

INDEX